MEMOIR

OF

MRS. HARRIET L. WINSLOW

MEMOIR
OF
MRS. HARRIET L. WINSLOW

THIRTEEN YEARS A MEMBER OF THE AMERICAN MISSION IN CEYLON

REV. MIRON WINSLOW

GYAN

Published by

GYAN

Gyan Publishing House
5, Ansari Road
Daryaganj, New Delhi-110002
Phone: 011-47034999, 9811692060
E-mail: books@gyanbooks.com

Distribution Network
gyanbooks.com
India, USA, Canada, UK, Australia, France

ISBN : 978-81-212-3773-4 (PB)
First Published, New York, 1848

2nd Impression 2020

Printed at: Gyan Press, Delhi.

Memoir
Author: Rev. Miron Winslow

MEMOIR

OF

MRS. HARRIET L. WINSLOW,

THIRTEEN YEARS A MEMBER

OF THE

AMERICAN MISSION IN CEYLON

BY REV. MIRON WINSLOW.

PUBLISHED BY THE
AMERICAN TRACT SOCIETY,
150 NASSAU-STREET, NEW YORK.

PREFACE.

The wishes of his associates abroad, and of the friends of missions at home, induced the Compiler to attempt the preparation of this memoir, though it was undertaken amidst the distractions and multiplied engagements of a visit to his native land, which the claims of the heathen forbade him to protract.

The favor with which it has been received, especially as "introducing the reader into the daily trials and enjoyments, the hopes, labors, and disappointments of the missionary life," and bringing into view those parts of the picture not usually presented in published journals and reports, with the peculiar light and shade given by the delicate touches of a female hand, has led to its careful revision: those portions which seemed less important being omitted or condensed, and giving place to new and valuable matter, which, through the kindness of correspondents and friends, has since been obtained.

In an Introduction by the Rev. James H. Evans to one of the two reprints of this work in England, from which it has also been translated into French, he notices the mass of missionary intelligence it comprises; the ease and simplicity of its style and narrative of occurring events; the example it affords of early consecration, and patient, self-denying activity and perseverance in the service of Christ; the illustration of the usefulness, responsibility and encouragements of christian mothers, and especially the wives of missionaries; the value to those abroad of mutual confidence, watchfulness, and fidelity; the riches of Divine grace bestowed on the prayers and labors of faith and love; and the exhibition it contains of the true principles of missionary effort, on the success of which depends, under God, the hopes of millions thronging the pathway to eternal perdition, every one of whose souls has a worth which no human thought can conceive.

It was to deliver *such*, "drawn unto death and ready to be slain," that the efforts detailed in this volume were made, and the life, of which some account is given, was consecrated to their good. And if this imperfect memorial, by one who, willing to pay a tribute of affection, feels himself also "a debtor" to the heathen, shall kindle a spark of missionary zeal in one youthful breast—or throw the least light on the path of any follower of the Lord Jesus to a foreign land—or excite in any heart a throb of pity for a dying world, or an emotion of sympathy with the suffering Saviour in the "travail of his soul," his labor will not have been "in vain in the Lord."

CONTENTS.

MEMOIR.

CHAPTER I.

Her Early Life.

Conversion—Juvenile letters and journal—Communion with God—War with Great Britain—Taste for literature—Wadsworth's mountain—Society and school for the poor—Death of a brother—Letter and journal—Journey in New England—Efforts for the salvation of young friends—Visit to the city of New-York.

There is a charm in native simplicity, and a value in the record of facts in christian experience and the missionary life. These, it is believed, will be found combined in the following memoirs, and especially the correspondence, of one who wrote with no view to the public eye; but whose active mind and glowing affections induced her, for the promotion of her own walk with God, and in frank and unreserved communications with dear friends, to express the joys and sorrows of her heart, and delineate the varied scenes through which she was led.

HARRIET WADSWORTH LATHROP was born at Norwich, Connecticut, April 9, 1796. She was the second child and the eldest daughter of CHARLES LATHROP, Esq. and JOANNA LEFFINGWELL. Her father was a graduate of Yale College. Her immediate ancestors were pious. Her maternal grandmother was a daughter of Mr. JOSEPH COIT, a devout and consistent christian; her father's mother, ABIGAIL HUNTINGTON, happily exemplified the "meek and quiet spirit" of the Gospel; and her great-grandfather Lathrop lived a life of prayer, in which he often sought mercy for his children and children's children to the latest generation.

In Harriet's early days she displayed unusual energy and perseverance, with sometimes an undue inflexibility of purpose; but she was under the care of a judicious mother, and influenced by the example of a mild and dutiful elder brother. She had also amiable younger brothers and sisters, who, with a kind and excellent father, formed a domestic circle of much loveliness, adapted to cherish the best affections of the heart; and an interesting circle of youthful associates, some of whom have proved the brightest ornaments of society, exerted a happy influence in the formation of her character.

In connection with her fidelity, and in answer to her prayers, spiritual blessings began to descend upon her father's family before she left the country; and while far hence toiling for the heathen, God gave her the joy to learn that *all* its members had publicly professed Christ. Three of her sisters, Mrs. Charlotte H. Cherry, Mrs. Elizabeth C. Hutchings, and Mrs. Harriet Joanna Perry, followed her to India, the bodies of the first and last of whom now rest with hers at Oodooville, in the island of Ceylon.

The grace of God early appeared evidently to sanctify and seal the subject of this memoir for himself, some notice of which we happily have in a brief sketch found among her papers.

"In the summer of 1808, when I was 12 years of age, weekly evening meetings were commenced by our pastor, which were held at the houses of the parishioners. Being a new thing, they attracted notice, and were generally well attended. Some special interest in religion was about the same time manifested among a few middle-aged people, and some even among the youth. I first attended these meetings to accompany my mother, who often put into my hands such books as she thought might do me good. About this time she gave me Hawes' directions for obtaining the new birth. I examined them, and determined strictly to observe every thing which he recommends, yet seemed to gain nothing. It then occurred to me that I could not make myself better, so I went to God; and whenever I looked at my rule of duty, prayed that He would constrain me to observe it, and do all that was required. I daily meditated over this book, likewise reading the Bible, and retiring apart to pray. I was often deeply affected, and my numerous offences filled me with confusion.

"Our evening meetings became more interesting. I was not willingly absent from one. Sometimes I prevailed on some of my young friends to go; but they seldom inclined to do so without their parents. The religious interest now increased among a few young ladies much older than myself, and they held a meeting by themselves, which I was permitted to attend with a pious lady in our neighborhood. She sometimes conversed with me on our way, and often caused me to weep, though I know not that she drew any thing from me respecting the state of my mind. I had never spoken of it to any one, for indeed I scarcely knew myself what I felt. I saw my sins, and that they made my best friends unhappy; but I had not seen their true nature as offensive to a holy God. Yet I looked upon my companions as not standing in the same need of a new heart that I did, and therefore was not so urgent to turn them from folly as I afterwards became. Although sometimes grieved at their unkind remarks, I was principally intent on attempting to make myself better.

"Sometime near the end of Autumn, at a meeting in the evening, the 55th chapter of Isaiah was the subject of remark, especially the first two verses, '*Ho, every one that thirsteth, come ye to the waters*,' &c. Here I was for the first time overwhelmed by a consideration of the goodness of God in offering salvation to lost sinners. I felt my need of such a Saviour as is provided in the Gospel. In this state of feeling I returned home, and could not any longer conceal my anxiety. My dear mother inquired why I was weeping. I replied that I was a great sinner, and that evening felt more than I ever did before, that I was wretched and must perish for ever. I said but little, and she left me after saying only a few words. My anxiety increased. I felt willing I thought to do any thing, to be any thing, if the Lord would receive me as his child. I seemed to expect some special revelation from Him of my adoption, and often prayed that some angel might come and give me the so-much-desired assurance. I did not find myself amended of my faults. I only saw and felt them more, and knew that God must interpose and change my heart entirely, or I should continue to grow worse and worse.

"According to the advice of Doddridge and Hawes, I privately dedicated myself to God in a written form, resolving to be his alone, and his for ever. I seemed to receive a blessing in this act, and was greatly encouraged to persevere, and not to cease striving until I obtained. It appeared to me an awful step that I had taken; I had promised to be the Lord's; to lead a new life; to devote myself and my all exclusively to his service, and I dared not go back. Yet I knew not how to go forward. This carried me more frequently to the throne of grace. I had for some time observed three stated seasons of prayer each day; now I set apart a fourth, and generally nothing would prevent my observing them all. It was a busy time. Our house was filled with company, and sometimes I could not find a retired spot except in the garret, which often witnessed my importunity with God. My parents, not then professedly pious, and knowing little of my feelings, said nothing, but carefully avoided doing any thing that might hinder the work of God. No one spoke to me with any particularity, and I felt no freedom to speak to any one; so that I had no counsellor, no guide, but the Bible and the Holy Spirit.

"In the month of January, 1809, I received a letter from a dear friend at New London, saying that she had become anxious for her soul, and exhorting me to think of another world. This greatly encouraged me. I had one companion, one dear friend with whom I might take sweet counsel. I lost no time in replying to her letter. My earnestness had before been increasing, and I now felt new strength. One Sabbath noon, in the early part of the month, I was engaged in prayer as usual, when suddenly I nearly lost all my encouragement, and I believe ceased speaking; but soon recommenced, feeling that I could do nothing else. I seemed then to have new confidence in God, and the language, 'All things whatsoever ye shall ask in prayer, believing, ye shall receive,' caused me to open my mouth wide, and I trust to plead with that faith which is never rejected. A sweet peace was shed abroad in my soul. I felt assured that the Lord had heard my cry, and had not despised my prayer. Never can I forget the feelings with which I afterwards joined the family circle, the happiest of the happy. I longed to open my mouth to declare what the Lord had done for me; but I could only gaze on my parents, brothers, and sister, with new affection, and retire to weep by myself and pray. I went in the afternoon to the house of God, where every thing was new, every thing seemed to bid me welcome, and to say, 'The Lord of Hosts is in the midst of us.' For a number of weeks I enjoyed in silence this new world, into which I seemed introduced, though my solicitude for my friends was very great.

"In March our pastor called at the house, shortly after I had expressed a wish to my mother to unite with the church, if I were not thought too young. He said but little. Knowing my previous fondness for dancing, he inquired if I could relinquish that amusement for the sake of my Saviour. I expressed myself willing to make any sacrifice if I might be numbered among God's children. My beloved parents now examined anew their hope, and became convinced of their duty to profess their faith in Christ. Accordingly on the 9th of April, 1809, [the day on which she was 13 years of age,] they, together with myself and a female domestic, were propounded for admission to the church, and the third Sabbath following we sat down at the table of the Lord. It was a season never to be forgotten. I had taken a new stand, and the eyes of all were upon me. A child of my age never before was known, in that place, to come out from the world by a public profession of Christ! I had many acquaintances and friends, young, gay, and attractive. I received many cautions from the wise and good; but my connection with the world often made it necessary for me to reflect on the language of Christ, 'Whosoever shall be ashamed of me, of him shall the Son of man be ashamed when he cometh in his glory with the holy angels.' My dear brother was a valuable counsellor, and he was always at my side, jealous for the honor of God as well as for my christian character. My course was generally uninterrupted, and I had much religious enjoyment."

The written dedication and covenant here mentioned, was frequently afterwards renewed with great solemnity, and, as she thought, with profit. This renewal, indeed, constituted almost the closing act of her life, for only a few hours before her death, and the last time she wrote her name, while unaware of standing so near the eternal world, she subscribed the same document, which, twenty-five years before, she had with many tears, and who can doubt in faith, presented to the Lord.

It may not be easy, now that so many of the young are joining themselves to the followers of Christ, to estimate the degree of *christian decision* required in thus separating herself from her associates, having no individual of her age to whom she could freely speak on the subject most dear to her heart. This may have been one cause of her love of retirement, and perhaps of the habit, which seems to have continued through life, of comparing herself with the standard of *the Bible*, rather than with the experience of other christians.

It is known that she early commenced a diary of her religious exercises, and that in the year following her admission to the church, she prepared, for the use of her mother, a short account of her experience and trials; but in a season of illness, near the close of 1813, she destroyed both.

The following letters, obtained from those written by her during this interval, (for she preserved no copy of her correspondence,) show the state of her mind, and her concern for the spiritual interests of her companions:

TO A YOUNG FRIEND.

"*January* 19, 1810.

"It is true, my friend, that my feelings and desires are in a considerable degree changed since you were here, but should that diminish my affection for one who has ever been so dear to me? No, it should rather increase it; and I assure you that it does. What inexpressible pleasure would it give me, could I be a humble instrument in the hands of God in bringing you to him. By many religion is thought to be gloomy, calculated only to make us unhappy. Ah, my friend, such people are entire strangers to it. I never knew what real happiness is, until I found by experience that

'Wisdom's ways are ways of pleasantness, and all her paths are peace.' You have yourself witnessed what a blessed consolation religion is in the hour of death. I entreat you, my friend, seriously to inquire how the matter stands between God and your soul. Do not say, I am yet too young, I may put off repentance a little longer. 'Now is the accepted time, now is the day of salvation.' "

In October, 1810, we find her attending school at New Haven, and thus writing to her mother "bitter things" concerning herself:

"You say justly, that it is owing to my short comings in duty, that I am sometimes cold and destitute of spiritual life. I do not doubt it. But it is not only *sometimes*, but always, that I am accompanied with clouds and thick darkness. You will say that I do not go often enough to the throne of grace. I know that very well. When I had time and place I neglected it, and now that I would perform my duty the opportunities are denied me—and is it not just? Were it not for unbounded mercy and love, I should not now be lifting up my eyes in the land of the living. I think I have been going the downward road a great while, instead of growing in grace daily; and if my heart deceives me not, my earnest prayer is for more grace. But, alas, 'MY PRAYERS'—what are they? Had they been offered in sincerity, I should ere this have received an answer of peace.

"Do, mamma, remember me, that I may not bring reproach upon my parents, and the holy name I have professed; but may rather so grow in grace as to be made a peculiar child of God. I am almost discouraged. You say I must examine my heart. Whenever I attempt it, it is shut from me. It is all sin, that odious sin, which I pray God may not make him hide his face from me for ever. There is 'balm in Gilead,' and a 'Physician there;' but he has gone from me.

"Return, O holy Dove, return,
"Sweet messenger of rest;
"I hate the sins that made thee mourn,
"And drove thee from my breast."

TO A FEMALE ACQUAINTANCE.

"NEW LONDON, March, 1812.

"I have just returned from the Alms-house, where I attended the funeral of a very aged woman. Her husband was lying upon a bed from which he has not risen for several years; yet his countenance was the picture of resignation, and his whole deportment seemed to say, 'Thy will, O Lord, be done.' My dear friend, may we remember that, young as we are, we too must die.

Dear N——, do we not conform too much to the world? How frequently do I think there is no excuse for me, and I will certainly try to grow wiser; but my resolutions too often prove momentary, and without effect on my life. 'O that my head were waters, and mine eyes a fountain of tears,' that I might weep day and night for my sins. I have a book which I wish very much you to read; it is 'Wright and Hawes.' Do read it, and consider it as addressed to *you*."

The occasion of the above date being at *New London*, was that her father had been appointed clerk of the County Courts, the records of which were then kept there; but their safety, during the war with Great Britain, soon required them to be removed to Norwich, whither the family returned in the summer of 1813. The assistance frequently claimed in transcribing, was probably one means of Harriet's acquiring a fair, legible hand, and writing with uncommon ease and rapidity, a talent which she not only employed with great advantage in the business of the mission, but at all times felt at liberty to use for the enjoyment and spiritual benefit of herself and others.

Near the close of 1813 she recommenced her diary, which was continued almost daily until she left America. A few extracts will show the progress of her mind and her religious experience.

"*November* 11, 1813.—There has been a storm this evening. The wind was high. It was a most welcome sound to my ears. Did I not feel for those who are exposed to the inconveniences of such weather, I could hail the days when all without is dreary and boisterous, as more favorable to my happiness than any other. Then it is that I have no society but that of my own heart and a gracious God. Then have I a more lively sense of my dependence on Him, of my nothingness before Him, who is all in all."

"*March* 11, 1814.—Yesterday morning I walked with cousin L. We had some conversation on a subject dear to my heart. She is what I would be, and to believe it possible I shall ever be like her would be a great consolation. She has been to me a most useful friend. She has convinced me that were the love of God my ruling principle I should not have suffered as I have done the past two months. Could I regulate my heart by the Divine will, I should not be so much disposed to hide myself from every eye; but I feel continued weakness, and am deficient in every good thing. Yet why do I indulge this gloominess. I will be up and doing. There is forgiveness with God, and with him there is plenteous redemption.

He will not cast off any who come to him with humility, confessing their sins. To his throne of grace I will go, and if I perish it shall be at his footstool."

"*Thursday*, 16.—This day has passed but tediously. At evening we had a large party in our small parlor. Instead of receiving company, I could most gladly have retired to my chamber, and given vent to feelings which almost overpowered me. I was, however, obliged to assume an appearance of gayety which but ill suited me."

"*Sunday*, *April* 3.—This morning Doctor S. preached from Job, 20 : 5, 'The triumphing of the wicked is short.' I cannot doubt my claim to the christian character, as revealed in the Bible. I feel assured that 'old things are passed away,' and that where was once darkness is now light in the Lord. I have confidence in God. I believe his whole word. I rely solely on the Saviour of sinners for justification, adoption, and sanctification. Still I am perplexed on every side. Remaining corruption causes me to cry aloud for help. I feel that I have gone astray, have wandered, and loved to wander. It grieves me. Oh my God, I ask of thee strength. I ask for that divine love which will make me count all things but loss that I may win Christ. I beseech thee let me not live for myself alone. Enable me to be useful to all around me."

The following extracts show that Miss L. did not confine her views to herself, though she had many internal conflicts.

"8th.—This day has been appointed by the Governor for fasting, humiliation, and prayer. I have humbled myself before thee, Oh thou Most High. I abhor myself, for I am vile; my case, Oh blessed Father, is before thee. Thou knowest all my desires. Thou knowest every wish of my heart. I feel assured that thou wilt not cast me off, when I entreat thy favor. My sins rise like a cloud, but I will hope in thy mercy. Oh my soul, behold thy Saviour on the cross, dying for thy sins. See him rise from the dead, and ascend to heaven; calling upon thee to deny thyself, to take up thy cross and follow him. And how canst thou be inactive? How canst thou again grieve him by rebellion? Oh, dear Redeemer, forgive me. Give me not up to hardness of heart and to unbelief. Reprove me. Oh, humble me by afflictions if necessary, but sanctify them to me. Make me to feel thy chastening hand, if I otherwise shall not love and obey thee. For others I would also pray. Our country, O Lord, is in a deplorable state. Thou canst save it from destruction. Oh spare us in love. May we yet be a peaceful and a happy nation. Bless the poor the afflicted, the sick, and the destitute. Oh revive thy work in this part of the land. Cast not away from thee my dear, my beloved town. Thy judgments have been upon it in a peculiar but merited manner since this war; but, Oh God, let it still be spared.

"30.—Many times within a few of the last days I have exclaimed, 'thanks be to God who giveth us the victory, through our Lord Jesus Christ.' I adore him for his most wonderful works. Had he not appeared for me, I should most surely have perished in despair. Now I rejoice that not a secret thought is concealed from him, because I am convinced that, knowing my weakness, he will give me strength.

'In Him, not in an arm of flesh I trust,
'In Him whose promise never yet has failed,
'I place my confidence.'

"To-morrow is appointed for the communion. Oh my God, give me, I beseech thee, a believing, humble heart, and grant the blessing of thy presence in every soul which may partake of this feast.

"*May* 1.—This day I have enjoyed sensible communion with God. When first seated at the table, the belief that with all my selfishness I was numbered among the chosen of God, humbled me while it made me happy. The hope that I should meet around the throne of the Lamb all who were with me on this interesting occasion, and not these only, but absent friends, was balm to my wounded spirit; and though, but a few moments before, I was doubting my good estate, I could now rejoice in God my salvation, and wonder at his condescending love. I longed to have done with all sublunary things and be at rest.

"*June* 6.—Intelligence has reached us, that on the 31st of March the allied armies entered Paris. The nations of Europe are now at peace. Oh my God, give me a thankful heart, and grant the best of blessings to those who are so signally delivered from the horrors of war. May they learn war no more. May a similar blessing soon visit our unhappy country; and may the consequence be a humbling of every rebellious heart.

"*July* 23, *midnight*.—The past day has been one of apprehension, of trial. My dear aunt J—— is very low. In consequence of being called to attend her immediately after rising this morning, I omitted my morning devotions, and when reminded of my omission in the course of the day, I still deferred going to God, which caused my heart bitter sorrow.

"30.—Aunt J—— died between one and two o'clock. The preparation for her funeral devolved on me. I feel more as though a mother was to be interred than an aunt."

"*At New Haven*, *August* 10.—Last night Norwich was in great consternation. The alarm guns were fired, and an express arrived from New London, stating that the surrender of Stonington Fort was demanded. This news gave universal alarm. I however left home this morning for New Haven. At Colchester met many soldiers with sad countenances, repairing to their place of rendezvous. It was a painful sight. At New Haven found friends well, and received a cordial welcome."

The mind of Miss L. was early interested in the state of the heathen, as is shown by frequent references in her diary.

"21.—When I reflect on the multitudes of my fellow-creatures who are perishing for lack of vision, and that I am living at ease, without aiding in the promulgation of the Gospel, I am almost ready to wish myself a man, that I might spend my life with the poor heathen. But I check the thought, and would not alter one plan of Infinite wisdom. I could, however, cheerfully endure pain and hardship for them, and for my dear Redeemer. Has he not given his life for multitudes now perishing, as well as for my soul? And Oh, how basely ungrateful and selfish in me, to sit down quietly in the care of self, without making any exertion for their salvation. But what can I do? A weak, ignorant female. One thing only do I see. My prayers may be accepted. Yes, I will plead with my heavenly Father, that he may be a Father to the poor benighted heathen."

The following extract alludes to the lamented Rev. Dr. Payson:

"*Monday*, 22.—Spent this afternoon and evening at Mr. S.'s, with uncle and aunt L. Met Mr. and Mrs. Payson. If there ever was a good man on earth, Mr. Payson seems to me to be one. He appears truly humble, and much engaged in religion; and possesses much of the manner and countenance which I love to fancy belonged to St. Paul. In conversation this evening, he confirmed me in an opinion which I have sometimes ventured to express, that all ought immediately to repent, and that we should neither pray with a wicked heart, nor omit prayer; but pray with a holy heart."

A letter to a dear friend with whom she continued at times to correspond during her life, shows something of her early taste for polite literature. It should be remembered, that the remarks on the poetry of Lord Byron were made before his more exceptionable works were published.

"NEW-HAVEN, Sept. 2, 1814.

"Most welcome was a letter from my dear L. last week; and let me request you never to think that a letter from you can prove an intrusion, even though I be much occupied by a sick room. I am pleased to learn that you are 'enthusiastically fond of poetry.' In this we shall find a similarity in our characters. I have seen nothing *new*, but the 'Feast of the Poets,' that pleased me very much. Lord Byron's productions you have undoubtedly seen. Do you agree with me in admiring them very much? I was unwilling to be pleased with any thing that could proceed from a character like Lord Byron's; but found it impossible to read without being delighted with almost every page. At the same time, I found much to condemn. Unchristian sentiments, conveyed in such a garb of loveliness, have unquestionably a very pernicious tendency; and much as I admire these books, I would gladly hear that there is not one copy remaining on the earth. Scott must please every lover of the muses. Of his poems, the 'Lady of the Lake' is my favorite. A greater degree of sweetness and simplicity, I am sure, cannot be found in any work. And where is there a description more beautiful than he gives of Matilda in Rokeby? The poor old minstrel, too, interests my feelings very much. The lively pathos in the lines,

'Lives there a man with soul so dead,
'Who never to himself hath said,
'This is my own, my native land,'

like almost every thing I meet with concerning *home*, 'that dearest, sweetest spot,' I now recollect as one part which particularly interested me. *Cowper* and *Young* have always power to make me forget myself, and wholly absorbed in their delineation of the human character, especially where they contrast it with infinite purity. Of such writings I can never be weary. The more I read, the more excellent they appear. I like *Thompson* very much, and know not why I have read his 'Seasons' but little. For amusement only there is nothing that I would sooner read than *Shakspeare's* plays. His witches have always the power of bewitching me. Shall I go on to name the beauties of Campbell, Rogers, Goldsmith, Southey, Burns, &c. &c. No, I fear I have already made myself tedious to you. I cannot, however, fail to notice 'Cumberland's Retrospection,' which I think admirable, considering the advanced age of the writer.

"I do not envy any their situation or their enjoyments, but if such a passion should find place in my heart, the object of it would be the leisure and the inclination to read all valuable and interesting books. Inclination I have too much of for my peace, while the opportunity is beyond my reach.

"My friend, when fancying that some great enjoyments are withheld from us, are we not apt to forget the numberless unmerited blessings which we daily receive, or to view them as things of course, which God in justice confers upon us? Perhaps I ought not to judge of others by my own experience, but from some observation I infer that all of us are ungrateful for mercies enjoyed; and that we have always something unattained in view, which we fancy would promote our happiness. This is certainly the case with me. I am too much addicted to 'castle-building,' but it is not solely that I may increase my own *happiness*. I seek principally such changes as may promote my usefulness, and in these I should find my greatest happiness."

The following letter to her mother shows how early her thoughts were turned to a missionary life, though not of course with any definiteness of object. To appreciate her feelings, we must bear in mind that Foreign Missions were then but little known or thought of in this land; it being but four years after the organization of the earliest Foreign Missionary Society in this country.

"New Haven, Sept. 13, 1814.

"If the weather was good, I should probably be at this moment preparing myself to go and hear an oration, instead of writing to my dear mother. Were *every* privilege denied me, I might murmur; but how can I now, when I am permitted to converse a few moments with my best friends. Truly, I have cause only for rejoicing. Even when sorely oppressed with a sense of my depravity, and the feeling that there is no good thing in me, that all my thoughts and actions are sinful, I have reason to rejoice; for the Saviour of sinners has condescended to draw peculiarly near to me. My darkest hours are irradiated with the light of his countenance. I can hardly reconcile it to the justice of God, that so vile a being as I should be under such favorable circumstances. I am almost ready to ask, Why was Harriet Newell taken from life, and a creature of so little worth as I am, continued here? Am I reserved for similar usefulness? I will encourage such a hope. Think not by this that I desire to become the wife of a missionary. I desire to spend my life in the service of my Maker, and however inconsistent with such a wish much of my life may appear, it is my most ardent desire. Often my judgment leads me astray, and often do I wander through thoughtlessness, but I am most thoroughly convinced that no service is so delightful as that of my Saviour—that no privations, no toils, no sufferings, are too great for his chil dren to endure for his sake."

The following notice of an excursion to "Wadsworth's Mountain," a few miles west of Hartford, the summer residence of Daniel Wadsworth, Esq. (after whose sister our young friend was named,) is inserted to show her early love for the beauties of nature. The excursion was made while she was on a visit to some friends in the neighborhood.

"*September* 26th.—After riding about seven miles, we found ourselves ascending the mountain through a forest, not of lofty pine, and towering oak, but of low trees with thick foliage, which seemed impervious to the sun. No variety of objects attracted our attention for two miles, when suddenly we found ourselves near a farm-house. It was built of wood, and in the gothic style. From this we proceeded to the mansion of Mr. W——, which appeared the seat of elegance and repose. We were cordially welcomed by himself and lady. A few moments were allowed us to rest. After admiring the structure of the building, and the situation of the rooms, we sallied forth in quest of new scenes. The elderly portion of our party took the direct road to the *tower*, but the younger preferred a more circuitous route, so as to lose none of the beauties of the surrounding country. We proceeded to the top of a formidable hill. Below, as far as the eye could reach, was a varied landscape of meadows, fields, groves, hills, villages, and water prospects; it was the most enchanting scene I ever beheld; but my astonishment when I ascended the tower, none but those who have been in the same place can well conceive. On the north, Mount Holyoke and Mount Tom (near Northampton) were visible in the distance, while to the south-east the prospect was grand beyond the power of my feeble pen to describe. Hills, mountains, valleys, villages, towns, and the winding river, all seemed confusedly blended together, 'the fragments of a slumbering world.' At the south was Mount Carmel. The distant view for fifty miles on each side of us was truly sublime; but that directly at our feet excited my most enthusiastic admiration. There was a small lake, with a mountain at each extremity; the high tower on which we were standing being at the top of one, while the other, scarcely less lofty, was crowned with primitive forest. On one side of the lake there was a delightful grove, and on the other, the walks and cultivated grounds around Mr. W——'s romantic mansion. After spending some time on the tower, we descended and wound our way through groves and enchanting scenery to the lake. We were taken in a boat to the opposite mountain, ascended it, and then returned to our friends at the mansion, where we were prevailed on to stay to tea, and received other kind attentions."

It is evident from some succeeding passages, that Miss Lathrop *desired to be useful.* By marking her subsequent path, we shall learn *how* those desires were carried into effect. The society to which she next alludes, and which she was instrumental in forming, was established for the *Relief of Poor Women and Children.* Under date of October 5, 1814, she writes:

" This morning I made *eleven* calls on business for the Society. Some were on our poor pensioners. Returning home alone, I thought much on the degree of enjoyment of this class of people, compared with that of those who move in a different sphere. They appear to be much less favored than we are, but there is reason to believe that some among them are more sincere christians than many among us. God has chosen the weak things of the world to confound the things which are mighty. These people have different comforts from ours, often nothing more than a subsistence for themselves and family for the passing day, but they are happy in present gratification. Doubtless they have some trials of which we know nothing. We, too, find perplexities and troubles. Every heart knows its own bitterness, and a stranger intermeddleth not with its joys.

"*October* 6.—This afternoon I went to the society meeting. I found pleasure as usual in attempting to do good. Oh that I had a heart to improve every opportunity of usefulness to my fellow-creatures; but *self* too much engrosses my thoughts, my time, and my labor. For *self* I sigh and toil, often regardless of the suffering multitude, and more frequently neglectful of the few who are in my own family, and who might be benefited by my exertions.

"12.—This morning friend N. Charles and myself took a ride to Canterbury. The country would have appeared to me very fine a few weeks ago, but now I cannot view it without sad thoughts. The association of ideas leads me to think of my latter end, of my decay—not sudden, as from life to death—but a lingering decay of powers which constitute my chief source of enjoyment in life, and which, when I become old, will pass to second childishness. But that time may never arrive. I will not embitter my present joys by anticipations of my future helplessness."

The following was written on commencing the instruction of a voluntary *school for the education of poor children:*

"15.—I have been studying some parts of my character, and find more cause for humility than on a cursory view I could have believed. I pray that I may not rest day or night, until I am better versed in self-knowledge.

"I am about to commence a school. May God make my motives pure, and prosper the work I have begun. Alas! do I not attempt this task more for appearance, than for the love of immortal souls? This question, O my soul, is of the greatest importance. I can never expect the divine blessing on my sinful actions, or on apparently good actions proceeding from bad motives. 'Search me, O God, and know my heart, try me, and know my thoughts, and see if there be any wicked way in me, and lead me in the way everlasting.'

"I ardently desire to devote my life to the service of my Maker; to be constantly mindful of my responsibility; to feel that I must live for others, and not for myself. Yesterday I renewed my solemn dedication of myself to the Lord, promising with his assistance to devote my time, the faculties of my mind, the members of my body, my talents, and my influence over others—

all to the Maker and Giver of every power. O Heavenly Father, accept of me, and let me not again return to the vanities of life with the avid ity which I have done heretofore.

"*November* 12.—No day of my school-keeping has been more interesting than this. Oh, that all who think their charities must be limited to a certain few, and that institutions of this kind are productive of no good, would spend a few hours with these interesting little creatures, see their engagedness to excel in their various employ ments, and witness their progress from one month to another. Sure I am they could not retain all their selfishness."

Besides her efforts in the society and school formed for the benefit of the poor and suffering, she often ministered personally to their wants, especially in the care of *the sick*.

While thus sacrificing herself for the good of others, she was called into the furnace of affliction by tidings received from her beloved elder brother, then a member of the senior class of Yale College; but it was to her as the "refiner's fire."

"*Nov.* 18, 1814.—This afternoon letters from New Haven state that Charles is no better, and he wishes to have mamma with him. Accordingly she left us this evening to go in the stage, in a damp, dark night, and over bad roads; but the same God who has supported us hitherto, will not now forsake us. Verily he is a friend in affliction.

"25.—Painful intelligence has arrived from Charles. He is very low, and we have reason to apprehend that the next account will be of his departure from this world of sorrow. Oh my God, wilt thou sanctify him wholly, and make happy his dying hour.

"26.—The day has been one of severe trial. Never was I so anxious for the arrival of letters. I went to school in a state of suspense. There, however, a letter was handed me, stating that our dear Charles is rather better. Oh my God, fill my heart with gratitude for this favor, and grant its continuance for Christ's sake.

"30.—And must it be? Am I no more to see the fond object of my love? Oh my God, suffer me not to murmur. In all thy dealings thou art kind. And is my dear Charles first called to commence the 'travel of eternity?' Oh, grant us support, and the sanctification of these trials to us all."

The violent fever with which this promising youth had been attacked, raged till December 3, when he was called from his preparation for the ministry, to the rest above, at the age of twenty. The following extract indicates true resignation:

"*December* 6.—What can I render to the Lord for all his goodness? Most severely has he afflicted us, but I trust it is in love. My dear parents returned yesterday in much better health than I had reason to expect, and are now tolerably comfortable, and composed. Did I not feel resigned to this bereavement, their composure would surprise me. That Charles has made a happy exchange, I have not the least doubt. For him I rejoice, rather than mourn. Yes, Oh my God, if thou wouldst grant his restoration to this family, to this fond, lacerated heart, in answer to its requests, it would be silent. I feel that he is taken from the evil to come.———I have been called away to receive the condolence of a friend. These friends are very kind, they prove that they are indeed our friends; but my selfish heart would seek loneliness, and indulge its feelings apart. I would summon piety to my aid, if a merciful God would grant me grace, and then return to the duties of the family with fortitude; but now, the continual offers of sympathy but renew the anguish they are intended to allay."

The friends of Job better understood the nature of affliction, when "they sat down with him upon the ground seven days and seven nights, and none spake a word unto him, for they saw that his grief was very great."

We next find Miss Lathrop seeking to guide a beloved female associate, inquiring for the way of salvation.

"NORWICH, December 24, 1814.

"After a delightful visit from ——, I improve a few moments in acknowledging the pleasure which your letter afforded me. You say, '*Many and earnest* have been my prayers that I might have an interest in the redemption of Christ.' What, my dear M——, is required of us but *a willing mind?* Those who earnestly seek, have the promise of him who cannot err, that they shall obtain. Says our Saviour, 'Blessed are they who do hunger and thirst after righteousness, for they shall be filled.' 'Come unto me, all ye that labor and are heavy laden, and I will give you rest.' 'Ask and it shall be given you, seek and ye shall find.'

"But you may reply that 'the sacrifice of the wicked is an abomination to the Lord.' Can it be that those are the wicked ones here mentioned, in whom God has put *a desire after holiness?* When one feels willing to take up the cross and follow Christ through evil and through good report—willing to sacrifice her dearest earthly enjoyments if he will take a seat in her heart, I think it cannot be that her offerings are unacceptable to a God of mercy. May I not hope that such is the case with my friend? Then will I say, that though 'clouds and darkness' are now about you, it will be for a season only; for never did God say to us, 'Seek ye me in vain.' He is more ready to hear and bless us, than we to ask any good. But he requires of us a surrender of *the whole heart*—there must be no reserve—an entire approbation of all his dealings, and earnest desires that we may be enabled to conform to *them*, and not that they may be altered to suit our present gratification."

Again we find her resuming her charitable efforts, which it must be borne in mind, she was then pursuing almost *alone*. Tract distribution, which she employed with other means, was then in its very beginnings in this country.

"31.—I am almost discouraged with the little improvement which the children make in the school; but if by 'precept upon precept,' by prayer, or by any other means, I may be permitted to do good to *one* of them, it will reward all my endeavors. I felt to-day more than usually engaged in my duties. After school, called on Mrs. I——; found her not well and three of her children sick. She did most truly claim my sympathy. I gave her a tract, hoping for the blessing of God on her perusal of it.

"*January* 6, 1815.—I have this afternoon visited a poor sick negro woman, and derived more pleasure in contributing to her comfort, by reading in the Bible, than I could have found in the most splendid worldly entertainment. What can equal the pleasure of doing good ? Oh for a heart and the power to do good continually, to devote my whole life to the service of my Maker.

"27.—This day until three o'clock was spent in soliciting charity with my friend L., and in visiting the poor and sick. Could my days all pass thus, methinks 'the cares of this world, and the deceitfulness of riches' would not 'choke the word, and render it unfruitful.' O God, I pray thee enlarge my sphere of usefulness. Give me power and desire to do good continually. This evening I spent at the reading meeting. Returned home, not very well either in body or mind; but God is good. 'I will still praise Him, who is the health of my countenance and my God.'"

On hearing of the proclamation of peace with Great Britain, she writes:

"*February* 6.—This afternoon most glorious news has reached us. And may we indeed be permitted to enjoy the blessings attending the restoration of peace to our suffering country. To God be all the glory; O, eternity shall tell the gratitude and joy which fill my heart. May I never forget this day. May I never cease to praise the Lord for his goodness, and may not one soul be unmindful of the source from whence flows all good."

A letter to her friend in H——, shows that death was sometimes anticipated by her with desire.

"NORWICH, March 13th, 1815.

"I am told that Miss H. is in town, and will return to Hartford in a few days. I trust she will take a letter to Louisa. Your last was most welcome. What can I say that will give you half as much pleasure? You ask the character of that dear friend who has been taken from me. Can a sister describe him impartially? He was all that my fond heart wished him. He was dear to me by every tie which mutual affection and entire confidence could form while on earth. Now, my love to him is of a more exalted kind. Is the sweet belief that he is permited,

'With unseen ministry of angel power
'To watch the friends he loved,'

mere delusion? Be it so. I will cherish it as a precious solace. My friend, there are seasons of weakness when feeling triumphs over reason and religion. Such is the present one with me. I have been most forcibly reminded of my loss to-day in the death of Mr. W. Will you believe that, on first hearing the tolling of the bell, I com plained, 'Why am not I permitted to join these kindred souls, to add another to the trophies of redeeming love, and behold the unveiled glories of Immanuel?' Not often do I 'chide the lingering moments,' but there are times when my soul is distressed by this cumbrous load which chains it to earth, when it longs to fly away and be at rest. But I am ever quieted by the reflection that the appointments of Infinite Wisdom, though inscrutable, are always right. Every thing that is in the power of highly valued friends to confer upon me, 'to tempt my tarriance here below,' I am permitted to enjoy; and truly my life is pleasant. I have constant reason to be filled with gratitude for innumerable temporal blessings, and what is of greater value, a peace of mind 'which passeth all understanding.' Why then am I dissatisfied? I am not; but to be perfectly freed from sin, and to be arrayed in the spotless robe of Christ's righteousness, is a privilege so glorious, so transcendently superior to all the combined pleasures of earth, that I must languish for it. Were I not on every side so vulnerable, in all my duties so *imperfect*, I would cling more to life.

"What you say of *prayer* exactly meets my feelings. Most truly it is a glorious privilege; and when our petitions are not limited to ourselves, but we carry the case of every dear object to Him who knows their wants, and will be inquired of for the supply of them, we find it most consolatory. If any whom we love have never bent the knee or lifted the heart in supplication to their Maker, how sweet to plead for blessings on their heads! On the whole, were we disposed to appreciate our trials and blessings justly, we should find the latter much to exceed the former; and what though disappointment constitute a large proportion of our checkered lives, this is not our home. We are but journeying to a better country, where all tears shall be wiped from every eye."

Again the ardor of her soul is expressed in her closet:

"*March* 30.—Oh, my soul, shout for joy, tune thy harp to notes of praise, and live ever in the celebration of Jehovah's excellencies. For such sweet foretastes of eternal felicity I can never be enough thankful. Oh, sing aloud and tell of God's wondrous works to a sinful depraved descendant of the first transgressor. I could dwell ever on the mount, and thus find a heaven here below. Oh, my poor fellow-beings, how my heart yearns for your salvation. Why will you not hear and live? Blessed Saviour, pour out thy Holy

Spirit on all thy children this night. Grant that, with all the energies of our souls, we may supplicate thy favor for poor lost men. Oh, save by thy mighty power. Magnify thyself on the earth. Remember those on whom the glorious light of the Gospel has never shone. May *the heathen* sing of thy mighty works. Oh, my Saviour, come near I pray thee, and bless all souls as thou dost mine.

"*April* 9.—(Her birth-day.) Again does a revolving year find me in the land of the living. Sad vicissitudes have marked its course ; but consolation has so mingled with grief, that it has been one of the happiest years of my life. A year this day, two dear friends, now gone, were pilgrims here ; but though what are termed *real calamities* had not visited me, I was then laboring under most distressing conflicts. God be praised that they no longer destroy my peace ; but I feel liable to something similar. Yes, my weak soul, thou art less than nothing to accomplish thy purposes. I must trust implicitly in God, for he only can make me holy.

"I have commenced this interesting period with a resolution that I will set apart *a season of the last evening of each week to pray for the outpouring of the Spirit in this town.* Have proposed the plan to several friends, who approve and will follow it. Thus may the consciousness that friends are asking the same favor with ourselves, at the same time, animate and warm our hearts. Oh, heavenly Father, condescend, I beseech thee, to be glorified through us unworthy creatures. Hear the feeble voice of our supplications, and grant us more than we can ask or think. May this year be wholly dedicated to thee. If my life be continued, enable me to realize constantly that the vows of God are upon me.

"*May* 11.—I have made a visit to Mrs. K——, who was with my dear departed brother in his last moments. It has revived many painful recol lections.

> 'And is he gone? how oft on sudden solitude
> 'That fearful question will intrude.'

Why am I so selfish? True, I am afflicted, but God is now magnifying himself on the earth. For this let me rejoice, and forget my sufferings in the happiness of others. Gracious Saviour, continue thy glorious work, and let no false zeal, no semblance of christianity where it does not exist, mar the beauty of thy cause. Move our hearts to pray continually, with increased faith, for the prosperity of Zion.

"*Monday* 15.—This afternoon accompanied my grandmother Lathrop to visit aunt P——. She is going down to the grave as a shock of corn fully ripe. I have enjoyed the visit greatly. Returned home alone at twilight in a most peaceful, happy frame, thinking thus: Why am I not one of the happiest creatures in existence? Would I exchange situations with the rich and great? Oh no, they may envy my joy. Why is it, Oh my God, that I, so weak, so frail, so altogether depraved and vile in the view of a holy God, am thus distinguished?

"*July* 30.—I again tried to-day, as repeatedly before, to establish *a female prayer-meeting*, but was unsuccessful—from an unexpected source was disappointed. I beseech thee, O Lord, open to me some other door of usefulness. I feel that I could do any thing, frail and imperfect as I am, that would lead sinners to repent. Oh Lord, graciously be pleased to hear the feeble voice of my supplications, and make me an humble instrument in thy hands of good to the souls of men

"31.—Gave a Tract to a poor woman, who, on reading the title, 'Sin and Danger of Neglecting the Saviour,' burst into tears; and, as soon as she could speak, said, 'I see this every day.' She attempted to thank me, but could not. Oh that I may be made the means of good to her soul. She must soon go down to the grave. Save her, Oh God, from endless wo."

The following note to the estimable female friend whom she addressed December 14, gives intimation that the Lord was raising up a coadjutor in her labors of love, while the two succeeding paragraphs, under a later date, intimate that she was not backward to summon to effort any available energies.

"Believe me it is not idle curiosity which makes me long to know if you have not determined that, let others do as they will, *you will serve the Lord* even in the ways of his appointment. Although your letter to L—— expressed no expectation that you should accompany the young ladies in commemorating the death of Christ, it increased my hope that you would soon follow their example. I believe you are sensible that it is a great *privilege* as well as *duty*."

"August, 1815.

"You are among us a *new heir* of glory. Do not, I beseech you, when comparing yourself with those around you, rest satisfied with attaining a degree of sanctification equal to us. *The word of God* must be the only correct standard of faith and practice. I think it is unprofitable to compare our frame of mind with that of other christians; the witness must be in ourselves if we are the children of God."

"It has been proposed that all those professing

christians in N—— who feel the importance of having a shaking among these dry bones, should, if possible, be engaged in prayer for this object at 12 o'clock each day. The idea that many voices are at the same time mingling upon the altar of God, we trust will give animation to holy desires, and fervency to divine love; and, my friend, is there any thing to which *our hands, our voices, and our hearts* should not be devoted that promises any benefit to immortal souls?

"Poor —— is very sick. This dear sister needs your prayers very much, that her faith fail not. She is more severely tried than any can conceive who do not daily witness her sufferings. I need your prayers, that in all God's dispensations I may subscribe a hearty *amen*, be fitted for his service, and be made faithful in it."

We now accompany Miss L—— on an excursion made chiefly for the benefit of her health, in company with her mother.

"WOODSWORTH'S, MANSFIELD.

"*October* 17.—I leave the conversation of my mother and friends to recall the occurrences of the day. Nothing worth recording occurred in our ride from Norwich to this place. Here we now are, after a comfortable repast, seated around the fire-side of a brother, in the best of bonds, as by his conversation I venture to believe and feel. Truly, christianity is lovely, whatever may be its outward garb. Oh that we could find it at every step.

"There is some prospect of rain to-morrow. May we say with the good Shepherd, 'It will be such weather as pleases me.' Although I am surrounded with the beauties of nature, my thoughts have wandered to the dear home which we have left; but I am weak. Assist me, Oh my God. I pray for strength of mind to resist every emotion which is incompatible with supreme love to thee. May I seek to glorify thee in every thing, and live only to serve thee.

"SPRINGFIELD.

"18.—We left Mansfield this morning at eight o'clock, and after a cheerful ride through forests of pine, &c. we proceeded on a good road to Coventry, Ellington, Enfield, and Springfield. Again have we been most kindly sustained by a good Providence, and permitted to welcome the 'evening shades' in circumstances of much comfort. Oh that we may render unceasing thanks for such manifestations of love.

"NORTHAMPTON.

"19.—Here we arrived at sunset, after a ride of twenty-five miles. Our course was sometimes on the banks of the Connecticut, sometimes on the sides of the mountains, and at others between lofty *cliffs*, with ranges of mountains before us, covered with thick foliage, in the inexpressibly rich garb of the season; the river being on the right hand, and the variegated forests on the left. The scene was delightful, and in some places even magnificent beyond description."

The journey was continued through Pittsfield to Canaan, N. York. The closing record of it is,

"28.—Last evening, through the goodness of God, I was permitted to return to my beloved home, after a most delightful journey; and found friends here in good health. Although unattended, we have met with nothing to disturb us, but every thing has been pleasant. Oh that I were more grateful, more wholly devoted to Him, whose I have resolved to be in all things, and at all times."

The following is an illustration of her careful notice of the *anniversary* of days on which events of especial interest to herself and friends occurred:

"NORWICH, December 4, 1815.

"MY DEAR M——, This is to me a most solemn and interesting season—one year yesterday since my dear brother entered on the scenes of eternity. Last evening I spent with *three* of his *class-mates*, and for a moment could hardly check the rising murmur, Why is it thus? But immediately rejoiced that he is happily removed from this *wilderness of wo.* It is easier *to say* that we are resigned to the dispensations of Providence, than *at all times to feel* perfectly so. Time has mellowed the poignancy of my grief; but it has not lessened the estimation of my loss; or made me *feel* less keenly at times, that *I am left* 'to linger longer here and grieve'—while *my friend* is enjoying the glories of Immanuel."

In March, 1816, Miss Lathrop made a visit of some weeks to friends in *the city of New-York*, and the subjects which engrossed her mind and heart, the impulses she obtained in the spiritual life, and the practical use she made of them, especially in the organization of the *Sabbath-school* in the place of her nativity, beautifully exemplify the maturity and excellence of her christian character.

After describing the adventures of a voyage of two or three days by sloop; "the majesty and benevolence of God" displayed in the *sun rising* from the bosom of the ocean—"Tracts having employed her fellow-passengers at evening until about nine o'clock, when singing was proposed and all retired to rest,"—and having received the kind hospitalities of valued friends, we find her, the next day after her arrival, addressing the following letter to a beloved female associate, on the subject of *publicly professing her faith in Christ*:

TO MISS M—— H—— H——.

"New-York, 14th March, 1816.

"Dear M——, Your letter has been much on my mind, but it has not been in my power to give you a reply until the present time.

"You know that 'christians have doubts and fears,' but imagine that 'they are never powerful enough to eclipse their former views.' I believe, my friend, that christians in darkness often question whether there has ever been vital piety in their hearts—whether they have not fancied themselves to be something when they were nothing, and thus deceived their own souls.

"Again you say that you 'do not "grow in grace," are not enjoying the light of God's countenance, and running with alacrity and zeal in the path of holiness.' Let me ask you, my friend, if God has given you no more humbling views of yourself—no more sense of sin—and no clearer view of the infinite condescension of the blessed Jesus, and your obligations to devote all your time and faculties to his service? If this be the case, let me entreat you to *watch* and *pray*. If, on the contrary, by a more intimate acquaintance with your heart you find in it more depravity than you expected, and that it has more need of a Saviour, do not question his power or mercy to fulfil all his promises to those who ask of him the supply of their wants.

"You appear to believe that I cannot invite 'such a sinner' to the communion table. Were you *holy*, most assuredly I would not; but the Scriptures invite *sinners* to come to the Gospel feast. *There* is food for the hungry—refreshing grace for the weary and heavy laden. Can our christian graces be increased, while we avoid the use of those means which are expressly designated by the Most High as necessary to our advancement in the divine life?

"The inconsistencies of professing christians ought not to discourage you from obeying the command of Christ, if you are indeed one of the happy number to whom he has said, 'Do this in remembrance of me.' If God is *your* God—your supreme object of regard—while walking in the way of his appointment you may be sure of his assistance and support. With this portion, we should not fear, though all the earth should encamp against us. We know that all 'principalities and powers' cannot pluck God's dear children out of his hands, or separate them from his constant care, without which the best saint on earth will not be a consistent christian.

"I am sensible that it is *a great thing* to be a christian, and would not for the world influence you to take a step which would endanger your soul's best interest; but I would, if I have any influence, use it in exhorting you not to delay *a thorough knowledge of yourself and the faithful discharge of every duty*. It is in the path of duty that we may expect a blessing—out of it we have no right to rely on the mercy of Jehovah.

"I will not say, forgive my freedom—you encouraged me to do thus. To the goodness of God I commend you, with fervent prayer that you may be faithful; that you may devote your time, your talents, and all that you possess, to Him who claims them as your reasonable service.

"My friend, our time is short, we have much to do. Shall we who have hopefully obtained an interest in Christ rest satisfied with our present attainments, and indifferent about the welfare of precious souls around us? Oh no, let us separate ourselves from the multitude who live to do evil; and by a consistent walk in our profession of faith, manifest to all around us that we are christians in truth—thus being humble instruments of good. To this end let us pray for each other, as sisters meeting with the same temptations, subject to the same infirmities, and in constant need of the same *renewing grace.*

"I wish there may be *a praying society* in Norwich. L—— has the constitution which I wrote—not such as I could wish, but as well as I could do. Use your influence to effect the object, and I am sure you will never regret it."

In another note to the same, she says:

"You lament that your duties are so *imperfectly* performed. Alas, such may too truly be the language of all who have not stepped beyond the confines of earth. The *best* of mankind are 'unprofitable servants;' and I believe those who know their own hearts, will find in them so much rebellion and all kinds of depravity, that the subject of their greatest astonishment will be that such inconsistent creatures are permitted to have a place with the sons and daughters of the Most High.

"We must not then put off the performance of *duties* until we can perform them with *perfect love;* but if the Holy Spirit, witnessing with our spirits, declares our souls are regenerated, I think we may, in dependance on divine aid—not in the least on our own strength—go to the communion table, and sitting at the feet of Jesus, be transported even to the gate of heaven. Come then, my friend, not because you are strong and rich in faith, and zealous unto every good work; but *because you are weak*, and have nothing in yourself. Come, with *humble confidence* that he who bids you come, will not send you away without rich supplies of heavenly food. That you may be guided in this important step by the good Spirit of our God, prays your friend HARRIET."

TO HER PARENTS.

"NEW-YORK, March 28, 1816.

"You will rejoice to hear that N— F— has within two days obtained that confidence in God which she thought would *never* be her happiness—her tongue seems loosed, ready to declare what great things the Lord has done for her soul. She attends Dr. Romeyn's church, and considers his catechetical lecture yesterday as one great means of opening her eyes. These lectures have been greatly blessed.

"Rev. Mr. Spring and Rev. Mr. Whelpley have similar lectures; and Mr. Spring says, the commencement of the revival in his church was at one of these lectures. There is now a great number of his congregation who are very serious, about sixty of whom have obtained hope, and are expecting to unite with the church.

"The present state of religion in this city is very animating. In several places where we have heard of revivals, their commencement has been apparently traced to *prayer-meetings, and days of fasting*, appointed on account of the declension of religion.

"It has been said to me that there is unusual attention to religion in *Norwich*. Can this be true, and my friends not tell me of it? If indeed the good Spirit is passing among you, my dear friends, do not suffer him to depart. Whether it be true or not, do wrestle at the throne of grace for a blessing. Brother D——, I am not willing you should leave Norwich just at this time. Why may not you, or papa, call on Dr. S——, and pro pose a prayer-meeting for the members of the church on account of the declining state of religion; or if it may be so, on account of the *dawning* of a brighter day. *United prayer* is the means which God has more frequently been pleased to bless than any other. Do let me hear that you have met to pray; and on the same evening let me suggest that it would be desirable to request the prayers of friends at a distance from you. I find it has been apparently of great influence here and elsewhere.

"My dear *sisters*, why may not your Saturday evening exercises be repeated during the week? You may set apart days or hours of prayer among a few individuals. Oh that you may cast off restraint; let your tongues be loosed, and glory in the cross of Christ. This is a peculiarly privileged day. Now you may be strengthened and encouraged by the prayers of christians in other places; for I believe that many bear Norwich on their hearts at the throne of grace. I will insure to you many prayers in this city, if I may know a certain day, or evening, on which christians are thus engaged in supplicating the blessing of heaven. Do not delay, but write me immediately on this subject."

"*Saturday evening.*—O my dear sisters, how gladly would I make one with you to-night. I have thought much of you; that your hearts have been quickened by the good Spirit of God, that your prayers have ascended in faith, and have met with gracious acceptance. Would that we were wholly devoted. Do we 'seek *first* the kingdom of God,' for ourselves and others; or do we give to the world far the greater portion of our time and talents—leaving little for Him who hath redeemed us by his own most precious blood? Should we not tremble for our acquittal at the judgment bar, when so unfaithful in this life? Let not this consideration harden our hearts still more, but induce us to arise and shine in the glory of God."

TO HER MOTHER.

NEW-YORK, Sunday evening, March 15.

"DEAR MOTHER,—This has been a most blessed day. In the morning I attended Dr. Mason's church. It was their communion. I felt that my soul needed something to rouse and reprove. Rev. Mr. L—— preached on the subject of saying 'Peace, peace, when there is no peace.' He seemed a preacher sent from heaven. I was more refreshed, and I humbly hope, more benefited, than by any preaching I have heard.

"*Wednesday.*—I had never seen Mr. ELISHA COIT, and being introduced yesterday afternoon, he asked if I had ever before visited the city—then, instead of the usual question, 'How are you pleased with it?' he asked how I had been affected by the religious privileges I had enjoyed. This is quite like the man, and will give an idea what was the subject of our conversation, and that I feasted upon a few moments' familiar christian communion.

"*Thursday evening.*—This evening I was at Mr. Spring's session-room—had a most interesting meeting. I never saw an audience apparently so much affected. The good work continues in this church; new cases of seriousness are daily occurring."

Having mentioned her hope of deriving much benefit from the memoir of *Mrs. Isabella Graham*, and entreated her parents and friends not to despond as to the advancement of the work of God in Norwich, she gives an account of a meeting of the *Sunday-school Society*, which she had attended; mentions several examples of conversion reported; and states that 2,194 female children were under the care of the managers. "It is a most pleasing sight," she adds, "to see a hundred or more children coming into each church on the Sabbath with their teachers—most of them being those who have usually spent the holy day in the streets, if not in flagrant immoralities."

Having returned to her native town, she soon resolved on attempting *what she could;* and with the aid principally of a dear relative and friend, (now Mrs. P——, of New-York,) encountering discouragements and obstacles from the prejudices even of good people, now difficult to be understood, succeeded in forming *the first Sabbath-school* in Norwich. After going from house to house, pleading with children and their parents, they commenced their instructions with the number of *seven* scholars; and, as she at a later date familiarly wrote, "though the doors of the school-house were once barred against us, the number of pupils increased, and with them our interest and our hopes—the final result being no less auspicious for a few difficulties at the outset."

Early in June, she also writes to a beloved uncle, "Oh that I could give you joy by announcing a *general revival* here. We will, however, rejoice that a little number are about to "name themselves by the name of Israel." *Five young ladies*, and one lad aged sixteen, were yesterday propounded for admission to our church. Four of them are recent subjects of divine grace. If the angels in heaven rejoice over one repenting sinner, surely that six are hopefully added to the kingdom of our God, is ground for abundant thanksgiving and praise. Grandma Lathrop says she has never known so many attend religious meetings in Norwich, as at the present time. These appearances are favorable: could I see *christians* alive to the subject of religion, I would say they portend great blessings."

CHAPTER II.

Consecration to the Missionary Work.

Examination of duty as to missions—opposition of friends—grounds of her decision—joy in consecrating herself—private meditations on the subject—short residence at Litchfield, Conn.—letters—Dr. Griffin—visit at New Haven—Mr. Cornelius—Dr. Worcester—benevolent endeavors—efforts for the spiritual benefit of individuals—ordination of Mr. Winslow—designation to Ceylon—marriage—visit to Andover and Vermont—farewell notes—embarkation.

The question of her personally engaging in a mission to the Heathen was now brought before the mind of Miss L——, and received, as it claimed, her most serious and prayerful consideration.

It is to be feared that, for want of such careful examination and prayer, some enter the path into which she was at length directed—no longer new and untrodden by American females—without sufficiently considering whither it leads, or the spirit of self-denial which it requires. They go out, cheered perhaps by the smiles of friends, and encouraged by the approbation of all the churches, without reflecting that soon, amidst a people of strange speech, they will see these smiles only in remembrance, and hear the voice of encouragement only in dying whispers across the ocean; and that then, nothing but a thorough conviction of being in the path of duty, nothing but the approving smile of heaven can keep them from despondency.

It is time that the *romance* of missions was done away. It has been of use, perhaps, in exciting attention to the subject; but no attraction from its novelty, no impulse from its moral dignity, will bear up and carry forward any one, amidst long-continued labors of almost uniform sameness, which, though dignified as to their object, and their connection with the conversion of the world, are yet, in nearly all their details, most humble and forbidding. A young lady, who in this country may stand, perhaps, at the head of a large seminary, and take the lead in many benevolent operations, should either chasten her imagination, or invigorate her principles, before she goes forth to teach a few heathen children, or to exert an uncertain, it may be an unacknowledged influence over a handful of degraded and dark-minded female idolaters. By not doing this, some have unexpectedly found the sphere of their usefulness apparently contracted, rather than enlarged, by the sacrifices they have made; and in want of the excitement occasioned by the presence and the encouragement of fellow-christians, have been in danger of sinking into hopeless inactivity.

There are encouragements enough to any sacrifice—if what is done for Him who bought us with his own blood can be called a sacrifice—but, it must be from *principle*, and not mere *impulse*. Mere excitement will not answer. The mind must be kept *steady;* and there must be a willingness to take the more humble part of breaking up the fallow ground and casting in the seed, instead of gathering in the harvest, as well as some clear-sightedness of faith, to see in small beginnings germs of great and long increasing good. An ardent love for souls, and a deep sense of the constraining love of Christ, will support even a delicate female under any privation, and enable her to "rejoice in tribulation also."

TO HER MOTHER.

"Sometimes I feel an absolute necessity for determining whether I can leave all that my heart holds most dear on earth, and encounter the toils and hardships of a missionary life; but again I realize my insufficiency to decide a question of such importance. Indeed, I would not decide for myself. I cannot. I must trust solely to Him who has promised grace and strength. When I ask myself if I can endure a separation from such friends as mine, my answer is uniformly, 'We must be separated in a few days, and can I refuse to suffer a little for Him who has redeemed my soul by the sacrifice of Himself?' Oh, dear mother, I need your prayers."

TO A FRIEND.

"My heart is full this evening. Have heard a little too much this afternoon about my desire to be useful in the world,—and the first duties being in my own country. Were it proper that I should follow altogether the opinion of friends, in a case of this importance, I would thank them for counsel; but my own conviction of duty must determine me.

"A letter from cousin F. to-night, asks what I am about, and what are my feelings, and what my plans, and says, that although she 'cannot go all along with them, she shall view them impartially.' I should be glad if those whose approbation I value would permit me to rest on this subject; but friends in N. L. seem to have received an impression that I am going on a mission, and I fear, will never give their consent. But should that deter me? With the smiles of my heavenly Father, I must be happy though friends forsake me. Oh that I may justly estimate the blessings I have, and leave the rest to God."

TO THE SAME.

"On Tuesday I visited E. for the last time. She seemed hardly to be this side of eternity; and, although expressing a desire to die, manifested not the least evidence of love to God. I have rarely witnessed any thing which affected me so much. Her appearance was uncommonly interesting. I spoke to her, with a desire to ascertain on what she grounded her hopes of happiness after death; but to no purpose. On leaving her, I engaged to sit up the next night, but Providence ordered otherwise. My mind was filled with intense anxiety, and even horror, in view of her spiritual state for the following twenty-four hours. I may be asked how then I can think of witnessing multitudes of precious souls perishing together, without the least hope of their salvation. It would excite anxiety in me, if I did not consider the peculiar circumstances which attended this case, and that, probably, I may never again witness one so calculated to overwhelm the mind. Often do I exclaim, Oh for more faith, more fervent love. I feel more and more, that few are so culpable as myself. Duties stand thick around me, I see them at every step, and, Oh, how neglected!

"*Evening.*—Have just returned from a prayer-meeting. I find myself more interested in prayers, which make particular mention of *the poor heathen*, than others; and especially those which refer to the missionaries who have gone, and are yet to go. I feel a growing interest in this part of the human family. I sometimes indulge the belief that God is bringing me nearer to Himself, and that he keeps me more and more in dependence on his grace for every blessing of each day and hour."

In reference to the opposition of friends to the missionary undertaking, mentioned in some of the above and of the following letters, it should be remembered that the subject was then new; and in justice to these friends it should also be stated, that they afterwards, almost without exception, became favorable to the cause, and most of them its warm supporters. The difficulties in the way of forming the little societies, which are noticed, seem now quite unaccountable.

"June 5, 1816.

"I yesterday sent Messrs. Hall and Newell's letters to cousin F. whom you know I esteem as one of my very first friends, with a particular request that she would give me her opinion respecting them. She returned them the same day, accompanied by a letter, but said not one word about them. She merely touched upon the subject, by saying 'she could have no influence with me, and would not if she could, but would have me view *facts* with *coolness.*' I find myself censured, pitied, and condemned. Eliza C. I miss very much. Her heart is ever open, sincere, affectionate; and if my judgment seemed altogether erroneous, she would still feel for me and manifest herself my friend. L. not only approves, but I think would go with me with all her heart.

"You will rejoice to hear, that after this length of time, a few of us females have concluded to meet at Mrs. H.'s, next Monday afternoon, for prayer; and intend to continue to meet once in two weeks. It will not be a general thing, because very few are willing to make the sacrifice of feeling which is necessary. We are not, however, satisfied with doing no more to bring the church together, and have resolved on making an attempt to form a society of females, one object of which shall be to promote christian acquaintance. They will meet once in two weeks, and spend the afternoon together in some kind of work, making articles which may meet a ready sale, and appropriate the money to some benevolent object; perhaps to the education of heathen youth. A number seem already quite interested in the plan. We design not to give it much publicity, as societies of every kind encounter opposition.

"How shall I tell you how happy I have been to-day Seven of us met at M. H.'s this afternoon. We were enough in number to claim the promise, and I trust did so. We felt like sisters, and separated with the persuasion that it was good to be there. We have determined to meet once in two weeks, also every Saturday afternoon previous to the communion, and to have four days of fasting in course of the year. Next Monday we are to meet at Miss T.'s, to make gloves, &c. My plans being so fully realized, I know not how to be sufficiently grateful. We have made a little calculation by which it seems easy to raise $30. Do not fail to pray for us."

"July 17th, 1816.

"The volumes and Tracts were duly received. Those respecting missions I shall read with great interest. I know of no little book which you could have made so acceptable to me as Mrs. Rowe's exercises.

"You would have been pleased to see father engaged, one forenoon, in reading some of *Horne's Letters* to mother. They both seem much interested in them. Mother says I must tell you that the note respecting missionaries being married was written by some Andover student, who wanted to take a wife with him, but feared Mr. Horne might discourage her. Father says, 'You see, Harriet, what is Mr. H.'s decided opinion.' 'Yes, sir; but I see, too, what missionaries, better qualified to judge, say.' 'Ah, I have nothing to do with notes.' He often tells me that I shall, or shall not, want such and such things, when I have an ox to ride on; all in a manner which implies that he does not think seriously of my ever leaving this country.

"This week I have felt the magnitude of the object before me more than ever. It is the constant burden of my thoughts, and my prayers by day and by night."

"Norwich, (Sabbath evening,) 21st July, 1816.

"How gladly would I make you a sharer of my enjoyments this day. My scholars were never more interesting, and the woman of color has given satisfactory evidence that she has passed from death unto life. We have remarked her progress from Sabbath to Sabbath; but this morning she came evidently in a different frame of feeling, and has indeed cheered our hearts with a recital of what God has done for her soul. Is not this ample compensation for all the difficulties we have encountered in establishing this school. Oh that she may be one of *many*, who shall bless God for bringing them into it.

"I must mention one of my class, as having given me much pleasure. She is eight years old—was *very ignorant* of religious things when she came to my Saturday school, but improved considerably there. She has been, from the commencement of the Sunday-school, very attentive Last Sabbath I proposed to the children to have each one read twelve verses in the Testament every day with much attention, and remember something of what they read to tell me when they came to school. Among others, this girl complied with my request. She came this morning, and showed me *the whole of Matthew and fourteen chapters of Mark.* I questioned her from various parts of both, and she answered without hesitation to almost every question; such as concerning the birth of our Saviour, the miracles wrought by him, his transfiguration, death, &c. We now count about *forty-seven* children in the school.

"*Monday evening.*—After meeting with our praying circle to-day, you will suppose that I had no inclination to meet a large party this evening. I was unwilling to go, but mother said she would hardly ever request me to visit for her again. She had a particular reason for wishing me to go now. Of course I went; how insipid was every thing there. Nothing of consequence was said on the subject of religion, though a minister was of the company. The world has less and less charms for me. I wish to make religion the business of my life, and have nothing to do with the pomp of the world."

To her correspondent in Hartford she writes as follows:

"NORWICH, July 22d, 1816.

"I long to see you—never so much before. You speak of visiting me at *my own house.* Ah, my dear girl, do not wait for that period. It may never arrive; certainly not for years to come; and then perhaps it will be where your feet cannot tread. A candidate for the ministry who has given himself to the Lord, saying, 'here am I, send me where thou wilt,' must wait the direction of Providence. The last and most emphatic command of our Saviour after his resurrection was, 'Go ye into all the world and preach the Gospel to every creature;' a command evidently extending to all his disciples, to the end of time, but which has been much neglected. Our own country, it is true, is in many parts in a state of darkness; but all men are brethren. We may extend our views to other countries, where still greater numbers have never heard of a Saviour.

"My ears are often assailed by reports that I am going on a mission to the East or West; but I do not encourage them. There will be time hereafter to suffer much from the world, and something from *dear friends*, who I know would strongly oppose me. You will believe that my mind and heart are completely full. Indeed, it would be too much for me to sustain, were I not assured that if God has a work for me to do, with one of the dear messengers of the cross, he will support me and qualify me for it. I dare not think or act for myself. God has not yet thrown light upon my path. I wait for his good pleasure."

The following letter is to a sister of the Rev. Samuel Nott, Jun. who was a member of the mission at Bombay, and returned on account of ill health:

"NORWICH, August 19, 1816.

"MY DEAR DEBORAH,—How gladly would I fly to you and your happy family this evening, to congratulate you on the arrival of your friends. I have been with you in imagination, almost every minute since the news reached me. I have looked forward to their return with peculiar interest. To hear them recount their toils, and the goodness of God towards them, will I trust prove useful to me. I know not how I could endure a life of self-denial and of hardship; but in some favored moments I am enabled to consider every thing under the sun as vanity which has not a tendency to promote the cause of Christ; and often say, 'could I serve God without sin, I would esteem the longest life too short to suffer for Him, who has ransomed my soul by the most ignominious suffering and death.' If we are dissatisfied with God's requirements to take up our cross daily and follow him, and long too much for the termination of our pilgrimage, that we 'may undress and be with God,' are we suitably affected with the reflection, that our Saviour left the realms of bliss for more than thirty years, and condescended to suffer for us infinitely more than we can suffer for him? Surely such love demands a life of praise. But, I did not mean to intrude such reflections upon you at this time—when I began, I thought of you more than of myself; and my heart was too full to suffer me to sleep until I had attempted to express my feelings.

"*Tuesday morning.*—My dear friend, I do not find the ardor of my feelings in the least abated since last night. When you are reminded that I indulge the expectation of being more decided on the subject of the mission to India, by the assistance of your sister, my impatience to see her will not surprise you. Our little interview at your house has often recurred to mind. It will ever be remembered with thankfulness. Very few of my friends enter into my feelings on this great subject, or even tolerate them. When one does, I seem to consider it a particular indulgence. I said something about avoiding the subject with my dear mother. Since my visit at your house, she has rejoiced my heart, by voluntarily expressing her entire resignation and willingness that God should dispose of me in his own way. I now enjoy free communication with her, and find her uniformly calm and even cheerful. Let me beg your prayers, dear Deborah, that my motives may be simple and my eye single to the glory of God. The magnitude of the subject seems daily to increase. Within two weeks I have felt it more than ever, and nothing do I dread so much as that God should leave me to think or act for myself. I have cast myself upon an arm of love, and earnestly desire to have no will but that of my Saviour. Never did I so much need the prayers of christians, never distrust my own judgment so much."

"NORWICH, October 28, 1816.

"MY DEAR FRIEND,—I have put off writing as long as I could, in the hope of being more decided on the subject of missions. But now I know not what to say. You will perhaps think that I have had time enough to determine respecting my feelings and duty. Although the subject has been much on my mind for months, more perhaps than any other, I have never thought there was a necessity for *immediate* decision, until about six weeks since, when it appeared to me important to ascertain what were *my* feelings and opinions before knowing yours, lest I should be too much influenced by you. From that time I have more earnestly engaged in the work of self-examination. I have indeed 'been tried,' but on the whole thought, just before the arrival of your letter, that I was quite ready to hear your decision, and my duty would be plain. It is, however, far otherwise; I am much in the dark, and cannot feel established. When I shall, I know not; but hope it may be soon. This state of suspense is very trying. It is impossible to tell you what I have felt, and what I still feel and think.

"The great objections which appear to my going to the East, are the opinion of my parents, and my own health. Mother has made repeated attempts to write a few lines to you, but is immediately overcome by the subject, and cannot effect it. I have promised to tell you whatever she wishes to say. Her first concern, I believe, is for my health—she thinks that I cannot endure the preparation. Then the field at home is so extensive in which you might do *so much good.* Still she would not dare to influence you if she could. I said, 'If I go, it must be with the entire approbation of my parents.' Her reply was, that, viewing my health as she does, she cannot now see it to be my duty; but I might, if I thought best, attempt to prepare myself.

"At times my own judgment discourages the hope that I can ever be extensively useful. My heart may, by divine assistance, be qualified to feel, but my mind will, I am afraid, continue barren and unfruitful. This would not make me what you need. You cannot wish me to be the *companion* of your toils, without having it in my power to afford you assistance. It cannot be your *duty*, and certainly not your *interest*, to connect yourself with such an one. Nor can I, with any hope of happiness, put it in your power to do so. I do, however, sometimes think that as nothing great can be effected without encountering many difficulties, I ought not to be discouraged on account of health until I have made a trial, unless the judgment of my parents should oppose it. I have confidence that my mother would be supported by divine grace, if I were called to leave her; but she would still suffer much. I need not tell you that few mothers have such solicitude and affection for their children. I believe that I am willing to meet any suffering where self only is affected, but it is hard to wound *such a friend*. You will find that I am indeed undecided, and I know of no new view of the subject that I can take to bring me to a decision. God must be my helper. 'I can only give myself to him.'

"You requested an unreserved expression of my views on the subject. I suppose that this is right, but was at first inclined to regret the necessity of communicating them. I ought to wish not to influence you. It has been my constant endeavor not to do so; but mamma and you have now convinced me that whatever has any bearing upon the great subject should be taken into consideration."

TO A FEMALE ASSOCIATE.

"NORWICH, Nov. 4, 1816, midnight.

"To E—— methinks I could open my heart. Denied that privilege by the distance which separates us, I breathe out my full soul *alone*. And shall I complain? My Saviour endured his Father's wrath, and trod the wine-press alone. But I am not alone—my God seeth me, and truly he is my only refuge. Though clouds and darkness are still round about him, yet I am enabled to trust that he has not utterly forsaken me. You will perhaps say, that, as praying breath is never spent in vain, I cannot have been faithful or I should before this have discerned the path of duty—help me then, my dear girl. I know that I have done nothing well, that my purest offerings need the cleansing blood of Jesus; nevertheless, if there be *any thing* of sincerity in me, I do say from the heart, 'Here is thy servant, Lord, do with her what thou wilt.' Yet behold me, on the one hand, with an ardent desire to devote my whole life to the service of Him who has done so much for me, and an opportunity before me of being extensively useful; and on the other, the opinion and advice of dear friends urging me to be convinced that duty calls me to remain here, and more than this, the tear of maternal solicitude and affection stealing unbidden to the eye—and can you not conceive that my heart bleeds? Oh your prayers! They may avail much. I derive strength thus to urge you by the consideration that you are interested in the great cause, and would not have a brother or sister dishonor it.

"Very few friends speak a word of encouragement. On the contrary, the hackneyed objection is offered, 'we have so much to do at home,' not remembering that 'he that watereth, shall be watered also himself.' Has not this been exemplified in the *outpouring of the Holy Spirit* in this country since a spirit of missions was first excited in it? and does not our own observation constantly affirm that 'the liberal soul shall be made fat?' What was the conduct of the primitive christians when Christ commanded them to go forth and preach the Gospel, taking nothing with them, not even two coats apiece? Did they say, 'Lord, we would obey thee, but have dear friends at home who would be grieved to part with us, and whom we cannot leave: if thou wilt give us a work to do in the midst of these privileges we will perform it cheerfully.' No, rather did they forsake all, take up their cross daily, deny themselves, and live only for God. And shall not we be grateful to be counted worthy to suffer for Christ? I believe *my feelings* have been long decided, though perhaps not uniformly the same: it is now time that *my duty* was; but God's time is best. I desire to wait patiently for its arrival."

Notwithstanding the ardor and agitation of her mind, the following paper will show the cool deliberation and sound judgment, as well as enlightened, devoted piety, with which she examined the important question before her, and some of the steps by which she was led to a most satisfactory result. It was dated and solemnly subscribed, "*Norwich, November* 10, 1816, *Sabbath Evening.*"

"QUESTION OF DUTY RESPECTING MISSIONS.

"In examining this subject I have considered the disposition of my mind; my qualifications; the language of Divine Providence; and the teachings of the Holy Spirit.

"*The disposition of my mind.*—For *four and*

a half years, my prevailing desire has been to spend my life in the service of Christ. During the early part of this period, my plans for future enjoyment always centered in giving up all for Christ, and spending my days in a pagan land. Such plans, however, appeared like idle dreams, to cheat life of some of its dull hours; every thing within and without forbade the indulgence of such hopes.

"The perusal of '*Buchanan's Researches*' first excited my warmest interest for the salvation of the heathen; and while I had not the least idea of ever going myself to the Eastern world, it was my earnest desire that many laborers might be sent to introduce the Gospel among its thronging millions. When I questioned myself if I should be willing to go, were all obstacles removed, my uniform reply was, that no personal sacrifice was too great to make; but these obstacles would probably ever remain, and therefore I must think only of duties in my own country. The memoirs of Mrs. Newell, while they exhibited the sufferings of a missionary in glowing colors, were yet alluring, and my fancied scheme of happiness was more frequently resorted to, as a solace in my pilgrimage, though with no more prospect of being realized. No situation in my native land could I imagine so capable of affording me substantial happiness, but I desired to be useful somewhere; and as I was in the hands of Him who had seemed to fix my destiny, I strove to feel, that, could I be entirely devoted here, I would ask no more. In this state of mind, the pleasures of the world gradually became insipid and unsatisfying. The early removal of my brother, when about to devote himself to ministering at the altar, awakened anew the desire to consecrate all that God had given me to his service. In no other view did *life* appear desirable, for *this* only did I wish a continuance here.

"When, at length, it did seem possible that I should be called to forsake friends and native land, my great object was to observe *the leadings of Providence*, that I might not rush uncalled into so glorious a work. Having long believed that insuperable obstacles would prevent this happiness, I was the less animated by the possibility of their being removed. It was not, that being called to view the hardships attending a missionary, with more prospect of realizing them, I was intimidated; it was rather the difficulty of *determining duty*, which often checked my roving mind. I strove to lay aside every personal interest, and to fix my desires where I could be most extensively useful. At times the magnitude of the work, my insufficiency, and the trials attending such a sacrifice of temporal comfort, have caused me to shrink from what appeared too much for feeble nature to bear. In the main, however, I have desired to be grateful for being counted worthy to suffer for Christ.

"*Qualifications.* This subject has caused almost my only doubts. When I compare my love for immortal souls with that of our Divine Immanuel, and that of his early disciples, I am almost ready to say, If I were really called to a mission so much resembling that on which He sent them forth, I should possess more of their spirit. But I do feel *something*, though in a far inferior degree; and what power, save the Holy Spirit, has put the least degree of faith and love within me? I trust that God has implanted a holy principle in me—He will then add to it all needful grace—to Him be glory for ever. My *mental* qualifications are by no means adequate. In this I have support in the assurance that God's 'strength shall be perfected in weakness.' My *health* has been an objection of some magnitude; but, after consulting my physician, and learning that the effect of the voyage and climate is, on every constitution, uncertain; and after consulting Mr. Nott, who has been abroad, I am led to the conclusion that my state of health should not deter me. The inference from these and other considerations is, that if other objections are removed, qualifications must not be an obstacle.

"*The leadings of Divine Providence.* These appear in my being early weaned from the charms of this life—an ardent desire being awakened within me to renounce every temporal comfort for the service of Christ—in my having sent to me an unsought friend, who had a missionary spirit, at the very moment when I was about to believe that duty called me to other scenes; in causing my health to be better than it had been for several preceding years; in giving me pa rents who do not oppose, and in constantly giving me increased desires to devote all my powers to His service. These, united with many more indications that the Lord was leading me, which I *cannot* record, enable me confidently to believe that the work is all His own, and to Him be all the glory.

"*Teachings of the Holy Spirit.* By these I mean the impressions on my mind, which accompanied the examination of duty, from time to time; and these were manifestly towards this object:—when, in reading the sacred oracles, my heart was particularly warmed by contemplating the wide field of missionary labor, and the examples of holy men of old, who willingly suffered any privations and hardships for the sake of being embassadors of the Lord Jesus—when, in examining *objections*, they always dwindled to a point, if considered with the command of Christ,

'Go ye into all the world and preach the Gospel to every creature'—when the trials of this life served to excite a more ardent desire to be 'counted worthy to suffer for Christ,' rather than to have any effect to intimidate me—and when, in pouring out my soul on this subject to the Father of light, I realized more of that sweet peace in which 'my willing soul would stay'—and, finally, in so drawing me to the throne of mercy, that I could not leave without a blessing; and at length dissipating every doubt, and enabling me by the eye of faith to discover the finger of God pointing to the East, and with the affection of a Father, and the authority of a Sovereign, saying, 'Come, follow me'—'this is the way, walk ye in it;' and adding for my encouragement, 'I will never leave thee, nor forsake thee.'

"In view of all these considerations, and many more, I do believe that God calls me to become a missionary; and do, with this belief, resolve to consider myself as devoted to that service; and, as much as possible, to make all my exertions have an ultimate reference to it; hoping that God will qualify me, and make me a faithful servant for Christ's sake. *Amen and amen.*

"H. W. LATHROP."

The reader who sympathized with Miss L—— in the agitation of her mind, as expressed in communications previous to the last, will be happy in the calm decision to which she thus arrived; and will not be surprised that her next letter describes both a settled and *joyful* conviction of duty. But our friend was a child of faith and of the Spirit. She believed that God *could* make the path of duty exceeding plain. In proportion as the darkness around her was great, she looked above for light; and it broke upon her in the midst of obscurity, with a strength and clearness which forbade her ever seriously doubting, from that time, what was the will of God concerning her. It may be proper to add in reference to her health, that the fears of her friends were not realized, though it never was entirely firm. The compiler would also here say, that the subject of health, with the adaptation of constitution to the contemplated habits and climate, deserves, on the part of missionaries of both sexes, a more careful consideration than is generally given to it, and that the advice of judicious physicians, friendly to the object, should be sought and received with much deference.

"NORWICH, November 10, 1816.

"Had I ten thousand tongues, methinks they could not all express the gratitude I feel for 'light and comfort from above.' Oh 'let us magnify the Lord, and exalt his name together.' For many weeks 'I looked (and I thought earnestly) for light, but behold, obscurity; for brightness, but I walked in darkness.' The last week, however, God has been pleased to bring me, with more childlike dependence, to the foot of the cross, and there led me, step by step, until I have communed with him on his mercy-seat, with more delight, perhaps, than ever before.

"The grand objections of health and friends seem now to have become, comparatively, of little consequence. For the first, I am assured that my prospect of enduring the voyage and climate is quite as good as Mrs. Nott's when she left America; though the previous preparation might be a subject of concern, did I not believe that if God has a work for me to do in a heathen land, he will prepare me for it. The silent tear of parental affection and solicitude would indeed overpower me, had I not confidence that He who thus afflicts, will support my beloved parents. Surely, if I can trust in this Almighty arm for my support in so great an undertaking, I cannot question but my God will be their God. And what though we are early separated, and that under peculiarly painful circumstances, our journey here is but short. I feel an inexpressible pleasure in commending them to God, assured that they will be enabled to give up their child without regret, in the hope that she will do good to perishing souls:

Let them be constantly remembered in your prayers; and, Oh, my friend, may we be henceforth faithful to our own souls, as well as the cause of Christ. It is possible that we may yet be in an error; let us 'pray always, with all prayer and supplication, making known our requests unto God.'

"*Tuesday*, 12*th*.—Why am I permitted to feel so fully satisfied with regard to duty? If I did lean to this side of the question at all, I expected it would be with little faith, faint hope, and a mind rendered almost incapable of action by so much doubt and anxiety; but on the contrary, the transition from that unhappy state, to this of peace and joy, has seemed to invigorate all my faculties. I feel new strength, new ardor, and long to be even now at work. You will, perhaps, think that the subject of qualifications is entirely forgotten; far from it, my consolation and support in this is the assurance that God will 'perfect strength in weakness.'

"Mrs. Nott spent an afternoon with us last week. I have seen her several times. The duties of a female missionary are great indeed; but no matter how arduous, if God be my strength."

"December 1.

"You inquire what —— thinks of this subject now. I have of late, indeed always, avoided saying any thing to her myself, because I have felt unable to support any opinion with such an opponent. One evening last week I accidentally found her in mother's room, and she immediately forced me to sit down and enter into the subject. The whole weight of words possible to be set in order before me, were brought forward with the peculiar power she possesses. I finally told her that her approbation, next to that of my parents, was to me most desirable. She replied, 'Harriet, you will never have it, *never*, *never*, *never*.' Among other things she asked if the opinion of three quarters of my most respected friends would not influence me. I said, if, admitting the principle that *some must go*, they would get all the information to be obtained on the subject of missions, and decide that I ought not to go, it would have weight. She confessed herself ignorant, for she had never read a word on the subject. The next morning I sent over the Reports of the Prudential Committee since the second year, and have engaged her to read *Horne*, which is now with Dr. S. Do you ask if these things move me? I know not but I am obstinate or stupid; but amidst all, my duty still seems plain. My health was never better, and I am impatient to be now preparing for this great work. Although I say I am not materially affected by this opposition, you will not understand that it does not give me pain. It is trying, but God has hitherto granted me strength in proportion to my wants.

"*December* 6.—Grandmother last evening begged the favor of an arm to lean on in a ramble this afternoon.

"We called on a hospitable family where is a daughter lately married, whose husband has failed in business. A mother and sisters have received her with open arms, and are affording her every temporal comfort. How different this from the situation of a lonely and destitute female in a foreign land! But as heaven is high above the earth, so is a heavenly better than an earthly friend.

"The abode of a *widow*, in moderate circumstances, but surrounded by all life's substantial comforts, next arrested our steps. It was in a retired and inviting spot, but there were here no praying hearts.

"Domestic felicity now at length spread forth all its charms. In the midst of kindred and friends, days, months, and years glide away sweetly. Every wish is anticipated. The full heart can ask no more. A husband and family being made happy, the summit of duty and usefulness is thought to be reached. And could *I* live for this only? God forbid. While I have hands to work, and the heathen perish because the Gospel is not sent to them, my hours and days shall be employed for them. There is something forbidding to me in prosperity, as the world use the term; it draws the heart from God."

"*January* 19, 1817.

"Have had a delightful season this evening. The Lord has permitted me to come near to him, and to plead with uncommon earnestness. My wants multiplied, and I finally rejoiced to leave all with him, who needeth not to be told what is in man, and will not proportion his gifts to our scanty petition.

"I must tell you that my friend Mrs. L——, from N. L. has made me a visit. You may remember that she warmly opposed my contemplated undertaking. She says that my letter explaining my views of duty, &c. almost satisfied her that I was right, and now finding my health so much better than when she last saw me, her language is, 'Harriet, I will not make the least objection.' I rejoiced particularly in this, because she is one with whom I 'have taken sweet counsel' since our earliest years.

"You would help me to a grateful heart, could you witness my dear mother's conduct respecting this point of duty. It would seem that she made every objection so long as it could have any influence; but now, considering me decided, she is equally decided to present nothing which may increase my trial. Indeed she strives to help me in every way she can. I will almost say that she has caught the fire of missionary ardor; at any rate, I believe she evinces an uncommon share of *cheerful resignation.* In my own family I now hear no word of opposition. All will rather lend a helping hand than put any obstacle in my way."

The mind of Miss L—— was now *settled* as to her duty, should no unforeseen providence prevent, to leave home and country for a heathen land. She had resolved to do so. Her only reservation was, *if the Lord will.* She never took up the question again to *find reasons for going.* Her only anxiety was, when any providence seemed adverse, to know if God was *forbidding* her undertaking. On this point she held herself open to conviction. Again and again she said, "I shrink from no sacrifices, no trials; I only tremble lest I should rush uncalled into the service." There was no wavering, no indecision of mind. She had laid *all* on the altar, and only waited for the Lord to accept the offering. She looked upon a perishing world, and the question was what she could do, and where she could do most for its rescue. She only inquired, "Lord, what wilt *thou* have *me* to do?" and when she heard a voice behind her saying, "this is the way;" conferring not with flesh and blood, she immediately endeavored to walk in it. This is abundantly evident from her journal and letters to the time of her embarkation.

"*January* 16, 1817.—Have had much enjoyment of my Saviour this evening. Was at first very heartless, and it seemed for a long time that God would not permit me to come near his mercy-seat; but I could not leave praying, or rather articulating unconnected broken petitions. At length the Lord showed me that there was mercy even for me, a vile worm. I could plead with Him as with a father who heareth the cries of his child.

"18.—Have been meditating on the glorious labors of a missionary. It seems too much, that while so many are so much more worthy of this honorable employment, and so much better qualified to be useful, my heavenly Father should permit me to hope for the privilege of going to the heathen. Christ will strengthen me. But Oh may my motives be pure. Gracious God, suffer me not to bring any reproach on thy cause.

"29.—Have been much engaged in contemplating the work I so fondly anticipate. It has become a darling theme; so much so, that the thought of being finally obliged to relinquish it, would be far more painful than that of leaving friends and country for a life of trial and hardship.

"*February* 12.—My heart seems unusually enlarged; and I long to embrace, in christian love, all the world. Have been more assisted in prayer for perishing souls to-day than for a long time.

"18.—The wind howls round my retreat. Snow beats upon my window, and no cheerful ray illumines the footsteps of the traveller. Thus dreary, dark, and desolate is our way here below, until we see the light of heaven, which leads us upward. Such seasons are to me peculiarly sweet. I could, for my own sake, scarcely wish to see the earth again lighted up; so much is the prospect now in unison with my present feelings. I have been thinking on the days of other years, until my soul is sad; but it is a precious sadness. Among my subjects of thankfulness to the Author of my existence, I consider this one, that He has given me a disposition to relish those scenes of nature wherein his majesty is displayed; and that in these manifestations of his power I often find exquisite enjoyment.

"21.—If the tear of gratitude glistening in the mournful eye can afford pure enjoyment, I found it this morning in visiting the dying Mrs. D——. I think she evinces genuine repentance, and I must believe that she has obtained the pearl of great price. Poor old Miss C—— met me at the door and held me by the arm till I should tell her if it was true that I was going to India.

"To pity the weeping widow's wo is certainly my delight. And shall I not find these desolate ones in the sultry regions of Hindoostan? Now, alas, they know not the christian's God and Comforter. May I not point them to Him, and finally watch their dying hour with the interest of a sister in Christ? O yes, I may yet sit at the feet of Jesus, with a now wretched Hindoo female. God of mercy, let me, I beseech thee, realize this fond hope of my heart; and may I be qualified for extensive usefulness in that field.

"22.—This evening I have been looking into my heart. It was weary of earthly cares and earthly good. I looked abroad. The rapid gliding away of the great body of snow which has long covered the ground, reminded me how soon all worldly prospects will vanish. All I have on earth seemed held by a most uncertain tenure. 'The wind passeth over us and we are gone.' In the world I saw nothing to allure me; my whole soul was averse to seeing more. But when I turned my eyes above, the bright view was so enrapturing that I could scarcely think of being longer in the flesh. But I bless God that it is not with me as in times past. I believe I do not cling to life for the pleasure it brings; but if I may do something for the cause of my Saviour, I desire to see many days. Yes, a life of self-denial in a heathen land will claim my most ardent gratitude. While ruminating on the scenes of nature and the workmanship of God in the formation of my body and mind, I have desired to know whether the benighted Hindoos are susceptible of such feelings as I too often am. If they are, with their darkness respecting a hereafter, surely but few could endure existence. What peculiar cause have I for gratitude to the God of all grace, that he has granted me a balm for every wound. Will the longest life be sufficient to repay this mighty debt? God of my life, suffer me never to be impatient of my continuance here, but rather to desire a long life of entire devotedness to thy service.

"*March* 3.—Oh that I could never cease to magnify the Lord, and exalt his name. Have been to the alms-house. The poor infirm old ladies welcomed me with gratitude. One of them has long been anxious for her soul. For the last two weeks I have always remembered her in my prayers. I found her to-day for the first time rejoicing in hope. Another, a sister in the church, who has appeared to me very lukewarm, said that for three days she had experienced new feelings. For the same period I have felt an unusual interest in her case, and tried to pray for her. Have I indeed been assisted to plead for these precious souls? To God be all the glory. At first I feared to think that my prayers had been heard; but why should I not derive from this encouragement to 'pray without ceasing?'"

In the summer of 1817 she spent a few weeks in Litchfield, Conn. in the family of the Rev. Dr. Beecher, pursuing a course of reading that might promote her future usefulness. Her communications to friends show how her heart clung to the objects of her beneficence at home and abroad, and her regret that there *was then no Sabbath-school in Litchfield.*

TO TWO FEMALE ASSOCIATES.

"LITCHFIELD, Saturday evening, July 2, 1817.

"SISTERS M—— and E——. How refreshing it would be to spend an hour with you this evening; but I will be thankful for the privilege of writing.

"My external privileges here are indeed great, but these alone will never keep us near to God. Great as mine are, I have less enjoyment in religion than when at home. I believe it is owing to my mind being so much occupied with study, which is not calculated to excite devotional feelings, and not being engaged in those little *exercises of love* to souls which I had at home. You will understand me; if not now, you will when deprived of the opportunity to visit the alms-house, Mrs. D., and such people. While in these occasional visits we give pleasure to our fellow-creatures, and I hope sometimes do good to their souls, we are benefiting ourselves. I have been this afternoon to see a saint, who though poor in earthly covering, has a treasure in heaven, and hope to visit her often. Shall have opportunity to tell you more about her if I do. Likewise hope to tell you of a visit to the alms-house here."

TO THE SAME.

"July 19.

"I would excite your gratitude to the Giver of all good for his dealings with *two dear souls in this family*, just brought from 'the horrible pit and miry clay.' Their mouths are filled with praise, and I trust their hearts with love. They have been greatly tried; their stout hearts resisted long, until they were almost in a state of despair. Two days were spent in distress that I have never known exceeded under similar circumstances. He who remembered the 'wormwood and the gall' could not fail to feel much for them, but it was useless to try to administer comfort. They had a more able Friend, who had been tempted, and will succor those who are tempted. In his own time he appeared for them. They will, I trust, have ability to do good. They seem much concerned for their companions, talk with them, &c.

"Mr. B. says, if God should pour out his Spirit, I shall have found here the best school I can have. Pray for me, my friend, cease not to remember me in some of your precious moments when you commune with God. All the return I can, I give. May the Saviour be your Advocate. He will prevail.

"How stand Sabbath-school affairs? I am anxious to hear very particularly of them, especially respecting I—. Sometimes I flatter myself that she manifests more and more concern. Again I fear that this is not the case. Does your number increase? Has Mr. M—— joined you? Do the ladies call? Tell me all. I want, too, to know about the other societies. When you see Mrs. D——, do not fail to give her my love, likewise to all the folks we visited at the alms-house. I think much of that place; have enjoyed some precious seasons there which I would not exchange for all that I have found in the splendid drawing-room. Do you attend any conferences there now? I want to ask about many things more, but you must write all that you know I want to hear. Think of the 'golden rule' when you write. I need your letters with other friends, to relax my mind, and give me a little of that enjoyment which *late-found* friends cannot convey."

TO HER BROTHER IN OHIO.

"LITCHFIELD, July 22, 1817.

"MY DEAR BROTHER,—Before this arrives, you will have been informed, by Norwich friends, of the smiles of Providence in placing me in a situation so pleasant as Mr. Beecher's family. It is indeed more than I expected. Although I am not so many miles from home as you are, I feel my separation from our invaluable friends *very, very* much. I too am among strangers. Oh my brother, my dear Daniel, we are wanderers and pilgrims. But we hasten to our rest. It is good to have no *abiding* place in such a world as this; in which our Lord and Master had not where to lay his head.

"The missionaries, who have been so long waiting to go to the East, are at length ordered to sail in two or three months. This has brought the subject very near to me. God willing, I shall be among the next who go. When I take a view of life, and consider that our days are few, and that *youth* is emphatically the time to serve God, I wish the moment to arrive. But you know me too well, to think that I can be impatient to be removed from what my heart holds so dear. My dear brother, with one side of the picture before me, flesh and heart sink. Yet I fear nothing, except that the Lord should leave me to choose for myself; or that he has so left me. If you love me, *pray often*, *pray daily*, that this may never be the case."

"LITCHFIELD, August 19, 1817.

"MY DEAR MOTHER,—Surely it is something more than a simple emotion of joy that I feel to-night, after the receipt of so many precious letters; all others of which were not so valuable as yours. Never before did you tell me, in so many words, that you are satisfied in the decision which I have made; although your conduct has implied this, and given me the sweet assurance that God is gradually preparing you cheerfully to bid me a long farewell. Formerly, every letter from home riveted me more strongly to our dear family, and made me feel that it would be a bitter trial to part with you. How different my sensations to-night! I certainly do not love you less, but with the strength inspired by your composure, I could fly on wings of the wind, and think only of the happiness of being completely devoted to the service of Christ, with the entire approbation of my best friends. Oh, my dear mother, God has been with you in six troubles, and in seven. Yea, has he not always been at your right hand? In an hour of particular trial He will not, He cannot forsake you.

"I think I do feel more and more that I am highly privileged, and that you may congratulate me, or rather thank God. My dear mother, I have strength in your prayers. God will give to those who ask, and the importunity of a mother will prevail. I want to be more humble, to feel more the worth of souls, to be more dead to the world, and alive in God."

TO HER FAMILY FRIENDS.

"LITCHFIELD, (Monday Evening,) August 4, 1817.

"MY DEAR FRIENDS,—I have fully realized this evening, that, although our bodies are more than seventy miles from each other, our souls have been near together. And not only ours, but those of the children of God, in every land, who have been surrounding the mercy-seat. Even once degraded Hindoos have been lifting their hearts to their Creator. And may I ever sit with them, to listen to the glad tidings of the Gospel, and may I unite with them in pouring out my soul to God? I must hope so. The Lord has great blessings in store for the heathen who now sit in darkness. He will call many laborers into the vineyard. The time is hastening—it is at hand. Oh let us strive to be among his instruments to bring it on. When Dr. Buchanan was pleading in behalf of sending the Gospel to India, he said, 'Doubt no longer whether it can be established here—it is already established; it has taken firm root, and all your powers cannot hinder it'"

TO A FRIEND.

"LITCHFIELD, August 17, 1817.

"I spent yesterday afternoon reading 'Ward's view of the Religion of the Hindoos.' It deprived my mind and body of energy, and filled me with horror. The enormities of these wretched creatures exceed all that I had imagined. How can it be that christians have slumbered so long, when there is such exceeding depravity in the world? Well may we bless God that we live at this auspicious era, instead of a century ago. Is it not strange that they who have experienced the efficacy of a Saviour's blood, can think the sufferings of a missionary life too great to be endured? It must be from ignorance. They cannot know the state of the heathen, they cannot consider the worth of souls. It would seem that the stoutest heart must melt in reading the accounts of Ward. Happy are we, yea, thrice happy, if among the little number whom the Lord shall call to aid in the glorious work of evangelizing the heathen. Methinks I do begin to realize in some degree how great is our privilege. But still my heart is hard and strangely insensible."

It would be well, if the christian sentiments expressed in the quotation below, were really those of every pious parent; and yet, if truly pious—if they have the spirit of Him who sent his only Son on a mission to earth—what others can be cherished? Have they given their children *wholly* to the Lord, and do they still claim the disposal of them? May it not be said, 'Remember Ananias and Sapphira?' The mother who cheerfully resigned this almost idolized daughter, felt as tenderly as any mother, yet she has been enabled to give up, besides her Harriet, *three* other beloved daughters to the same blessed work, though she herself is left, in advancing age, a dependent and almost solitary widow.

"New Haven, September 3, 1817.

"From all my mother's letters, I think she is abundantly supported. Her last at L. overwhelmed me with emotions of joy and gratitude. I must transcribe a part. Speaking of a friend who came some distance to see her on my account, she writes, 'I enjoyed her visit much, because she talked on subjects particularly interesting. My friends mistake my feelings, when they studiously avoid a subject so near my heart as is your contemplated undertaking. I can think of it with composure, and speak of it with much satisfaction. She remarked that it was cause for gratitude. I am, if I may so say, partially thankful, that is, thankful for the *disposition* which leads you thus to devote yourself. How earnestly have I desired, and how fervently prayed, that my children might be the subjects of grace, and instruments of bringing souls to Christ; and now can I claim to choose the place *where*, and the manner *how* they shall serve this kind Master, who has so often answered my petitions, even to have given me the very things I have asked of him? No, my child, I believe I am saved from this inconsistency. I believe I am willing to leave to infinite wisdom to direct in all things; and as you are satisfied with regard to duty, I do not question about it.' Is not this change in our dear mother's feelings, and particularly her opinion of my duty, an indication that the hand of God has been in this thing?

"I have been to the celebrated *cave* in 'West Rock.' Ascending the mountain, we called on the inhabitants of the cave. They are a man, his wife, and three children. In approaching it, we threaded our way through a narrow walk, walled on each side several rods, and then almost crept some feet into a dark, dismal place. There was no light except through the opening by which we entered, and another which afforded a passage for the smoke. In one corner, on something which seemed a bed of dirt and stone, with a few pieces of carpet for a covering, lay a boy four years old, who had that day broken his leg, and an infant a few months old, who appeared scarce ly alive. It was much diseased—the mother had scarcely clothing enough to cover her, and her countenance indicated the lowest grade of vice. Yet she was not a heathen. Two Bibles, a Testament, and a hymn-book were there, all of which she professed to delight in reading. She acknowledged dependence and obligation, but not sin. I contrived to be left alone with her, and my feelings being much excited, I dealt plainly with her, and as I have been seldom able to do. She listened—was solemn, and confessed she was a sinner. Indeed, when I asked her to look back on the sins of one day, she started with a sort of horror, and said, 'I can't; they would more than fill this cave.' Her appearance, when alone with me, was entirely changed. People generally think there is scarcely a possibility of her reform, and so say but little to her. I never witnessed such a scene, never before saw human nature so degraded. This poor wretch had not even the external comforts of Harriet Newell in a season of trial, for with her no human being heaved a commiserating sigh at the period of nature's greatest anguish, in *a gloomy cave.* Oh your heart would have bled. With all, this woman had the tenderness of an affectionate mother. Her husband had received a blow on the head which almost killed him, and had gone to have it dressed. It was now sunset; she was three miles from town, with the prospect of her child's death in the night; no candle, and no wood to kindle a light. Who has made us to differ?"

In the following, allusion is made to a short tour performed by Mr. W. as an agent of the Missionary Board:

"NORWICH, November 2, 1817.

"My dear friend will not be unmindful this evening, that it is just one year since his duty to become a missionary was first made plain; nor can I forget that it was a time of darkness and distress with me. Happily the clouds are scattered. I see nothing from outward circumstances to discourage me, while you have already entered on your employment. Have we not every reason to sing of mercy, and to praise God? Yes, even for the darkness and doubt which almost sunk us to despondency before He was pleased to show the way in which He would have us to go. I cannot tell you how happy I am at your success in missionary labors. But it makes me feel more than ever that I am doing nothing for Christ.,

"In your wanderings my imagination has followed you in many pleasant rides, at the fire-side of some of the dear followers of the Saviour, and in the sacred desk. In all these, engaged for Christ and the heathen, I have thought you peculiarly happy. This has added not a little to my enjoyments, and I trust has brought me with more life and fervor to the throne of grace.

"I have been led to think more of our prospect, and the successive steps by which it has been placed before us, by the return of this season. The autumn had always many attractions for me. I love it still, independently of those associations which the occurrences of the last three years connect with it. The last season which I spent with my deceased brother, and the pleasantest of our lives, was just three years ago. Two years since another friend excited interest, and rendered the season particularly pleasant; and one year since I indulged the expectation of going to India. Now have I not reason to welcome the 'falling leaf' and the decay of nature's charms? Perhaps I may not spend another such season in my native land."

TO A SISTER FROM HOME.

"NORWICH, November 14, 1817.

"DEAR SISTER,—Your letter made me feel again, as I find myself feeling, perhaps too often, that in leaving all my friends I make no trifling sacrifice. Not, my sister, that I attach any merit to this. O no; the most cursory view of my heart shows me very plainly that my best services are but filthy rags. It is no merit; but it will be a great mercy if I am permitted to live and labor in a heathen land. Yet although I feel this, and am in some measure thankful, I am sometimes almost overwhelmed. The path does not appear unbroken by hills and mountains, nor would I have it. Difficulties often humble me; they bring me to the foot of the cross, which is indeed my highest exaltation. If it is the will of heaven to send me away, I shall be sustained. I fear nothing but going uncalled."

"February 17, 1818.

"I have just received a letter from Mr. Cornelius, dated at New Orleans, Jan. 13. It seemed written in the spirit of a missionary. He had been there only two weeks, yet had 'preached several times to large and attentive assemblies, and two or three souls were beginning to feel their need of Christ.' From the brethren at Chickamaugah he had just heard that *three* Indians had been hopefully converted after he was there. He says, 'When you go to the East, if that should be your destination, tell the brethren there that a star has arisen in the West.' He expects to leave New Orleans in March for the Indian country, and to take some promising youths to be educated at the North. This letter has cheered my heart. I needed it, or something else, to rouse my slumbering spirit."

"*April* 26.—I must call this a happy day Went early to school, where Mr. A. made us a visit. An increased number of scholars animated me a little. In the forenoon enjoyed being in God's house. At noon came home and offered my requests for brother L. Returned to school, where I prayed with the scholars, which seemed to give a zest to the remaining exercises. After meeting, attended to the adult school. Returned home and took tea. Taught C—— and E—— in the catechism, and read to them a sermon. Called again on God, and went to evening meeting. Was there refreshed, and returned home wishing the Sabbath would last always.

"*May* 22.—Little did I foresee, when writing last in my diary, that instead of meeting my Saviour at his table at the time appointed, I should be prostrated on a bed of sickness. On Sabbath morning, when alighting from the chaise to take charge of my scholars, I fell on the steps so as to fracture a limb and otherwise injure me seriously. I was, for a short time, in great distress, and thought myself dying, but had no particular alarm. Was removed, after fainting, and subsequently conveyed home. Suffered much, and anticipated lasting injury. I may say, in all this affliction I have had the presence of my Saviour. I desired to glorify God by patience under suffering, but did not succeed so effectually as I wished. I had some dark moments, though in the midst of them I had support. I wished to know the design of God in afflicting me at this time so severely. Perhaps it is that I may realize more the value of my friends in seasons of sickness, and know better what I am about to relinquish. But I believe that at no time did they seem so indispensable to me as to prevent the desire of devoting my life to the heathen, though by so doing I must part from them all.

"*July* 26.—My feelings have been tried, and my faith put to a test, by the proposition of my friend to go to South America. He says he can do nothing without first knowing my views. Sometimes he thinks he must go. His brethren incline to that opinion. He hesitates, not being satisfied what is the will of God. If he go on an exploring mission, I feel a deep persuasion that we shall not meet again in this life. But ought I therefore to object? I think not. May God grant me grace to say, as I ever have since first contemplating this subject, *If it be the Lord's will*—although I knew it would result in the death of my friend, I will oppose no obstacle."

The reference in the last extract, the spirit of which cannot but be admired, is to a proposal of some friends of missions in New-York and the vicinity, for two of the missionary candidates, then at Andover, to go on an exploring tour to South America. It was subsequently undertaken by Rev. Messrs. Brigham and Parvin.

"July, 1818.

"Since my last we have had some precious seasons with Dr. Griffin. He attended a meeting at our house on Wednesday. The lower part of the house was filled, even crowded. On one of the warm days he said to me, 'How is your health affected by warm weather?' I replied, 'I mean to find out this summer.' A day or two after, when the weather changed, he said, 'I thought much of you this morning, when I felt my system so braced by the cool air, and meant to tell you that if this summer should convince you that a warm climate is *unfavorable, you must yet go on a mission.* There is no need of relinquishing it; South America presents every variety of climate.' "

In September Miss L—— made a visit to New Haven, where she had the pleasure of meeting several friends of missions. It would be well if the remarks in her letter, on the neglect of the poor and ignorant around us, were not still applicable in too many places. Christians in general feel too little personal responsibility on this subject. It is easier to become impatient with ignorance, and indignant at vice, than to remove the one or reform the other. The subject of this memoir did not, in extending her views abroad, overlook duties to be performed at home; or in attempting to embrace a world in the arms of her benevolence, suffer the minor charities of the family, the neighborhood, the country in which she lived, to be neglected. The spirit of that missionary is to be suspected, who acts differently, and does not begin his operations at once where he is—endeavoring to widen the circles of his influence, like the widening waves, caused by the pebble thrown into the still lake, until they reach the most distant shores.

" New Haven, September 13, 1818.

" Mr. Cornelius came to me this morning and said, 'Dr. Worcester did not know who Harriet was until now. He will think more of you in future.' I had previously felt quite at ease before him, confident that he knew nothing about me. In our next interview he introduced the subject of missions. We took a walk together, and I began to fear him. He looks sharply and expects much of missionaries.

"I am surprised to find in this city so many ignorant people, who seem to have no means of instruction. The alms-house is a wretched place. It contains more than eighty souls, and but one of them gives evidence of piety. I have found two colored women, one of them in a dying state, who knew not what sin is. One of them told me she had heard something about Jesus Christ, but could not tell what. She had not, apparently, the least notion concerning his mission to this world, and said she never prayed. When I asked if she knew the Lord's prayer, in other words, 'Our Father,' she replied that she did not know, but would try to repeat it after me.

"The coming generation, we may hope, will not be like their fathers. Means are using to store their minds in youth with the first principles of the Gospel. But must *the present generation*, who are so rapidly going into eternity, be regarded as in a hopeless state, because they will not or cannot become members of Sabbath-schools? Surely there is great want of efficient means to instruct poor souls. I am concerned. How can there be *ease in Zion* when such multitudes live and die in ignorance at her very gates."

A few extracts annexed, will further show how *the true spirit of a missionary* continued to be exemplified by Miss L—— among those to whom she could be useful *at home*, though her mind and heart were so engrossed with the claims of millions perishing abroad. To these objects of her care she still extended her solicitude long after she arrived on foreign shores—addressing letters to the Sabbath-schools, and sending messages to the inmates of the alms-house, and others to whom her faithful efforts for their good, her sympathy and her prayers had greatly endeared her. Happily in the latter years of her sojourn in this land, God had raised up from her associates an interesting circle to co-operate in such labors, and join her in bearing the wants of suffering men, both at home and abroad, before his throne of mercy.

To N—— F——, one of this circle, who spent some time in New-York, she writes:

"You do sometimes think of our poor native town. Oh yes, in some of your best moments I trust we have a remembrance. Have you heard that our hopes for precious souls have recently brightened? A good work seems actually to have been begun in a distant part of the congregation; but the hearts of many, sickened almost by hope deferred, can hardly believe that it is so. Yet distressed souls affirm the presence of the Spirit. I fear lest professed christians should hold themselves back from the proffered mercy. They do not seem awake, but there is power with God. His sovereignty will accomplish all his purposes. In this I have strength—here hangs all my hope for those who are out of Christ."

Again she says: "The poor people at the almshouse still excite interest. Mrs. W—— seems stationary in her religious feelings, though she may make progress which I do not discover. Mrs. —— and Mrs. —— have expressed to Dr. S——, a wish to join the church. Our Sunday-school prospers, if the occasional addition of a scholar and attention to the lessons is evidence. We desire to see *present fruit* in the conversion of souls; but if I should never witness one such case, I should still have reason to bless God for the school. Good seed is sown, and in God's time it will be made to bring forth fruit.

"I am sorry to say that I do not know particularly the state of ——'s mind. Her deportment plainly declares that earthly treasures do not satisfy her, and that she seeks a better country. I am told that —— is inquiring. M—— is to make one of our number at the next communion.

"Letters from D—— mention that the Lord has a care over that part of his vineyard where he resides. Their meeting on the Sabbath continues, and so crowded, that they contemplate building a larger room. Two souls are hopefully born again, and a number express concern for themselves.

"You mention H——. He has not yet come out boldly on the Lord's side. My time is so engrossed that I see but few friends."

To Miss B—— T——, another beloved female associate, she writes, stating that the sum of $30, which they were again collecting for missions, was filled, and entreating her not to relinquish their little missionary society after her departure.

She again addresses the same friend in behalf of the circle of females who were accustomed to meet for prayer.

"You have not prayed in vain. No, the Lord has heard your prayers. Are you not greatly encouraged to persevere with increased ardor and faith? Yes, my sisters, take courage. There are still greater blessings in store for precious souls in Norwich. Never had you so little reason to faint, or be weary. God says, 'Open thy mouth *wide* and I will fill it.' O cast yourselves continually at his feet. Keep there, and pour out your hearts before him. He waits to be gracious. In my absence I have enjoyed precious seasons, while bending with you before his throne of mercy. It seems particularly the province of females to pray. In this way they may be eminently useful."

To Miss M—— H—— H——, another member of the same endeared circle, she writes—at one time expressing the joy and refreshment she had gained in their meetings for prayer, and drawing encouragement from the consideration, that as God should pour out his Spirit their numbers would be increased; then in reference to the next annual subscription to be raised; then to the Sabbath-school; then to the monthly concert of prayer; then to the church, having renewed their covenant; then informing of two hopeful conversions, and requesting prayers for a young lady who had sought religious conversation with her; then requesting prayer for herself, in reference to the missionary work; then alluding to a private concert of prayer observed monthly by young ladies; and then in reference to the appeal of Rev. Messrs. Hall and Newell, missionaries at Bombay, in behalf of six hundred millions of heathen, and asking what we do, and how far we deny ourselves for Christ and the perishing.

To another female friend, who in deep affliction had called herself *a backslider*, she writes, seeking to give spiritual encouragement: "If it be true that the best of christians are but partially sanctified, that they continually carry about with them a body of sin, is it not *desirable that they should know and feel this?* And is not their doing so an evidence that they are making progress in the Divine life? If we did not see our deformity, how could we go forward—we should want that stimulus, which of all others has most efficacy, *a sense of our helplessness!* That consciousness of remaining corruption which causes us to groan under its weight, and is sufficient to crush us, is directly opposed to a retrograde motion in the christian warfare—we cannot then go back. There is but one way—to press forward, through the grace of Christ, or die in the attempt."

An estimable female friend of Miss L——, who was then without hope in Christ, says, "From a number of notes which it was my privilege to receive from her, I enclose two, indicative of her untiring zeal for the salvation of souls at home as well as abroad, and thus far exhibiting the beautiful consistency of her christian character."

"NORWICH, (midnight,) Dec. 17, 1818.

"DEAR ——, If you knew how frequently I have thought of you of late with affectionate concern, you would wonder that I have not before this sent you a note. I have one lying by me which has been written several months, but no opportunity presenting to deliver it very soon, I concluded that it should be destroyed, and I would soon converse with you freely, as I wished. Every attempt to do this has been fruitless, and I now presume something on your kindness to excuse this intrusion. Need I offer any other apology than to express the simple fact that I long for your salvation. I have marked your deportment from time to time with much interest, and have been happy to observe that you do think christianity worth possessing, that you are almost, and I hope altogether persuaded to be a christian. The extent of your feelings I do not know, but think myself safe in concluding, that convinced of the immortality of the soul, you do not seek durable riches in this life, but are looking towards another, better world. The requisites to obtain an inheritance in heaven are doubtless plain and familiar to you. A candid mind cannot mistake them. It is a great thing to be a christian—so to adorn the doctrine of the Saviour, as by our example to win souls to him. Well may every one exclaim, 'Who is sufficient for these things!" Sovereign grace can alone effect it.

"I want to say to every inquirer after the truth, turn your face from the lives of professing christians—even the best are but partially sanctified—and look only at the example of Jesus of Nazareth. Regard his precepts, imitate him, and you shall have abundant peace and joy in the Holy Ghost."

"MY DEAR ——, You have not at any time been long absent from my thoughts. I have loved to place you before me as dissatisfied with the charms of this world and seeking an interest in the Redeemer. You find your heart 'a medley of inconsistencies.' Happy for you if you indeed see it *and feel it too.* Your remedy is in the God of heaven. This you know, but 'your desires are faint, are few; indeed you almost question if any of them are sincere.' It is true that we are often and most easily deceived. But we need not be. We can know ourselves. Especially we may know if we really love and fear God, if we will be honest in our examination.

"I would, if possible, help you to a perfect acquaintance with yourself and to taking a decided stand on the Lord's side. It is ground of thankfulness, that you are not insensible to the danger of those who are without God and without hope in the world, but it should excite deep solicitude that you are not already established in the faith. There should be no wavering, no standing still, or turning back. The object in view must be pursued with unremitting diligence. The Lord is not slack concerning his promise. He waits to be gracious, but he requires that we faint not, pressing towards the mark. It should be always remembered that if we are not *for God* we are *against him*.

"Dear friend, can I help you? I tremble at every thing like delay in this great work. Come now; all things are ready. To God I commend you. He demands our heart, our whole souls, and that *this day*, lest it be for ever too late. In haste, but with much affection, your friend,

"HARRIET."

To another esteemed female acquaintance she addressed the following tender and faithful appeal:

"DEAR ——, The interest that I have long felt for your best good I think warrants a plain and friendly communication before my departure from my native land. Indeed it would be opposing the dictate of conscience as well as affection to withhold the testimony of my experience to the vanity and injury of worldly pleasures and the sufficiency of Divine grace to ensure rational and permanent enjoyment. I recollect a conversation with you at Mrs. ——'s. You considered yourself happy. In the world you found much to amuse and to fill you with enjoyment—you sometimes thought of futurity, but it was not with dread—the employments of heaven were unlike those of earth, but your views on this subject were indefinite. This I believe was the substance of what was expressed; but we were interrupted when I wished to say much more. No convenient time has since offered, and now, dear ——, you must forgive me if I offend, and rest assured always, that the salvation of your soul is an object which I most earnestly desire, and for which I would spare no effort. But I trust you will not blame me; if you do, it will only increase my solicitude for your happiness.

"Permit me to ask if you are still satisfied with the daily round of amusements which present themselves; and if you are willing not only to spend *life* in this way, but even *eternity*? If this is the case, I entreat you seriously to inquire if you can thus indulge yourself from age to age? Is there not a limit to every earthly scene? And as this life is so small a part of our existence, is it not of the first importance to be prepared for enjoying another?

"Do not dream of heaven without a compliance with the terms of salvation. God is merciful, but he is likewise just, and 'it is a fearful thing to fall into the hands of the living God.' Look, dear ——, into the Scriptures: 'Except a man be born again he cannot see the kingdom of God.'

'He that believeth not, shall be damned.' 'Except ye repent, ye shall all likewise perish.' I could refer you to every page in the sacred volume which condemns the impenitent, but you may know this.

"Whatever the world may say, *christianity does confer happiness in this life.* There is not a real christian on earth, nor ever was, even though his lot be low, and he be stripped of every earthly dependence, who would exchange his interest in the Saviour, his rags and his poverty, for the pleasures of the *most happy, the most distinguished* of worldly men. Is not this fact a proof that religion is worth something—that it is worth every thing? If you would be happy in this life—be a christian; if you would secure a place at the right hand of your Judge in the final day, fear and love him now. Trifle not with your immortal interest. If it was so valuable to the Son of God, that he could leave heaven for a residence on our earth, accompanied by such unparalleled suffering, is it not worth your whole attention? The Lord by his Spirit warns you of danger, that your soul is rushing to its final perdition; resist not his strivings; be persuaded to to repent, believe and live. I shall often think of you with affectionate concern, and my first wish for you shall ever be, that you may seek and obtain that peace which belongs *exclusively to christians*. That the Lord may forgive and keep you evermore, is the prayer of your friend

"HARRIET."

To her sister, who was on a visit at New London, she writes: "I do sometimes realize that I shall not perhaps always be surrounded with earthly parents, brothers, and sisters. Well, if I have a heavenly Parent, and Hindoo brothers and sisters, there will be call for unceasing gratitude. Never forget me in your prayers. And here let me say that I know too well how visiting friends, as you are now doing, dissipates the mind. Without stated seasons of retirement and communion with God, we cannot maintain a regular consistent christian walk. Such a walk is never more necessary for you than at the present time. Seek and find frequent opportunities to present yourself more immediately before God, and maintain a heavenly frame of mind. This will enable you in some measure to discharge your duties, which may be various. Let not one, however minute, be neglected. And, my dear sister, ever remember that you are the Lord Jesus Christ's, and not your own. Let not trifles light as air engross that time and those affections which belong exclusively to God. Speak often of your Saviour. Let him never be wounded by your silence, through fear of a fellow-worm. And may God grant, in answer to your constant prayers and most earnest endeavors, that this visit shall redound to his glory in the best good of some immortal soul, and in your own advancement in the divine life."

In the autumn of this year, the designation of Mr. W——, as also of Mr. Spaulding and Mr. Woodward, was made for Ceylon. Their ordination, with that of the lamented *Fisk*, took place, the fourth day of November, at Salem, Mass.; and was a most solemn and interesting occasion. In the evening, after the ordination, *eleven brethren* were assembled, who had dedicated themselves to foreign missions. Among these, besides the four then ordained, were Parsons, who soon went with Fisk to Palestine, Temple and Goodell, who a year later joined the same mission, Bing ham, who went to the Sandwich Islands, and By ington, who went to the Indians of this country These joined hands, and standing in a circle sang, "When shall we *all* meet again." In a few months they were scattered to the four quarters of the globe, and ere long two of them, whose feet had stood on Mount Zion, rested from their la bors.—Dear companions of my earlier and later studies, ardent cherishers of my little missionary spirit, sharers in some of my most precious seasons of social devotion, may I at length sit down with you on the "*heavenly hills*," and I ask no higher privilege than to tread in your steps here, however painful and weary!

It was expected that the departure of the missionaries would follow soon after their ordina tion, but it was delayed for want of a passage.

"NORWICH, October 7, 1818.

"MY DEAR UNCLE WHITING,—It is now probable that I shall be called to leave my native land sooner than was at first expected. The illness of Messrs. Richards and Warren, at Ceylon, induces the Board to propose to strengthen that mission immediately; and we are designated to embark for that station as early as possible. This great work is now brought nearer to my mind than I could ever before regard it, and I trust it does not appear the less desirable. A long adieu to my kindred and friends will rend the heart. I feel *already* that it will; but at the same time the prospect of doing good to some poor heathen soul will fill it with joy; with God for our portion, even the wilderness would not be solitary; tossing on the tempestuous deep, we should fear nothing; a stranger in the midst of a strange people, we might have society; and above all, in preparing the way, in ever so small a degree, for the universal dominion of the *Prince of Peace*, would be a constant feast to the soul. I am sometimes ready to inquire who is there who would not be a missionary if the Lord directed, or even permitted it. But when I look *at home*, I wonder indeed that *such an one* could ever think of attempting so much. It has seemed like presumption to suppose that I have been thus called. Now the prospect seems more fixed, but I still consider it a 'wonder of mercies.'

"My dear mother is greatly supported in view of what is before me, and my family all bid me God speed. Should I be prevented seeing you, let me now say, comfort my parents when I am gone. I shall be but a few days sooner removed than I should if life were spent with them. It is only taking a different road to the same place of rest; yet nature speaks, and calls for the sympathy and affection of remaining friends."

"*October* 11.—This has been a precious day. Truly, one day in God's house is better than a thousand elsewhere. Mr. W. preached. I thought the Lord was with him and with the hearers. Oh! how different such a day spent in America, from one in heathen India. How do I look at this work now?—as I thought I should when brought so near? I believe that I have the same support from God, and the same conflicts between contending and opposing feelings.

"*December* 24.—My exercises have been pretty

uniform since the final determination to embark soon. I have generally some faith, though at times great weakness constrains me to shrink from the prospect before me. Yesterday and to-day I have felt this. It seems too much opposed to every natural feeling. Yet when I ask myself what alternative I would prefer, I find invariably, that of all stations and employments, those of a missionary are to me the most desirable. I would not relinquish the hope of engaging in them, for any thing else which this life presents."

In reference to her marriage, which took place at Norwich, January 11, 1819, there is the following notice in her journal while at Andover; to which place she went with her husband, on the way to visit his friends in Vermont; and where they were detained a little by his Sketch of Missions then in the press.

"*January* 30.—The feelings which engrossed me previous to, and at the time of our marriage, cannot be described. I believe that I had some just view of what I was doing. I was cheerful, and I hope grateful; at the same time when I considered how much meekness and patience a husband would need to bear with my infirmities, I could almost have said, 'Lord, save him from this trial.'

"This event, too, was to be connected with a trying separation. My dear parents and friends would soon see our faces no more. But the thought that the Lord had grace in reserve for them comforted me. We left home the third day after our marriage, and had a pleasant journey to Boston, where we visited some friends, and then came by Salem and Newburyport to this place. Friends were raised up to us of the Lord, and for his sake we were every where kindly received. Blessed be his name for ever. How much more should we love those friends who show us kindness for the Lord's sake, than though it were only for ourselves."

"ANDOVER, January 22d, 1819.

"DEAR PARENTS, BROTHER AND SISTER,—Your letter this morning deserves our most hearty thanks. To describe our emotions on perusing it is impossible. Why is it that we ever forget our obligations to Him who so constantly and so abundantly manifests his forbearance and love towards us? In your resignation—more than that—your cheerful acquiescence, we have fresh occasion for gratitude, and are encouraged to go on our way rejoicing. Dear father says, the afternoon after our departure was 'a sorrowful one.' It was in a degree such to us, notwithstanding we had much to make us comfortable. I trust it was not exclusively sorrowful either to those at home or those by the way. I considered that it was not a last parting, at the same time it *was parting*, and that, too, not under the most animating circumstances. But why talk of this? We shall meet again, yes, in a few days, and we shall be as we have been; and then, if we are the children of God, we shall meet *never to part!* O that He would sanctify *us all*, make us useful in life, and finally take us to Himself.

"*Saturday.*—This is the first morning the sun has shone since my arrival at A. Could my mother and friends see how comfortably I am situated this smiling day with kind friends, they would lift their hearts to God in thanksgiving, and call me insensible to His goodness if I indulged any gloomy feelings. I ought to be happy, as much as is consistent with carrying about this body of sin, and I am so if friends at home are. My enjoyment is still closely connected with theirs. But I feel that it is a privilege to be permitted to make any sacrifice for Him who freely gave his *life* for us."

It would be pleasing to follow Mrs. W—— in her notices of the journey through Massachusetts, New Hampshire, and Vermont, where she met, for the first and last time, many dear relatives, and had many affecting interviews with beloved christian friends, who never ceased to remember her and her mission with deep interest. She returned to Norwich near the end of March, and soon after received the long wished for information of a passage being engaged for India. The delay which had taken place, though trying in some respects, afforded the better opportunity for preparations to leave *home*, which are often too much hurried; but what was of vastly more consequence, it was the occasion of the valuable accession of *Dr. and Mrs. Scudder* to the mission. Her feelings and those of her family, in view of her immediate departure, are expressed in a letter to her husband, who had proceeded to Boston.

"Your letter from Boston was handed me this afternoon. I was overjoyed to hear of a ship to convey us to India. I can say with you, that 'no intelligence for a long time has animated me so much.' The family appeared to partake of my feelings in some degree. To us all I believe it was a relief from trying suspense, and consequently was welcome. This evening it has been mentioned at meeting, and fervent prayer was offered that we might be kept in all our way, and made instrumental of great good. Our dear father first led in prayer, and it was worth more than I can name to hear him. All present must have been astonished, if they were ignorant of the efficacy of grace. I was comforted, I hope I was grateful for such a father. Mr. G. and Mr. C. followed him and expressed all that I could wish. A letter from Daniel, at New-York, mentions his calling on Dr. and Mrs. Scudder, and finding them very interesting people."

Among the notes which she addressed to friends just before leaving Norwich are the two following:

"Thank you, dear M——, for your kind invitation. You are thoughtful, kind, abundantly. What shall I say? Only may Heaven return you a hundred fold for every benevolent feeling toward me and mine."

"You ask what you will do without my sympathy—rather ask what I shall do when deprived of you all. My heart sometimes sinks at the prospect. I wish it otherwise. It ought to be so. But, dear cousins, I have much reason for gratitude that I do feel so great a degree of happiness in this undertaking—that the sacrifices are made to appear so light, in comparison with the object in view. For this I feel daily that I am indebted, under God, to the prayers of friends."

FAREWELL NOTE.

"May you be blessed in this life with the richest communications of God's love, and may our next interview be on the right hand of the throne of God! We do not, we cannot part to meet no more. Spirits know no confinement; they may range the world, and from its utmost extremities meet and mingle prayers. We shall thus meet Yes, dear M——, our acquaintance with each other is but just begun; it shall be perfected in eternity—a long, a blissful eternity. We pursue different roads to the same final rest—to our *home.* God grant us his Spirit that we may devote our whole lives to Him; be spiritual; follow our Divine Lord, and finally have an abundant entrance to his kingdom. Dear sisters, farewell; we owe each other our fervent petitions day by day. Let us be faithful, and we shall find abundant reward in this and a better world. Again I say, farewell! We have taken sweet counsel together; often walked to the house of God in company:

'Our hopes, our fears, our aims are one,
'Our comforts and our cares.'

"The God of peace bless you more and more. Amen and amen.

"HARRIET."

Mrs. W. was accompanied to Boston by her mother. From that place she wrote as follows:

"BOSTON, May 31, 1819.

"I improve a few minutes, while dear mother has gone out with Mrs. C. and Mr. W., to write to my beloved sister and other friends at home. You have probably received our letter sent last Thursday, and may think it a little doubtful whether you see mamma to-morrow. She has about determined on returning then, notwithstanding our sailing is deferred till a week from that time. You will readily believe that she has been a comfort to us on this visit. I trust she will have no reason to regret that she undertook it. Indeed some seasons we have enjoyed here would have been prized by any of you. All our visits have been closed by singing and prayer, and all our social interviews have been just such as the soul needs to quicken it when languishing for want of spiritual communion and fellowship."

At length the mission band, amidst the prayers and tears of many friends who "accompanied them to the ship," sailed from Boston, June 8, 1819, in the brig Indus, Capt. Wills, bound to Calcutta.

CHAPTER III.

Voyage to Calcutta, and passage through Trincomalie, Galle and Colombo, to Jaffna.

Journal and Revival at Sea—Ascent of the Hoogley—beautiful scenery—drowning of the gods—missionary and other friends at Calcutta—passage to Trincomalie—brief description of Ceylon—Fort Galle—a Boodhist temple—Colombo—friendship of Sir Robert Brownrigg—arrival at Jaffna.

It will be perceived that Mrs. Winslow, from the time of her separation from her parents and family circle till her death, was accustomed to brighten the chain of affection, by writing, under successive dates, a summary description of scenes through which she passed; transmitting the sheet as opportunity offered. These *letters*, having thus in many cases *the aspect of a journal*, constitute some of the richest materials for tracing a connected history of her life.

The following highly interesting communication to her parents, in which we accompany her on the voyage to Calcutta, amid signal displays of Divine mercy, is of the character just mentioned.

"Brig Indus, at Sea, June 21, 1819.

"My dear parents expect the same unreserved communication from their absent child which they always allowed her when under the paternal roof. I feel that you have an irresistible claim to every thing in which I can gratify you without interfering with the more direct object of my life; and nothing within my power shall be wanting to compensate in some degree for the sacrifice you have made in giving me up to God and the heathen. To you, then, dear guardians of my life, I address what I may be permitted to write from time to time, concerning whatever interests me, with the assurance that you will exercise all that indulgence that you have hitherto done, and will remember that I can write to you, and to my brothers and sisters, what I could not to any one else. You know my feelings on this subject, and my objections to having any publicity given to what I write.

"And is it true that all our future communications must be by means of pen and paper? Will you no longer administer to the thousand wants of your child; no more listen to her complainings and rejoicings with parental kindness? Have your labors of love for her ceased; and shall she be deprived the privilege of alleviating your cares in the decline of life, when you will most need her presence and attention? Shall she no longer be an immediate partaker of your joys and sorrows? Ah no. But we can still be helpers together of each other's joys, we can still bear each other's burdens. Though separated, we may meet and mingle prayers and tears on the same common altar. You can still exercise the affectionate solicitude of parents, and I the love and gratitude of a child. The wide ocean will soon divide our bodies, but our spirits may meet and hold sweet communion. We will not then be cast down, but go on our respective ways rejoicing.

"I could say much of parting scenes. Those which most impressed my mind, and to which I must always recur with indescribable emotions, are the farewell seasons with my parents. The last sounds which fell on my ear from their lips still dwell in my soul. The other members of the family too!—but I forbear. It is enough that I have enjoyed you so long, that God permits me to leave you for his service. While I weep, I rejoice. To see you all, to be with you and to enjoy you as I have done (and surely no person ever found their home more pleasant,) I would not return. I have entered on the work so long desired; the object before me is worth a far greater sacrifice than mine, and I would press towards it.

"We sailed from Boston, as we expected when mother left me, on the 8th instant. The weather was fine. Many people collected on the wharf to witness our departure. A prayer was offered by Dr. Worcester, and a parting hymn, 'Blest be the tie that binds,' was sung by many. The spectators were solemn and apparently affected, and we, though our object was so desirable, could not bid adieu to our dear native land, our privileges there, and the friends so long bound to our hearts, without a struggle. There was, however, much quietude on every countenance. About ten o'clock the vessel moved from the wharf, and we bade a silent but affectionate farewell to one, to another, to all the assembled multitude. Dr. Worcester, Mr. Dwight, and some other friends, among whom was Mr. Winslow's brother Hubbard, accompanied us six miles out. Our pilot left us early the following morning, and about 11 o'clock we were out of sight of the American shores. Our captain and other officers were soon found agreeable and kind. Happy in each other, and happy in our prospect, we promised ourselves some enjoyment amidst the privations necessarily attending so long a voyage.

"Our accommodations are as good as we could expect, and our spiritual privileges great. The brethren have had a meeting to make some arrangement for religious exercises and for intellectual improvement. It is agreed that there be public worship on Sabbath morning in the cabin, and in the afternoon on deck; morning and evening prayers daily, a public conference on Thursday evening, and a prayer-meeting the first Monday in the month. In our rooms we are to have a missionary meeting every Friday afternoon; and a prayer-meeting on Saturday evening; besides meetings at other times as circumstances may render expedient. Every afternoon we are to meet immediately after dinner for discussion on theological subjects.

"The brethren have conversed and prayed with the seamen, and find them attentive. The sisters presented to each of them a Bible. Some Tracts have been distributed, and we have the satisfaction of knowing that they are read. It is very common to see one reading aloud, while a number surround him with eyes and ears open as though they would seize every word. Last evening Mr. W. and I walked on deck just at sunset, and observing five or six assembled to hear a Tract, we stopped and listened till the reader ceased, after which Mr. W. conversed and prayed with them. It was a pleasant season, and such as I hope to enjoy many times. We have had one missionary meeting and one prayer-meeting. Service in the cabin yesterday morning was conducted by Mr. W. and on deck in the afternoon by Mr. Spaulding. The occasion was interesting. Aside from the charm of novelty, it was delightful to see such an audience on the great deep.

"*July 23.—South of the equator thirty miles.* My journal has been interrupted by severe illness, of which Mr. W. will give you some account. My thoughts on a sick bed have very often travelled back to the friends I have left. Not one person of early and affectionate interest has probably escaped them. Awake and asleep, I have walked, rode, and held sweet converse with many whose faces I do not expect to see again in the flesh. Every day I have been with my dear family at the altar where God has permitted us to unite our hearts, and to mingle our thanksgivings and petitions.

"24.—A squall has just come up. I should like to have you see the confusion it occasions in taking in sail, &c. We run up and look out to see the waves. They come rolling on as though they would ingulf our little bark; but in a short time they are comparatively quiet, and leave it to 'walk the waters like a thing of life.' We can almost say that we have had an uninterrupted course of smooth and pleasant sailing, though one squall was so violent as to carry away our fore-top-mast, main-top-gallant-mast, and other spars, as the sailors call them. I have experienced nothing of that alarm and distress which severe storms must occasion.

"*August* 2.—This day is set apart by the brethren for fasting and prayer. I believe that the Holy Spirit has been in the midst of us; that he has encouraged our hearts, and strengthened us for our great work. We have observed the monthly prayer-meeting with multitudes who love our Lord and Saviour. It was some hours before our friends in America; but we are not prevented from thinking of them again at the time we imagine they are presenting their requests for us and for the world. You know not, my dear parents, how much I depend on your prayers. You cannot forget us. It is a delightful thought, that morning and evening our dear father prays for his absent children at the domestic altar. Oh may we hereafter unite our hearts and voices in those mansions from which we shall go no more out for ever. May all our household be assembled there. In that happy place you will not have occasion to regret that God called one of your number to himself before he had struggled hard and long against the storms of this world; that one other was permitted to labor among the destitute of our own country, and still another among the heathen for the welfare of precious souls—even though all this is just as they were qualified to contribute to your happiness in the decline of life.

"4.—To-day we have had pleasant weather,

and are now going at the rate of nine miles an hour. I have been sitting awhile this evening on deck with Mr. W. enjoying the scene presented by the moon casting her silvery rays on the waters, and a few scattering clouds, with here and there a star twinkling between them. I can give you no adequate conception of it. There are indeed many appearances at sea which mock description. The 'ocean on fire' is peculiarly grand. You have stood by the sea, and admired the waves dashing in white foam against the shore. Now fancy that foam to be rolling, sparkling, burning embers; or to be all ignited like a shower of fire in fireworks. The water seems to be liquid fire wherever it is touched by the ship, disturbed by the fish or any thing else, or broken by the wind. As you look at the crested waves rolling on towards the ship, you are almost ready to say, in a moment it must be in a blaze. But thousands and thousands, rushing forward with violence, dash harmless against the sides of the vessel.

"5.—The brethren meet in the forecastle every evening, and hold a general prayer-meeting there every Wednesday evening. They have also religious exercises on Sabbath morning before our service in the cabin. There is continued encouragement from the attention of the seamen. Two or three have manifested some concern for their souls. Four of them cannot read, but will probably learn a little before we leave them.

"6.—I have been on deck this evening. Saw the moon slowly appear from behind a cloud near the horizon, and thought how often I have watched her first appearance at the door of the 'red house,' with one and another whose faces I can see no more. We may, however, fix our eyes on the same orb; we may gaze at the same heavens filled with the display of the wisdom and power of Jehovah; and if we can all say, 'This awful God is ours,' it is enough. I am willing to leave you with such a Protector, such a Friend.

"7.—We have new occasion for rejoicing today. About 10 o'clock a vessel was discovered approaching us. When she had come within two miles of us, I went up to wait the result. You cannot at all conceive our emotions when we saw unfurled, as she approached, the flag of our beloved country. Captain W. exclaimed, 'Ah, she's a yankee.' We found it was the Lady Adams, on a whaling voyage from Nantucket, twenty-two months out, and now bound home. We had just time to close the letters which were written. I have not mentioned our daily union of prayer for the seamen. This evening one of them was selected as a special subject of prayer for a week.

"8.—This morning a *dolphin* was caught about four feet long, in shape something like a salmon. Its appearance is very beautiful. In the water it is silvery, when caught and dying, it displays most of the colors of the rainbow, varying every moment. Cape pigeons have been flying about us for several days. One was caught to-day with a fish-hook and bait. They keep us company to pick up what is thrown out from the vessel. They resemble doves a little, but have longer wings and webbed feet. Their plumage is very soft, and under it is an uncommon share of down. The flesh is something like that of the robin, but harder and stronger.

"9.—Captain W. just now called me to go on deck and look at what are called the Magellan clouds; seen only on this side of the equator. They are very distinct to-night, as the sky is clear. Two are white, and near the milky way, and one black, directly in that bright girdle. The first are probably collections of stars, the other a more vacant space in the heavens. They are apparently near the pole, as two of them revolve round the third. I have not felt the air so piercing before; should call it cold at home, though we are not in so high a latitude as you, by eight or nine degrees. I am seated in my room with the door shut, and my old black silk coat and plaid cloak on. We have no fire, of course you will suppose we need the warmest clothing.

"14, *Sabbath.*—We delight to think and talk of our dear friends at home on this precious evening, and would inquire how it is with you; but, 'the winds and waves tell all the same unvarying tale.' Could my voice reach you, or could I by my pen excite in your bosoms one more emotion in behalf of those who go to the heathen, could I induce one more petition for them at the throne of grace, how would I plead with you, my dear friends. You think of, and pray for us, but you do not know the extent of our wants. We want *more faith*, more *humility*, more ardent love for souls. I say *we*, because it is common to use the plural in such language, and it is perhaps true of us all, though I would place none of our little band on a level with myself. Yesterday afternoon at our meeting, there seemed an uncommon spirit of brotherly love, and we believe the presence of our Saviour. It was one of the pleasantest seasons of christian communion we have had on board.

"16.—This morning we were called on deck by the sound of *land, hoa!* You can know little of our feelings. Nearly ten weeks the great waters had bounded our prospect. We were really delighted, although the object before us was only a small island properly called *Inaccessible.* It is so high as to be visible fifty miles. Its circumference is two leagues. A little distant, another and larger one presented a bold and majestic front. It reminded me of East Rock in New Haven, or seemed as that would appear if you could give it the same aspect at a distance as when riding at its foot. This island resembled the other in its roughness, as the clouds over it cast a shade, admitting some rays of the sun here and there amidst surrounding darkness. Between these two islands were two others which resembled stacks of hay. As we were gazing at this interesting scene a very dark cloud arose. The waves literally gathered blackness, and a squall of wind and rain obliged us to retreat to our cabins. This has furnished some variety for to-day, and gives a little tone to our languid spirits. The weather, on the whole, is very favorable to our rapid progress towards the heathen.

"18.—I could now tell my dear parents some thing more of a sea-life than when I last wrote. We had then boisterous weather, but this week it has been trying. Last night I did not sleep at all, indeed for several nights have slept but little. Repeated squalls and strong wind have raised the sea so much as to keep our vessel tossing with violence. The motion is like the rocking of a cradle, when it is thrown far over each way so as to roll the child from side to side. Every thing loose is thrown about. Chairs and other articles of furniture are constantly travelling to and fro. There is no such thing as rest. I wish I could give you any just notion of the scene on deck this morning. The waves were what is called 'mountain high.' I never saw any thing so grand,

and said to Mr. W. that I would willingly suffer much at sea to witness such a display of the power of Jehovah.

"26.—The last week our progress has been very rapid. Saturday night we had a gale which Capt. W. called severe. In the last fortnight we have come the distance of America from Europe. We are not, however, impatient for the end of our voyage.

"At this time, when we were almost desponding, we are made glad by the hope that one of the seamen is a subject of grace. Mr. S. has been in the habit of giving two of them instruction in navigation. On Monday when he went to the forecastle for this purpose, one of them said, 'I must give up navigation for my Bible ; I find I have neglected that too long.' He was convinced of his sin and danger while at the helm in the gale on Saturday night. Mr. W. after conversing with him last night, thought he appeared well. He has been a decided infidel. When he found that missionaries were to be on board, he cursed them and said, 'am I to be shut up with these creatures so long? I cannot even take a civil oath without being mauled at the elbow by all the holy brotherhood.' This man was the week before last selected as the special subject of prayer. His name is Brown. There are several others of whom we hope good things.

"28.—After a trying day from violent weather, this evening has been among the most precious of my missionary life. I have felt more than ever before that I can rest my eternal *all* on God, and fear nothing. Enjoyed our prayer-meeting very much.

"30.—Could my dear parents participate our emotions this evening in behalf of the precious souls around us, how would they bless God that he called their children to the heathen. We do believe that fruit will abound to his glory. Mr. W. after some conversation with the youngest sailor, the only one whose prospect is something better than to be always before the mast, is almost ready to believe he is a christian. The last fortnight his views of sin and of the character of Jehovah have been more affecting, and he gives some evidence of a change of heart.

"Two others are subjects of apparent conviction. The weather last night was more boisterous than before. We had a tremendous storm of lightning, rain, and hail, succeeded by an almost entire calm, which left our ship to be tossed on the waves with great violence. The principal danger to be apprehended in this voyage is from the calms which follow high winds in this region. The vessel then is in great danger of foundering. It is knocked about on the mountain-waves like an egg-shell. I cannot say that through all the storms I have been unmoved. I have often trembled at the display of God's power. In few things is his power and our weakness more manifest than in a severe thunder storm at sea. You can have no adequate conception of the scene, and it so baffles all description that I will not attempt one.

"*September* 3.—This is dear H. J.'s birth-day. When at Andover, Dr. Woods said to me, 'Your heart will often ache to see the little folks.' He was right; yet *I would rather see them in Ceylon than in America.* Dear sisters, I desire most of all that you be good children, that you love God, be kind and affectionate to each other and to all around you.

"Our missionary meeting was this afternoon a refreshing season. Could you know our dear companions as we do, you would rejoice that we are so favored. You must know something more about these meetings, as they are the pleasantest we have. The special object of them is to mention any deficiencies that we have observed in each other's conduct in course of the week, and to remark upon them with the freedom of brethren and sisters. Nothing has tended more to unite us as members of one body.

"4.—This afternoon, after the theological discussion, Mr. S. proposed that Mr. W. and I should remain with them to read the Bible. We enjoyed the season very much, and I could not but think of many hours I have spent with the children of God in unprofitable conversation, when if they had been employed in reading the word of God I should be a better missionary. It has been well said that the degree of our piety may be measured by our attachment to this book.

"8.—The brethren have had an interesting time with the seamen. It was the general prayer-meeting in the forecastle. The sisters met at the same time for prayer. Most of the seamen came together. The most abandoned was there, who said last evening when one of the brethren spoke particularly to the others and not to him, 'then you leave me to perish.' He has been more profane for a few days, evidently attempting to harden himself in sin. One said to him, 'I have been thinking much of you, and am afraid you are becoming hardened.' 'So,' said he, 'you give me up for a lost sheep. I have done all I can to be a christian, and cannot. I am no worse than others.'

"11.—It was agreed this evening to set apart Monday afternoon as a season of thanksgiving to God for the mercies with which he has accompanied us so far on our way towards the heathen; particularly for his preservation of those who have been sick, and for his display of mercy towards Brown, the man mentioned as hopefully regenerated.

"Some *albatrosses* were caught to-day. From

the extremity of one wing to the other they measured six feet. The first mate told me that he had caught those that measured fifteen feet. I have secured some of the feathers to make fans for Charlotte and Elizabeth.

"13.—Our season of thanksgiving this afternoon was precious. The brethren talked of the way by which God directed them, till they were persuaded that He called them to the heathen. Occurrences altogether providential, but in themselves trifling, led them step by step to the important result. I too could say I knew not at the time what many things meant which are now intelligible. The change in the state of missionary feeling in the seminary at Andover is great since they first inquired what was their duty. Then, almost four years ago, when Mr. S. and Mr. W. entered the Seminary, there was but one missionary there. At the close of the year there were three, at the close of the second year, six, and of the third, eleven. There were then no missionaries in the field except Judson, Hall, and Newell, as Mr. Nott was on his return. What hath God wrought? How different are the circumstances under which we are now placed from what we could then expect. Bless the Lord, O our souls, and forget not all his benefits!

"14.—The general prayer-meeting in the forecastle was well attended this evening. Brown appears to gain strength every day. The second mate said to Mr. W., I believe there is *one* good man on board, and that is Brown. They who are at all convinced of sin think much, and our hopes for them continue. *Our* meeting this evening has been pleasant. Our absent friends are never forgotten on these occasions.

"15.—Brown has had a little difficulty—he says, 'I find it harder to get along than I thought I should. I have served Satan so long and so faithfully, that he is loth to give me up.' We are again gratified to have the testimony of the officers to his correct deportment. The man who has been so profane said to one of the brethren yesterday, 'I am afraid that I am heading the wrong way.' This was an acknowledgment that surprised us all. He likewise came on deck to the meeting last evening, when his watch was below. Another says, 'sin sticks pretty close, but I hope to get the weather-gage before long.'

"28.—Solemnity still rests on every countenance, and we believe the work of God is ripening. The three officers are distressed for their souls.

"29.—This morning we had a prayer-meeting in the cabin before breakfast. Appearances through the day much like those of yesterday. This evening we have been 'forward.' We found the seamen assembled, as it was the time for their general prayer-meeting. The concern increases. The officers and Captain Wills came; also the steward, cook, and cabin-boy. Only the man at the helm remained behind. It was a new time. The Holy Spirit was present and seemed to shake every soul. The first officer expresses some hope that the Lord has appeared for him. He, however, can only say, 'whereas I was blind, now I see.' The others are deeply distressed. After evening worship in the cabin, we had a meeting for thanksgiving.

"*October* 1.—I have felt to-day as though I dare scarcely think or act. I would like to hide myself where I could *see* what God is doing, and yet be in no danger of hindering the work. It is not merely a still small voice speaking to one and another, but a mighty rushing wind which fills all the place. We had a prayer-meeting before breakfast, and our missionary-meeting this afternoon. They were precious. It seems as though every word spoken through the day was accompanied by the Spirit of God. The sea has been calm since the Sabbath, and the sun and sky emblematic of our spiritual state. Clouds have appeared above the horizon threatening violent wind and thunder; but they have hung round for a time and sunk again behind the blue waters. The sun has remained bright, and never, I believe, did the Sun of Righteousness so cast his beams into a little world on the waste of waters. I would describe the scene presented this evening, but you can never form an idea of it. We all went 'forward.' Every seaman, and the whole ship's company, save one man at the helm, were present. The subject of remark was, 'Now is the accepted time.' There seemed a general feeling that the Lord was passing by, and whoever *would* might obtain forgiveness. The first and second mate, and clerk, were appealed to for their testimony that 'now *is* the accepted,' the best 'time,' and with melting hearts and eyes each said, 'I feel it.' Captain W. prayed and addressed the meeting with a solemnity and feeling which melted us all. I never felt so much as though God was indeed present, as though angels were hovering over us to carry intelligence to the courts of heaven, of 'prodigals returned,' and 'heirs of glory born.' On retiring we stopped 'midships' to sing a hymn of thanksgiving. The clerk came up and joined in it. To our surprise we found him indulging a hope in Christ. After half an hour's conversation, we united in prayer that God would not suffer him to rest on any false foundation. The second mate then came up to be welcomed as a brother in Christ. His distress had been greater than that of any of the others. While we were conversing with him, the cabin boy came from below. He could not sleep, but wanted to go to God. Another prayer with singing closed our interview.

"While we were there, Brown had been praying with the men 'forward.' Mr. W. and I remained a while on deck. Never did the moon shine more pleasantly. We thought we should like to write on it, '*A Revival at Sea,*' that you might participate our joy. Never was a ship's deck a more solemn and awful place. In our meeting Captain W. spoke to the seamen of the temptations they would find in Calcutta. He said, 'Would you go with me to church, through the *bazar*, where three thousand seamen would ridicule you, and call you long-faced, praying fellows?' All said, 'Yes.' To the question, Do you love God? one replied, 'Yes, in every shape that I can think of Him.'

"2.—One day like this is indeed worth a hundred lives of 'pleasurable sin.' The three officers, and one or two of the seamen, have a new song put into their mouths. It is a common remark now among the sailors, 'What a place! never did I see such a forecastle.' The first mate has a pious mother, whose prayers are at length, we trust, answered. The second mate's mother hoped this would be the best voyage he ever made. He replied, 'I expect to hear some praying, and have a little fun with the psalm-singers.' The clerk has pious parents. He too made himself much amusement as to the missionaries. The first mate says, 'I feel more like a child than a man; I go about the deck crying and laughing.' The others say, 'If this is religion, it is happiness more than I ever knew before.' They are about among the seamen exhorting them to taste and see that the Lord is gracious. Poor Amy, the woman of color, thinks she was never a christian, and is deeply distressed. She spent the whole of last night in singing and praying.

"4.—It has been agreed to devote this day, which is the first Monday of the month, to thanksgiving for God's wonderful mercy towards us. At 3 o'clock we had a sermon by Mr. W. from the text, 'Give God the praise, we know that this man is a sinner.' Think you that such a scene was ever witnessed on the great deep? A whole ship's company assembled with a song of praise, and to unite with thousands in prayer for the prosperity of Zion. I thought of an expression of one of the seamen last week, after the captain's first most feeling address, 'A heart that won't feel now, must be as hard as that anchor.' In the evening there was another meeting with the seamen, when the origin and design of the monthly prayer-meeting were explained; and they were exhorted to feel that they might do something to advance the kingdom of Christ. In this, however, the brethren were anticipated, for they had been talking together about how they should do good to their fellow-men.

"There are some striking things to be marked in this revival. The hand of God was apparent in the manner of the earlier convictions. The first mate had lifted his harpoon to strike a fish on the Sabbath. It occurred to him, suddenly, that he was breaking the commandment of God, and his hand fell. He says, 'all the sins that I ever committed came into my mind.' His life has been often preserved in a signal manner, in the midst of battle and in shipwreck; and he called himself a barren fig-tree, which would have been cut down but for the interposition of Christ. Now, he seems to grow daily. The second mate was struck with conviction while at work in the rigging. One of the seamen was seized with alarm in a severe storm, and for the first time felt himself to be a sinner. The cook heard two seamen talking about the excellence of religion, and said, 'let me alone now till I have done eating,' but they continued, and he added, 'may God Almighty send down his Spirit and convert every body on board.' He had been awfully profane, and this was said with no meaning. The recollection of it followed him to bed, and occasioned great distress, till he found relief at the throne of grace.

"9.—We have continued occasion to bless the

Lord for his wonders here. Meetings and frequent conversations with the new converts are continued. A fresh breeze is carrying us swiftly towards Calcutta; if it continues, three or four days will find us at the head of the bay.

"12.—Our habitation, dear friends, is a *Bethel.* Is it not in answer to your prayers with many other christian friends in America? Continue to pray much for us, and for other missionaries, and the heathen. Will you not induce others to pray more? Oh that every pious heart would awake to this subject; that there might be continual wrestling in our churches, till nations are born in a day, and the world filled with the glory of God.

"14.—This morning Captain W. suggested that our prayer-meeting should have in view our preservation amidst the dangers which surrounded us. We had seen neither sun nor sky for four days, and he could not determine where we were, especially as the wind and sea had driven us to and fro. The aspect of the heavens was very threatening, and the season of the year gave reason to expect bad weather. It was, besides, more and more evident that we were near some shore; probably the western, to which we were fast driving, although repeated soundings found no bottom. The prayers accordingly had reference to our situation, and it seemed that while we were speaking the Lord heard. The clouds were in a great measure scattered, the sun appeared, and at 12 o'clock it was found that we were nearly 100 miles farther northward on our course than the captain supposed; and though there is no moon by which to ascertain the longitude, he thinks we are likewise farther east.

"18. *At the mouth of the river Hoogley.*—We have been tossed about in every direction since my last date. We now find that we came near being driven on the western shore, and once narrowly escaped a reef. I cannot give you particulars. The course up to the pilot-ground is very blind, and the sand reefs extend far into the bay. The Lord interposed for us, and last night, when we had no prospect but to go out again to sea or be driven upon a reef, about 10 o'clock we came suddenly on three pilot brigs. At 1 o'clock a pilot was on board. We anchored for the night, and now at 7 o'clock a fair wind is carrying us rapidly toward the river."

"CALCUTTA, October 24, 1819.

"MY DEAR PARENTS,—You will rejoice to hear that after a residence on the water of *one hundred and thirty-three days*, we are in the midst of friends, and on a heathen shore. My emotions on seeing the natives were much as I anticipated. Many of them came to us in boats to sell fruit, or to obtain fire that they might smoke; and two of their boats were attached to our vessel as tenders. The navigation of the river is so dangerous as to make this necessary. Vessels are sometimes lost by being driven on shore by the tide and current.

"The dress of the natives, you have often been told, is only a piece of cloth around the waist. Some, however, have a cloth thrown over their shoulders, or wear something like a tunic. Their hair is generally very black and oily. It is cut in various ways, usually most of the head is shaved. We were, of course, a little shocked to see people so nearly naked; but in a moment the recollection of their spiritual degradation filled our minds and hearts to the exclusion of every thought of their external appearance.

"On Tuesday at two o'clock we were off Calcutta. The wind, which generally blows from the north-east at this season, was for two days from the southward, so that instead of being in the river two or three weeks, as we expected, we came up in less than forty-eight hours. We had much bustle and confusion to get our trunks in order to come on shore in so short a time, and scarcely indulged ourselves to look at the banks of the river, which are very pleasant. Delightful country-seats, surrounded by the most beautiful scenery, on the very brink of the river, with here and there a group of Hindoo cottages, presented a charming prospect to eyes that had seen nothing for many weeks but a waste of waters.

"Soon after we were at anchor Mr. W. went with our good captain on shore to find a house which would accommodate us all, as he and we were alike unwilling to be separated. In their absence we were informed that the holydays of the natives closed that day. We soon saw on the shore directly opposite to us, great multitudes approaching the water with a horrid din of music, conveying their gods to throw them into the stream. We could discern nothing of their appearance but that they were the size of a common man, and about the waist were painted black. They were held over the water some minutes, while the noise of various musical instruments continued, and then plunged in to float down with the current. Near to them was a bedstead in the water, from which a sick person had been washed or taken off by the birds and fish. This ceremony of drowning their gods was observed hundreds of miles above us, by millions of these wretched beings at the same time. The idols came floating by us through the day.—Through the night we could see fire-works and hear music from the shore. Almost the first thing I beheld after I arose in the morning, was a dead child floating by. Within an hour three other bodies came down with crows upon them. Dead bodies are devoured by birds or fish soon after they are thrown into the river. The crows are particularly busy. They are not very large, but as they are not allowed to be killed, they are very numerous, and almost fill the air in flocks."

The first land that presented itself was the island of Saugor, where it was painful to recollect that for ages mothers had assembled annually to offer their infants in sacrifice, by throwing them to the shark; but cheering to know that the horrid practice had been for some time abolished by the British government; and to notice it with gratitude, as one of the tide-marks of ebbing heathenism.

Ascending the Hoogley, the scenery presented on each side of the river is very uniform, as the banks are low and the whole country is level; but it is pleasant, indeed almost enchanting, to those who for months have been at sea, especially if they have never before visited a tropical climate. "'Tis the land of the sun." The brightness and transparency of the atmosphere, the luxuriance and freshness of the vegetation, the entirely novel character of almost every tree, shrub, plant and flower, the mud or bamboo huts of the natives scattered along the banks of the rivers, or under the shade of palm-trees, and contrasted here and there with some more respectable mansion of brick neatly stuccoed, or a stone temple lifting its white dome amidst the green foliage of a cocoa-nut grove, or under the spreading banian, all attract and yet bewilder the fancy. The spectator finds himself in a new world; and as he advances above Diamond harbor, where all the large East-India-men lie; having, on the one hand, the extensive botanic gardens of the East India Company; on the other, splendid country seats, or garden houses; and opening before him, Calcutta itself, the "city of palaces," with its fort of a thousand guns, its magnificent government-house, and forest of shipping—the whole view is at once so picturesque and so grand as to call forth the highest admiration.

The *drowning of the gods*, or throwing them into the embraces of the goddess Gunga, the river Ganges, is a very important ceremony among the Hindoos. In course of the holydays mentioned above, is the Doorga-poojah, or festival of the goddess Doorga. At this time every respectable native has an image made of this goddess, which represents a woman with ten arms. It is usually as large as life—made of clay baked, and beautifully painted, as well as elegantly dressed and adorned. After being consecrated by a

Brahmin, the goddess is supposed to come down and animate it. The idol is then placed in some convenient part of the house, and worshipped seven days, with offerings of incense, flowers, and food, attended by prostrations, feasting, music, and dancing ; and is then conveyed round the streets of the city in procession, with music, and thrown into the river, after being stripped of its dress and ornaments, which are *given to the Brahmins!*

"At eleven o'clock we came on shore to our own, or rather our captain's hired house, which we found very pleasant. A spacious dining-hall extends through the house on the second story, having at one end two windows with blinds from near the ceiling to the floor. At the opposite end are two doors leading into a wide verandah or portico. On both sides of the hall are lodging and sitting-rooms. Around the house, and connected with it, are stores for goods, called *godowns*, on the flat roofs of which we can take a pleasant walk just at evening. These houses are such as are occupied by merchants and other temporary residents in the place.

"We had just time to see where we were when dinner was ready. It was pleasant to be once more seated at a table where we were not obliged to hold our plate and cup to keep them from rolling about. While engaged at our acceptable meal, Mr. and Mrs. Lawson, of the Baptist connection, and Dr. Johns came in to see us. They received us as christian friends, and invited us to take up our residence with them, but we were too pleasantly situated together to remove. An invitation was likewise received from Dr. Carey for two of us to go to Serampore to his house, and also from an American gentleman. We did not expect to find ourselves thus surrounded by friends in this land of strangers. On Thursday we breakfasted at Dr. Johns'. A conveyance came for us at six o'clock. You will think this rather early at this season, but the people of Calcutta rise very early. The air is more pure and cool in the morning than at any other time. Dr. J. who is now a practising physician here, has a delightful residence on a pleasant street at a distance from the bustle of the city. Around it are winding walks and shrubbery.

"26.—The desire to see the practices of the poor heathen, and to return the politeness of friends, makes every hour full of employment. We are receiving every proof of kindness from the missionaries of the established church, from Mr. Townley and others of the London Missionary Society, and from the Baptist brethren stationed here and at Serampore. The face of things is greatly changed since the first missionaries came from America to the East."

For some days Mrs. W. was seriously ill, but speedily recovered; and on the eve of leaving Calcutta, we find the following cheerful expressions of gratitude to christian friends, and of interest in those on whom so rich blessings had descended in the Indus.

"*November* 8.—Our friends here have been very kind, especially Mr. and Mrs. Newton, who are from America. To other Americans, and some English friends, particularly the Rev. Mr. Thomason, one of the chaplains, and his lady, we are also much indebted. To Captain Wills we shall always feel that we owe more than we can ever repay. May God reward him. He feels much at the prospect of our leaving him so soon, and we shall find it very trying to part with him and the other officers and seamen. The officers give increasing evidence of being born again. At the recollection of what God has done, we are encouraged to devote ourselves more entirely to our work.

"CALCUTTA, Nov. 9, 1819.

"DEAR MR. G——, You will hear of our reaching Calcutta in health, and how the Lord smiled upon us while in the Indus. Your heart will rejoice, and you will lift it up in thanksgiving to the God of grace. Is it not wonderful, that to us, *even us*, was so great privilege given? The recollection of it fills us with wonder and admiration. And now, after being three weeks in port, where is every temptation, to see most of the ship's crew, and all the officers, content to remain in the vessel, except when there is religious worship on shore, and collecting their companions from other vessels to attend meetings on board, is indeed enough to astonish all who witness it. Several of the crew, and the first mate and clerk, have been to this port before with our dear Captain Wills, but never could he get them to a place of religious worship. Now they have been with us to the house of God with as much apparent hungering and thirsting for the bread of life as any you are accustomed to see. The first Sabbath after our arrival, all but those it was necessary should remain in the vessel came in the morning to our house, and went with us to Dr. Carey's chapel. It was a novel scene to all. They have ever since been regular attendants. The first convert, Brown, is a striking example of divine grace; he does not hesitate to pray among his companions, and even when officers of other vessels are on board. You would be astonished, notwithstanding all you know of the power of grace; to hear his petitions, so full of meaning, yet so concise, so appropriate, and so spiritual.

"I could write long about these interesting objects, and I believe not be tedious to one who loves the soul, but must deny myself. God only knows if they will continue to run well. You will pray for them; you will induce others to pray for them."

The subsequent life of the two mates, the captain's clerk, and at least two of the seamen, is believed to have given evidence of the reality of their conversion. The work was indeed glorious. A change of character in even a few of those who "go down to the sea in ships," and visit almost every heathen nation, and are thus the "epistles" of christian lands, "known and read of all men," is of great consequence in its influence on the conversion of the world.

On the 10th of November passage was taken for Ceylon in the ship Dick, of London, bound to Trincomalie and Columbo.

"*November* 27.—We are in a large commodious ship, and have every thing, of a temporal nature, to make us comfortable. In the most important things we are favored beyond our expectations. The principal cabin being devoted to us, except at meals, we have family-prayers there together, and can at any time hold social meetings. On the first Sabbath after getting to sea, it was proposed to the captain to have preaching on deck. He replied that it would please him. Accordingly the ship's company were assembled, and Mr. W. preached. All were very attentive. The seamen were early addressed privately, but there was no public meeting till Sabbath evening. They were nearly all present, and appeared to hear the word with gladness. All the officers regularly go forward to the meetings, which are continued every evening, and they appear ready to hear any thing on religious subjects. The first few days after we embarked we were much disturbed by the language used on board, so unlike that to which we had been accustomed on the Indus; but I have not now for many days heard an oath, and the brethren remark that there is a great change in that respect."

The high lands near Trincomalie were in sight before dark on the 27th. The harbor is rather difficult of access, but when entered, is one of the finest in the world. It is the rendezvous of the British navy in the East, being the admiral's station.

The island of Ceylon is by nature the fairest perhaps of the green isles of the tropics, concerning which it may well be said without any uncommon poetic license,

"*There* every prospect pleases,
"And only man is vile."

A great part of it, particularly in the interior, is still uncultivated. The conical hills, the high and abrupt mountains, the deep, dark valleys are covered with primitive forest, or thick jungle almost impenetrable to the rays of the sun, and inhabited by elephants, buffaloes, leopards, bears, hyenas, deer, jackals, and monkeys. But the maritime parts are generally well cultivated, and present an inviting appearance, though in the flat country it has much sameness. At the south and west are the lofty and waving groves of cocoa-nut trees skirting and embroidering all the shore; and at the north, particularly in Jaffna, those of the tall and erect palmyra with its tufted crown of fan-leaves always green, embosoming and covering almost the whole district with its more than one hundred and fifty villages. The sight of such groves under a tropical sun is "like the shadow of a great rock in a weary land." Near the western coast you have the rich cinnamon gardens for miles in extent, and in the interior a great variety of noble forest trees lining the sides of the mountains, sometimes to their very summit, six or seven thousand feet in height, apparently the more vigorous the farther they are out of the reach of the heat below, and the more luxuriant in their greenness in proportion as they approach nearer to the sky. Their foliage being similar to that of promiscuous forest trees on the plains of temperate climates, but never all falling off at once, and seldom fading, gives to the whole scenery the aspect of perpetual spring. The island lies nearly between 6° and 10° north latitude, and 80° and 82° east longitude, and is separated from the continent by a strait about 30 miles wide.

The principal towns are Colombo on the western side, Trincomalie and Batticaloe on the eastern, Galle at the south, Kandy in the interior, and Jaffnapatam at the north. The circuit of the island by the most direct road is 763 miles, and the distance from Galle at the south, to Jaffnapatam at the north, is 294—Colombo being 72 miles from the former and 222 from the latter. From Colombo to Kandy is 72 miles, and thence to Trincomalie 116, but there is a route across this part of the island 22 miles nearer. The island is in shape much like a pear, the larger end being at the south. It contains 24,664 square miles, and according to the census of 1831 had a population of 950,917, now much increased of whom 6,664 are whites, including, besides the English, who are not numerous, descendants of the Dutch and Portuguese. There are also a few thousand native Mussulmen, called Moormen

The mass of the population is composed of the Cingalese of the interior and southern parts, and the Tamulians, who are mostly in the northern and eastern districts; the former being Boodhists, speaking Cingalese, the latter Brahminists or Hindoos, using the Tamul language. There are scattered over the island forty or fifty thousand native Roman Catholics, who have many churches. Their priests, including the vicar-general, who is changed once in three years, are at present *seventeen* in number, and are most or all of them from the Portuguese settlement at Goa. There are many thousand nominal Protestants, especially among the Cingalese of the maritime parts; but, except those connected with the mission stations, they differ very little from the heathen among whom they dwell.

Mrs. W. after having described the scenery presented on approaching Trincomalie, of which she says, "the hills stretched along the coast much resemble those of our native country," and having given a view of the harbor, continues her journal.

"*December* 3.—We had been at anchor but a few hours, when Captain H. returned from the shore with the Rev. Mr. Carver, a Wesleyan missionary. He met us with the kindness of a christian brother, and urged our going to his house. The brethren went with him to make some arrangements about our proceeding to Jaffna. They had no encouragement that a conveyance could be procured direct from this place for us all, either by sea or land. No native vessels coast that way during this monsoon, and it is impossible to procure bearers or palankeens enough for all to go by land. To-day we learn from the collector that arrangements may be made for some by this route, and the others must go round by Colombo.

"After dinner we walked out to the esplanade to view the eminence on which is the principal fort, and to look at the waves by moonlight lashing the sandy beach. We had just arrived in sight of the water when our fair lamp was covered by obtruding clouds, but it soon partially re-appeared and cast that kind of light and shade over the scene which inspires a pensive sadness. We wished to ascend the rock, but had not strength. On the brow of the precipice is a monument erected to the memory of a Dutch lady who threw herself from it into the sea below. She went there to take a last look of a ship which was conveying away her husband and friends. The ship in going round the rock was wrecked. In a paroxysm of grief she threw herself into the same gulf which had swallowed up her friends

"4.—Last evening we left Dr and Mrs. Scudder on shore, expecting to see them again this morning, but coming on board we found preparations making for the ship to sail immediately. We were early outside the bay. There was much confusion on board, and very little sleep during the night, as we had, in addition to our own number, several military officers with their families as passengers. It was pleasant to be on land yesterday, and I felt a little dread of the water, but now am happy to be again on the dark blue wave. A fresh breeze is wafting us swiftly to our port."

The next day the ship came to anchor at Galle. The view as you approach this place, indeed all along the coast from Trincomalie, is varied and imposing. The hills and mountains are seen rising above the water in almost every shape, as cones, pyramids, and irregular piles of buildings, much like the fantastic forms sometimes assumed by heavy clouds in the west at sunset. Behind the fort of Galle is a very high hill or mountain called the hay-cock, and around are scattered peaks and bluffs of almost every variety of form. The fort or fortified town incloses a great number of buildings, most of them low and in the Portuguese style. The streets are narrow, but hard and clean, and the widest of them lined with venerable shade trees, a little resembling in appearance low branching oaks. Among these is the bread-fruit tree. The whole shore is rocky, and the surf rises in most places very high when the wind is strong from the south. None but the native boats could ride in the swell at all. Their construction is curious. They are, like the Indian canoe, made of a large log hollowed out; but unlike that, the opening at the top is very narrow, and boards perhaps a foot in width are lashed to the edges all round to prevent the water from entering the boat. Being so high and narrow, it would immediately upset, were it not for an outrigger made of a small log lying on the water parallel to the boat at the distance of two or three yards, and attached to it at each end by a bent pole curving upwards so as not to dip in the water. The boat cannot upset, and though almost buried in the swell or surf, it rides safely, and may carry a small sail.

"*December 7. Fort of Galle.*—This morning the Rev. Mr. M'Kenny, a Wesleyan missionary, came on board and kindly conveyed us to his house. He and his wife are agreeable, and appear zealous for the cause of God among the heathen. We feel quite at home with them. He has under his care several flourishing schools. In some respects the prospect of bringing these poor idolaters to a knowledge of the truth is encouraging, in others it is dark. Their confirmed habits and the evil example of most Europeans are the grand barriers; and these are more formidable than you can easily conceive. In looking round upon all this Eastern world, I should ask with despondency, 'Can these dry bones live?' were it not for the promises of God. These are the life and strength of a missionary amidst his greatest discouragements.

"9.—This afternoon we visited *a Boodhist temple* situated on an eminence in the midst of cocoa-nut trees. It being twilight, an old man went before us with a torch. The moment I entered the building a sort of horror seized me, so that I approached with trembling the hideous figure called Boodhu. It is made of potter's earth baked and painted, and is eighteen cubits long and proportionably large. It is stretched on a platform. A variety of flowers lay around it, which had that day been brought as offerings. A small stone image of the same god stood before the one lying down, and at the feet was Vishnu with a blue face and a distended bloody mouth. On every side were paintings of different gods. In the outer room were representations of kings, and of important events in history. At the door were images of two giants and of two lions placed as guards. Notwithstanding all the descriptions of these temples which I had read and heard in America, I had no proper idea of one. Returning home we had a pleasant walk by a canal, on one bank of which were both rocks and shrubbery, and on the other mud cottages swarming with children, who ran out in crowds to see us pass by. A part of the road lay by the seashore, where we had a fine view of the angry surge foaming amidst the rocks and sand.

"*Sabbath*, 12.—Where are the Sabbaths I once enjoyed? Their memory is still sweet. A part of to-day I have been refreshed. This morning went with Mr. W. to a school. The building is on the top of a hill. Below we could see a small sheet of water near a white cottage, also winding paths, cocoa-nut trees, and abundance of jungle near the side of the hill in the valley below. The prospect was charming. Mr. W. preached, through an interpreter, to about seventy boys, with their teachers and some of their parents. Previous to this, however, the interpreter read prayers in Cingalese. The responses were repeated by the boys with much animation. They likewise sang with spirit. Some of these little creatures scarcely moved their eyes from the speaker during the sermon. Their answers to questions put to them displayed a good degree of acquaintance with the Scriptures. Probably in most of the Sabbath-schools in America you would not find children better informed on religious subjects. Some of them write and read very well. When we came away they all rose and bade us farewell. I have seen nothing in India that interested me so much."

After having been hospitably entertained eight days at Galle, the party were summoned on board ship, and sailed for Colombo, where they arrived on the fifth day. In passing along the coast there was a fine view of Adam's Peak in the interior of the island, whose conical top rising boldly into the clouds, which often rest on the sides of the mountain, was now covered by them, and then appeared distinctly above them all, as a blue tent hanging in empty air.

One of the most singular sights presented on approaching Colombo, is the great number of fishing boats. Sometimes not less than five hundred sai in a morning, stretch out to sea so far as to appear only like ducks sitting on the water, or be entirely out of sight, though the weather is boisterous

Colombo is a fortified town, or a fort, a mile and a quarter in circumference, defended by three hundred heavy cannon; inclosing several hundred houses, including a large custom-house, a church, and the king's house, or residence of the governor, with wide and open streets On landing, all were most kindly invited to the house of the Rev. Mr. Chater, a Baptist missionary. The season did not admit of their going immediately to the northern part of the island by sea; but after a little delay they proceeded by the inland navigation to Jaffna, in company with J. N. Mooyart, Esq. a warm friend of missions and a magistrate in that district. The brethren previously waited upon the governor, Sir Robert Brownrigg, then about to leave the island, and *obtained an official permit for the reinforcement to join the mission.* Their arrival in season for this was very providential, as the successor of Sir Robert would not, there is every reason to believe, have granted their request. They had also opportunity to see something of the missionary work at Colombo, and to meet most of the missionaries from different parts of the island.

"*January* 16, 1820.—Mrs. S. and I went with one of the Wesleyan brethren to two of his schools this morning, and were much gratified by their appearance. These brethren have about *twelve* schools in and around Colombo. They promise much good, but when I see missionaries, habituated to the use of words beyond the comprehension of the ignorant, attempting to instruct children, I am more and more convinced that *females* also should be employed among the heathen.

"*February* 1.—This is a great day; the governor embarked this afternoon. I went to the government house in the morning with Mr. W. Many people were assembled. Among them was a large school of orphan children who have been supported by Lady Brownrigg. When the governor and his lady took leave of the people there was much emotion. Almost all wept. The poor children sobbed as though their hearts would break. It is to be feared they will not find another such friend as Lady B. Her ladyship, while her mind was so much engrossed, was kind enough to send an apology for not having called on us. Last week the governor had a levee. He then expressed to the brethren his approbation of our mission, and said many kind things of the missionaries.

"The Wesleyan brethren have a conference here at this time, and the church missionaries are met on business of their mission. At our table to-day were *fifteen* missionaries.

"*February 4, Friday evening.*—Left Colombo about 6 o'clock P. M. taking leave of our kind brother and sister Chater, after a season of prayer with them and some other missionary friends. We reached the place of embarkation in the evening. The scene was gloomy. Our passage was through a thick wood. In some places the river appeared scarcely wide enough to admit our boats. A fire on the banks only served to make visible the thick darkness around."

They proceeded through Negombo and Medupia, thence over a portage of nine miles into Chilaw lake, and through Andepan, Putlam, Calpenteen, and Manar, upwards of 200 miles, amidst many inconveniences—sometimes finding a shelter in the frail *rest-house*,* where the traveller is expected to furnish his own bed, and to cook his own *rice and curry*,* now amused by monkeys

* There are no inns in the country, and the "rest-houses" are mere sheds, or at best empty rooms, in which a traveller may *rest*, but he must furnish his own provisions, as well as bed, and most of the utensils for cooking. The cooking is, however, a very simple operation. An earthen pot, placed on three stones, and a little fire kindled beneath, serves to boil his rice; and in another smaller vessel, also of brown earthen, his "curry" is prepared. This is the staple food of India, and is easily cooked, whether you stop at a rest-house, or by the side of a road, or on the bank of a river. The curry is made of coriander, cardamon, and a variety of other aromatic seeds, ground up with tumeric (a yellow root) to powder, to which red peppers, onions, and garlic are added. This compound being mixed up with melted butter, or the milk squeezed from scraped cocoa-nut, is simmered with a little butcher's meat, fowl, fish, eggs, or vegetables cut up fine, and perhaps previously boiled. This forms a condiment of which a small quantity is eaten with the rice. At the rest-houses milk may often be procured, and sometimes eggs. Most of the natives have only one *full* meal a day, but *then* they eat an enormous quantity. Common laborers will carry heavy burdens in the sun, from morning to night, without taking any nourishment in the meantime. They look very thin; but see them after they have eaten their rice, and you might think they had swallowed a pumpkin.

playing on the trees; then disturbed by an alligator; and occasionally in fear of elephants and buffaloes, though sometimes making a repast on the milk of the latter—and on the 16th were approaching Jaffnapatam, when Mrs. W. says,

"I will not attempt to tell you what are my feelings at the thought of being within one night's journey of our future home. I confess that I have felt some degree of impatience to be there. The wandering life which I have led for more than a year has wearied me, and I could now be happy in the meanest place that I could call *my home.* We have met with much kindness every where, but no where have we felt *settled.* My health, and that of all our company, has been uncommonly good during this journey; for this we feel thankful to our gracious Benefactor.

"17, Thursday.—This morning at 7 o'clock we reached Jaffnapatam, and went immediately to Mr. Mooyart's empty house, he not having arrived, till we could get conveyances to our friends. We had soon the pleasure of seeing Mr. Meigs, who came to conduct us to Batticotta, and accompanied him to the house of Mrs. Driberg, a pious widow, where we breakfasted and dined. Saw there Mr. Knight, church missionary at Nellore. At evening, when about to leave for Batticotta, Mr. Poor also came in from Tillipally.

We rejoiced greatly to meet these dear brethren, whom we had learned to love for their works' sake, and with whom we were to be so intimately associated."

CHAPTER IV.

First year in Ceylon—to the Governmental Restrictions.

Origin of the Ceylon mission—first missionaries—political and religious notices of Jaffna—description of five mission stations—free and boarding-schools—death of Rev. Mr. Warren—first impressions of Mrs. W.—the language to be acquired early—the banian-tree—self-examination—houses of the Tamulians—happiness in the decision to enter on a mission—missionary trials—darkness and blindness of the heathen—cheering accessions to the boarding-school—violent prejudices—persecution of Supyen—Hindoo system of transmigration and fatalism—absurd methods of appeasing the gods—dishonesty—death of Mrs. Poor—governmental prohibition of a press, and of future additions to the mission.

The Rev. Samuel Newell, of the first mission sent out by the American Board of Commissioners for Foreign Missions, having been, with his colleagues, forbidden by the government of the country to remain in Bengal, and having, at the Isle of France, buried his estimable companion, whose history has done so much to awaken an interest in the missionary cause, visited the island of Ceylon, which is a dependency of the crown, and not in possession of the East India Company. Being favorably received by Sir Robert Brownrigg, governor of the island, he visited the district of Jaffna with a view to establishing a mission there; but at the request of Rev. Messrs. Hall and Nott, who, after a long struggle, had succeeded in establishing themselves at Bombay, Mr. Newell re-united himself with their mission, at the same time recommending to the Board to establish a mission in Ceylon.

The second mission of that Board was accordingly established in this inviting field; the Rev. Messrs. Warren, Richards, Meigs, and Poor, (in company with Rev. Mr. Bardwell, who joined the mission at Bombay,) having arrived at Colombo in March, 1816, whence they proceeded, under the countenance of the governor and Sir Alexander Johnstone, to Jaffna.

The district of Jaffna, itself an island lying at the northern extremity of Ceylon, is about 40 miles in length by 15 in breadth, with many islets near it; forming a surface of 1,220 square miles, and having a population of about 170,000, of whom about 650, descendants of the Portuguese and Dutch, are reckoned as whites. The population are chiefly of the sect of *Siva*, though some are followers of *Vishnu*, which two gods, with *Brahma*, form the Hindoo triad.

When, about three centuries since, the Portuguese formed their trading establishments in Jaffna, they destroyed many of the heathen temples, built many chapels and churches, and induced or compelled many natives nominally to embrace the Romish faith; and when the Dutch followed them in 1656, they attempted, in a manner somewhat similar, by governmental influence, to introduce the protestant religion. They did not allow the heathen temples to be rebuilt; forbade the public ceremonies of idolatry, and made the profession of christianity a qualification for all important offices; while they repaired the churches built by the Portuguese, and erected others. But this soulless religion, gradually declining for 140 years, till 1796, when the English took possession of the island, had at that time nearly expired; and as the natives were now allowed the free exercise of idolatry, they rebuilt their temples in great numbers; and when the American mission was commenced, if we except a few native protestants and descendants of Europeans in the town of Jaffnapatam, where Christian David, a native preacher, was laboring, and two Wesleyan missionaries had been recently stationed, *the whole district was a wild waste of heathenism.*

Having obtained permission of the government, the first American missionaries took possession of the mouldering walls of the churches at Batticotta and Tillipally; and on the arrival of the reinforcement, in like manner gained possession of the three churches at Panditeripo, Oodooville, and Manepy. The walls of the church at Batticotta were of stone, four feet thick, and 170 feet in length by 56 in width.

These five stations lie within a circuit of about 20 miles; Batticotta being seven miles westward from Jaffnapatam. From Batticotta you pass northward four miles to Panditeripo; thence five miles to Tillipally, which lies on the main road from Jaffnapatam to the sea at Kangy; thence on this road southwardly, through many populous villages, five miles to Oodooville, the church, which is of brick, standing three-fourths of a mile west of the main road; thence two miles southwest, to Manepy; and thence westward four miles again to Batticotta. In making this circuit you pass over open fields for rice or dry grain; or through villages of continuous gardens, where are the mango, plantain, orange, lime, and other similar fruit-trees, and towering groves of the palmyra, cocoa-nut, and other palm-trees—the low rice fields being, in the rainy season, covered with water, which is soon hidden by the waving grain; and the higher grounds, in that season, mantled with the greenest verdure, while in the dry season, except as cultivated by irrigation, they appear arid and burnt with the sun. Messrs. Richards and Meigs were assigned to Batticotta, and Messrs. Warren and Poor to Tillipally.

Besides attention to the necessary repairs, and preaching the Gospel, through an interpreter, until the language was acquired, "publicly, and from house to house," the missionaries had succeeded in establishing *free-schools** of boys in a number of villages, it being impossible, from the prejudices of the country, to induce girls to attend. In these schools native teachers were of necessity employed—but on the condition of their renouncing the badges of heathenism; attending

* In the small native schools, attended by the sons of the more respectable classes, and kept perhaps under the shade of a tree, or in the verandah of a small house, the children learn the letters of the alphabet by forming them in sand spread before them as they sit cross-legged on the floor, until they are able to name them from an olla leaf on which they are written with an iron stile. Little attention is given to spelling, as all the letters have their own proper sound, and none are silent. They proceed to *commit to memory the words* of the elementary books and the dictionary, and then go back to analyze the lessons; separate the words, which are printed without spaces between them; and in some degree to understand their meaning.

preaching, with the children, on the Sabbath; using christian books, and being at all times under the direction of the missionaries. At Batticotta and Tillipally about *fifty* boys and six or eight girls had also, with great difficulty, especially from the prejudice of *caste*, been induced to reside on the mission premises as *boarding scholars*. Four young men, employed as interpreters, had become hopefully pious, and some lads of the boarding-schools had manifested a serious conviction of the truth of christianity.

The mission, however, had been weakened by the illness of Rev. Mr. Warren and Rev. Mr. Richards, both of whom were compelled to spend some months at Colombo to avoid the rainy season, and then to visit Cape Town, where Mr. Warren died, August 11, 1818. He was a native of Marlborough, Mass.; a graduate of Middlebury college; left the study of law for the theological seminary; became a devoted missionary, having opened, at Tillipally, a small hospital for the natives; and departed in the calm assurance of faith, saying, "Is this death?—Yes, this is death. Give my love to them—tell them to be faithful unto death—farewell! Come, Lord Jesus, come quickly."

Such, in some of its more prominent aspects, was the state of the mission when joined by the reinforcement. The impressions of Mrs. W. on her arrival, she expresses in the following letter to her parents:

"TILLIPALLY, February 19, 1820.

"I am almost too happy, my dear parents, in being on missionary ground. At all the other stations which we have visited I have been disappointed; but here my anticipations have been more than realized. Yesterday, after a pleasant day at Batticotta, we all came to this place. Could the dear friends of missions in America witness what I have this day, they would not think their benevolence injudiciously exerted. Early this morning I went into the church to attend prayers with the children of the family and others. After prayers, the boys were arranged in the yard for us to see them all at once and hear their names. Among others were Porter, Dwight, Worcester, Woods, Stuart, and Putnam.

"I then went with Mrs. Poor to the store-room, where she gave out supplies of food for forty-three children, and her own family, for the day. As it was Saturday, when all bathe, the children each received a lime, to squeeze and rub over their heads before bathing. A cook is devoted to the boys to provide *rice and curry* twice in the day, and *congee*, rice gruel, once. There are eight girls, the two oldest 'take weeks' in preparing their food. This evening we went to see them at their meals. A long mat is spread out, on which they all sit cross-legged, with a large plate, or plantain leaf, full of rice and curry before them. Before they begin to eat, all fall on their knees, and one of them asks a blessing. Every night they pray together before they go to bed, and have a prayer-meeting one evening every week

"Some interesting circumstances attended the admission of a little boy about four years old. He appeared one morning in the dining-room, and Mrs. Poor inquired what he wanted. He replied, to get some ashes from the temple to rub on his forehead. He had wandered from home, and thought the church a temple, where he might get ashes to paint his forehead, according to their custom. He was received into the family, and it was afterwards found that he had no parents or near relatives living. A number of these boys give evidence of some concern for their souls, and one of them named Niles, they are almost ready to believe, is a decided christian. At this station one young man has been admitted to the church, and two at Batticotta. Another was a candidate, but his friends came and forced him away.

"20.—Mr. and Mrs. Mooyart came last night to spend the Sabbath with us. Mr. W. preached to about three hundred hearers, most of them children. Dr. S. took an interpreter and went out to spend the day in talking to the people wherever he could find them. This afternoon Mr Poor and Mr. W. went to a small '*rest house*' to address a mixed congregation. The sisters in the meantime met to pray for the presence of the Holy Spirit with them. It was pleasant once more to have this privilege. After tea, the children and servants all assembled in the dining-room, to repeat the lessons of the day and attend prayers. I must say, that for propriety of behavior, quickness of apprehension, and readiness to repeat their lessons, they are not at all behind children in America. Several of the oldest boys sometimes accompany the brethren as interpreters when they talk to the people."

Reminded, by the children which she found around her, of her former charge, Mrs. W. now wrote to the Sunday-school in Norwich, giving them intelligence of what she had seen, and animating them in the pursuit of sacred knowledge.

"22.—Mr. W. and I came back last evening to *Batticotta*. The brethren have to-day had a meeting for consultation, and it is determined that we remain here, and Mr. and Mrs. Spaulding at Tillipally, until the station at Oodooville can be prepared for us to live there together.

"28.—I continue to feel myself at home, and have, I trust, some gratitude to God for bringing me to this place. The *language* of these heathen now claims my attention. It is difficult of acquisition. The missionaries who have been here so long are not masters of it; though they are able to preach in Tamul. It seems almost a mountain to me, but you know I have loved study, and I do not at all shrink from it. I only feel as though I could not wait so long before I begin to talk to this perishing people.

"Yesterday was very pleasant. We had preaching in the house, the church here not being repaired. Mr. W. preached in the forenoon; in the afternoon he went out among the people; and Mr. Meigs had the children together, to inquire what they remembered of the sermon, and to talk with them. This is the course every Sabbath. I was much gratified by their appearance. They repeated more of the sermon than I ever heard a class of children repeat at home. There are twenty-seven boys and two girls in this family."

The acquisition of *the native language* should be the *first* object in the labors of every foreign missionary. Without a knowledge of the vernacular tongue, he can have little unrestrained intercourse with the people, little sympathy with them, and but a partial access to their minds. Of course the good accomplished must be limited, and discouragement, if not even a relinquishment of the missionary work, may ensue.

It may be stated also as a general truth, that if the language is not obtained to some extent, or a good beginning made, in course of *the first year*, it will never be obtained. All the strength and zeal of a missionary fresh from a temperate climate, and warm from the bosom of the christian church, and all the inspiration of novelty on his first arrival among the heathen, are necessary to carry him through the difficulties of an Eastern dialect, so as to make it familiar to him in speaking and writing. Nor is it less necessary for *the wife* of a missionary to begin well in this respect. Liable as she is to be interrupted by family cares, it is the more important for her to make thorough work at once, in getting such an acquaintance with the grammar and structure of the language as may enable her to classify and retain the words she hears. Around such a nucleus a great amount of knowledge will gather almost imperceptibly, and a sufficient acquaintance with the common dialect, at least for common use, may be gained without much subsequent labor.

It has been said that no one can live among the natives of a country without acquiring their tongue; but the fact is, that adults who continue to speak English in their families, may live in India among the natives for years, and hear their conversation daily, without learning any except the most common words, if they do not study enough to call up their attention to what they hear. If they are *obliged* to understand what is said, as in case of having none around them who speak English—and it is very advantageous thus to shut themselves up to the language—they may learn a good deal without the use of books; but some study will still be requisite to turn their knowledge to any account in communicating religious instruction. In consideration of the greater ease with which a foreign language is acquired by those not much advanced in life, and especially the *pronunciation* of almost any of the Eastern dialects, which is very difficult, missionaries should be sent out *comparatively young*. If going to a new station where much will depend on the maturity of their judgment, some of them at least may well be older; but where they go to reinforce stations already formed, or in company with those who may be depended on for counsel, that they may get the language easily, and assimilate readily to the climate, as well as have some years of expected life before them, they ought not to be much above twenty-five years of age.

"*March* 7.—Returned last night from Tillipally, where I went on Saturday. The Sabbath was communion season, and all our band came together, except Mrs. Meigs. We who have lately joined the mission were regularly received as members of the church, and came with the other brethren and sisters to the table of our Lord under the most interesting circumstances. Many of the poor heathen remained after the public services were concluded, to see what was to be done. One native convert sat with us, the others were absent."

The subject of this memoir did not for a moment consider her spiritual interests safe because she was a missionary, nor neglect her closet on account of having many duties out of it to perform. Her private diary through the whole course of her life in India affords abundant proof of her effort to keep her "heart with all diligence." It frequently records spiritual conflicts, and mentions occasional seasons of darkness—for she was always inclined to judge herself severely, and to dwell, too much perhaps, on the unilluminated side of her own character—but more generally it speaks of great peace in believing, and of her once darkened soul being "light in the Lord."

"*April* 9, 1820.—Twenty-four years have I

lived in sin. The first wish of my heart accomplished, to be on heathen ground, I am no less a sinner. Eleven years since, I professed my faith in Christ, and I have not the fervor of my first love. Well may I tremble. The more I look into myself the more I am convinced that God is pleased to try me in a peculiar manner. I would record my temptations, and some of my sins, but fear I should be unfaithful, and so injure more than benefit myself. Perhaps my conflicts were never more severe, but the power and goodness of God sustain me. Every *outward* thing might make me happy all the day long, but when I feel my spiritual bondage, I am in anguish. Oh that God would deliver me; Oh for a view of his glory as I have seen it; for that faith which enabled the apostle to glory in his infirmity, that Christ's own power might rest on him."

"*April* 15.—Last Monday I accompanied Mr. W. to *Oodooville*, to see the ruins of the old house and church which are to be repaired for us. The house was once the residence of a Franciscan friar. The walls only are standing, and they are much injured by time and the intruding *banian*.* The country around is nearly all cultivat-

* The banian-tree of India frequently springs up on the top, or in the crevices of old walls, into which it protrudes

ed, and presents a pleasant prospect of rice-fields and palmyra groves, in the midst of which are villages swarming with population. The house is small, but we expect to occupy it with Mr. and Mrs. S. until the funds of the mission will admit of enlarging it, or building at another station.

"You may think it time for me to introduce you to our present habitation, that you may fancy yourselves visiting us occasionally. It is a long single-story house, with a verandah in front. There are out-houses in the rear, and a garden. The house has four front rooms and four narrow ones back. The one that we occupy is in front at the south end, and is sixteen feet square. There are placed most of our possessions, and we still find abundant room to turn ourselves round. The floors are made of mortar. The

its roots so as to throw them down. They must be cut out, or such walls are soon destroyed. One species of this tree has the singular property of sending pendant shoots from all its branches towards the earth. These may be seen suspended in bunches, as small cordage, or singly like larger or smaller ropes, many feet in length and of a uniform thickness. They swing in the air until grown so as to reach the ground, when they take root, increase in size, and stand as supporters and nourishers of the branches on which they before hung, and send down other shoots to increase the common stock. Thus the tree spreads itself, and some scores, of every dimension, eventually surround the original trunk, and cover perhaps an acre of ground.

walls are stone, plastered and whitewashed. The roof is after the fashion of barns in America, and covered with palmyra leaves. The rough dark colored timbers and leaves are seen from below. These roofs afford a harbor for insects and squirrels, and sometimes serpents, which occasionally fall from them. I think much less of my exposure to them than I did at first. There is but little danger, and they can do no injury not permitted by our heavenly Father."

The houses of the Tamulians in the country, except such as are mere huts, have usually a court in the centre, open to the sky. Narrow pent roofs, supported by posts and covered with the large fan-shaped leaves of the palmyra, or the braided leaves of the cocoa-nut, are thrown over each of four low mud-walls, enclosing an area perhaps forty or fifty feet square. These roofs project on the outside, so as to form a verandah all round the building four or five feet wide; and on the inside, another of perhaps twice that width, looking towards the open court in the centre, in the manner of a low gallery. The floors of these are of hard earth or brick, and raised two or three feet from the level of the ground. The outside verandah is used for sitting, working, and sometimes sleeping; while the inside may be divided into enclosed apartments, of which there is usually one at least, where the most valuable articles and stores of the family may be locked up, but is most of it left open, or separated only by temporary partitions. It is the parlor, dining-room, and bed-room of the family, comprising perhaps two or three generations, and many collateral branches. Here they sometimes form a social circle at evening around a smoking lamp, though such family scenes are not very common; here they sit cross-legged on the floor, with their food before them on a leaf or brass plate, conveying it to their mouths with the right hand, without the use of knife, fork, or spoon, the husband taking his portion first and the wife eating after him; and here they sleep almost promiscuously, spreading a mat on the floor, and wrapping themselves in the clothing they wear through the day. This consists principally, among the men, of a strip of cloth two or three yards long wrapped round the loins, and occasionally another or a muslin shawl thrown over the shoulders; and among the women, of a piece twice as long wrapped round the waist, with one end thrown over the bosom and shoulders so as mostly to cover them. The lower castes however are not allowed to cover the upper part of the body. The men sometimes wear a shawl or handkerchief wrapped round the head, and sandals on the feet. Both sexes wear jewels in their ears and rings on their fingers; and the women wear a profusion of beads, bracelets, armlets, plates on their hair, clasps round their ancles, and ornaments on their toes. These are all of gold or silver, while the rings in their ears and on their fingers are frequently set with precious stones; and the gold plates on the head and breast with pearls. These jewels constitute a great part of their property, especially that of the females, and as their fashions do not change, are handed down from generation to generation.

"*May* 14.—I have been ill, but am now convalescing. When you hear of my want of health, you may imagine me disappointed in my plans of usefulness, and looking back to my father's house with regret. I am disappointed, and it is peculiarly trying to be an invalid where so much is to be done; but I think that no disappointment will induce me to regret a step taken so deliberately, and with so much evidence that it was the will of God. I have not once felt it necessary to put the inquiry, 'Am I in the path of duty?' It has been uniformly plain since my first decision, and should I be unable to do any thing here, I can still rejoice that to me was given the privilege to come to the heathen. Malleappah, our interpreter, and Amy, the colored woman who came with Dr. S. from America, have joined the church. There are some things encouraging among the people; but a missionary would soon faint in this desert spot if he had not the sure word of God to support him. It is vain to attempt to describe the stupidity and ignorance of these heathens, and to show how they are 'wedded to their idols.'

"*June* 27.—I have spent a fortnight at Nellore, near Jaffnapatam, in the family of the Rev. Mr. Knight, in the hope that a little change of air, and riding morning and evening, would be favorable to my health. The effect was equal to our expectations. After my return, by the kind solicitation of Mr. and Mrs. Squance, Wesleyan missionaries at Point Pedro, about twenty miles distant, we were induced to make them a visit, and try the sea air. A fortnight was spent with them very pleasantly, Mr. W. pursuing the study of the language with Mr. S. who is a laborious missionary. We returned from Point Pedro on Friday—spent the night at Nellore, and stopped at *Oodooville* the next morning.

"Finding that Mr. and Mrs. Spaulding had taken up their abode here, and were somewhat settled, we concluded to stay over the Sabbath. The pleasure of being at our *own* station so animated me that I almost forgot my bodily infirmities, and thought I could cheerfully submit to almost any inconvenience to remain here. After dinner Mrs. S. and I made some windows, by weaving palmyra leaves, basket-fashion, across small cords which Mr. S. and Mr. W. had extended from side to side of window-frames constructed by themselves.

"For a few days the work at the station has been interrupted for *want of funds*, and as the treasury is now nearly exhausted, we concluded to occupy the house without floors, doors, or windows, except of our own making. As there are no cellars in this country, a rough floor of earth is easily prepared. We shall be quite as comfortable as we expected to be when we left our native shores. Our congregation to-day consisted of about two hundred men and boys, and five women. We are much gratified to have any women attend public preaching, it is so contrary to custom. I may now hope to be *at work*. Employment, you well know, is my life, and idleness here, I can assure you, would be a sore trial.

"Our dear brother and sister at this place are very happy; Mr. S. says, 'I never was so happy before.' Dr. Scudder is repairing the old buildings at Panditeripo, about five and a half miles from Oodooville, which he designs to occupy very soon. So many of us are here, that we think it a duty to extend ourselves as much as possible. I hope that the christian public will enable some of us to go to the neighboring *continent*, which presents a most interesting and extensive field for missionary operations.

"*July* 8.—A good congregation assembled to-day. Mr. W. preached *at home*. Your hearts would have melted to see these heathen hearing an account of the mission of our Lord to this world, with every mark of pagan indifference exhibited in their faces; some trifling, others asleep, and only a small proportion giving any attention to truths on which their eternal all depends. Oh, it is trying beyond description. Instead of being received by this people with open arms, as a messenger from God to lead them to his kingdom, the christian missionary is at once regarded with jealousy and scorn. The trials of a missionary in India are not so much bodily sufferings; they are grief at beholding this wretched idolatry so entwined around the heart, and leading such multitudes captive to Satan;—they are disappointment, when, at the close of a day like this, he is obliged to inquire, 'Who hath believed our report?' Many say, 'give us every day enough to eat, and we will hear you preach.' They know no wants beyond those of the present moment. Eternity is to them an empty name. They who are so wicked that they cannot appease their gods by offerings at the temples, or doing charity, or performing some ceremony or penance, have no worse prospect than to inhabit the body of some inferior animal after death. Hardness of heart, stupidity, indifference and attachment to a religion which forbids the indulgence of no passion, however base, are indeed formidable barriers to the success of a missionary.

"OODOOVILLE, August 14, 1820.

"MY DEAR PARENTS,—How shall I tell you of the joy and grief which your letters, and those of other near friends, have occasioned. Mr. Garrett arrived last Thursday. We should have been very happy only in seeing *him*, but our joy was greatly increased by hearing from so many who are dear to us. To see the handwriting of my dear parents, after this long separation, filled me with too much emotion. I opened one letter after another, but could not read them. If I attempted it, I was obliged to lay them entirely aside, and take one from a more common friend, which would affect me less. I could scarcely believe, what I found to be the fact, that almost every other letter was read before I got through with one page from my dear family.

"27.—Yesterday morning thirteen women came to our house with burdens on their heads. While they rested themselves in the verandah, Mrs. S. and I went to speak to them of Christ. Their reception of us was not very encouraging, and they soon told us that they did not wish to know any thing about the Saviour. We tried to engage their attention, until we found every attempt fruitless. They called to one another to go, and with a levity which deeply grieved us, went their way. This is a fair specimen of the manner in which we are received by most of our sex. When they sometimes appear attentive, we may unexpectedly find every opportunity embraced to turn aside their heads and laugh.

"In the evening we went out into the neighborhood. The first two women whom we saw were respectable and of high caste. They were very civil, and engaged to come to our house this afternoon to hear something very interesting that we had to tell them. A man who stood by, said, 'No, they must not go; they have many relations, and cannot go without them.' The next house that we visited was in a cluster of huts, where quite a congregation of women assembled on hearing our voices. Several promised to attend meeting. Ten of them, with two others, came this afternoon, when no men were present. They were very attentive while we told them what induced us to leave our friends and come to live among them, and tried to convince them that the soul will not inhabit the body of some animal after death, but live for ever with God, or with wicked men and devils. One of them asked, 'Shall *we* go to heaven or to hell?' You may judge how deeply interested they felt in this question, when I tell you that we had scarcely begun to reply before they became restless and went away. This is more than we commonly have to encourage us. Few will listen attentively for the shortest time. They know nothing, and fear nothing. Their mental degradation is indescribable, and they are contented with it. What then can we do? I do feel that the ignorance, the hardness, the careless ease of these stupid, deaf heathen, continually presented to view, constitutes our greatest missionary trial."

"*September* 12.—I cannot fail to record," she says in her private journal, "that the Lord has been most gracious to me. Last Sabbath I sat at the table of the Redeemer. Never had I such emotions when looking towards Calvary. There was some indistinctness in my views, but there was a fullness of sweet peace, of assurance, of joy in the presence of Christ, and in the holiness of all around him. It seemed another place than this world. My wretched bondage to sin was forgotten, or rather the thoughts of it were swallowed up by a sense of *his* presence and *his* glory God was there, heaven was there. It was the atmosphere of the redeemed. Blessed be God, the memory of it still refreshes me.

"22.—The last week I may well call the pleasantest of my missionary life on heathen ground. On Monday morning one of our day-scholars came with *twelve boys* to live with us. Soon after a respectable man brought two of his sons, and gave them to Mr. W. and myself with much ceremony. He placed a hand of each in ours, and said, 'They are no longer my children, but yours. You are their father and mother.' We received *nine* of the boys. The care of them devolves on me, and I cannot tell you with how much pleasure I direct their studies, and attempt to give them religious instruction, besides supplying their daily wants. I could not but say to Mr. W. while we looked at them to-night, seated on the floor, each with a plate of *rice and curry* before him, from which he was ready to help himself with his right hand instead of a spoon or knife as soon as a blessing should be asked, could our dear friends at home see these children, some of the best feelings of their hearts would be gratified. You will not wonder that they already seem peculiarly near to me. I desire to feel more my responsibility."

The cheerfulness with which these children were placed on the mission premises, is a striking contrast to the prejudice at first exhibited. For a time, the boys were received on condition of their food being cooked and eaten on the premises of a good caste heathen; and when it was required that they should eat within the mission enclosure, they resisted for some days, but at length consented to return, on condition of having a well of water by themselves. They were told that there were three or four wells within the yard, either of which they could have. They must then clear one out. It was in the rainy season, and the springs high, so that when they had worked hard a whole day in drawing out the water, it was scarcely at all diminished. But they sagely concluded that they had drawn out as much water as there was at first in the well, and it was of course pure and suitable for their use. They remained contented, and gradually lost these absurd prejudices.

As an illustration of *the opposition of parents*, the case of *Supyen* may be mentioned, an intelligent Tamul lad of nineteen, whose father was wealthy, and connected with one of the temples near Jaffnapatam, but allowed his son to attend the school at Tillipally. Having there professed his belief in the Bible, his father was much alarmed; and when he next returned home, caused him to be confined, and kept for a time without food. He then ordered him to perform certain heathen ceremonies. Supyen refused, and when shut up in a dark room, made his escape, and fled to Tillipally; where he told Mr. Poor what had befallen him. He took a Testament, and pointing to the 10th of Matthew, from the 34th to the 39th verses, said with tears, "*that very good.*" His father hearing where he was, sent for him, and as he did not return immediately, came himself and took him away. They were no sooner out of sight, than his father stripped him of his good cloth, put on one so poor as to be disgraceful to him, placed a burden on his head, as though he was a slave, and beat him frequently with a slipper, which is very disgraceful among the Hindoos, until he reached home. Every art was then practised to make him renounce christianity. His relations said the missionaries had given him some medicine to make him a christian, and asked what it was? He replied, "the Gospel of Jesus Christ." A great variety of drugs were put into his food to turn him back to idolatry, and an idol feast being made by some of his young friends, he was ordered by his parents to make the customary offering to the idol. When the time came, he entered the little room where the idol was enthroned, pulled off its ornaments and kneeled down to pray to the true God. One of his companions looking through the curtain saw what was done, and told his father, who punished him severely, and sent him for a time to Kandy, in the interior.

Afterwards his father changed his conduct, and lavished caresses upon him. He showed him his various possessions, and told him he should have all, if he would give up the idea of being a christian, and if not, he should be an outcast for ever. Supyen chose banishment from his father's house, saying, "I do not need house or land if I have an interest in heaven." He attempted to go to Tillipally, but was followed and taken back by force. They then tried to bring him under engagements to marry a heathen girl, but he would not consent. He even tore the contract when offered him. In short, they put his feet in the stocks, beat him, caused him to be conveyed to the neighboring continent, and at length wearied him out, so that he signed a recantation of christianity. His father is since dead, and he for some years has seemed settled down in heathenism.

"*October* 8.—Another Sabbath, with its privileges, even in this heathen land, calls for thankfulness. I have not told you of our employments on this sacred day. Before breakfast we meet for social prayer, with our beloved brother and sister S. in concert with some friends who remember us on this day, at sunrise. After breakfast one of the brethren goes out and invites the people to attend preaching; the other makes preparation for the service, and hears the scholars of the several schools repeat their catechisms and portions of Scripture. The beggars come to the door, and Mrs. S. or I talk to them, and give them something to supply their more pressing wants. The morning service is over about noon. At one o'clock is our daily union of prayer, in concert with all the missionaries in this district. At two the boys of our family, and our domestics, are called in to give some account of the sermon, to repeat their lessons, and to be instructed in religion. We take dinner at three, after which the brethren go out about two miles, different ways, to preach again. Mrs. S. and I always design to be at liberty to see the women who may come at this time. Generally more or less are here. After they leave, and before our husbands return, when the sun is about setting, we spend a season in prayer together, for the blessing of God on the labors of the day, and especially on one of our boys, whom we have selected as a particular subject of prayer. After family prayers at evening, if not before, we feel that it has been a day of labor; and yet we seem to have done very little. Much less can be done in this warm climate, without impairing health, than in America.

"The women who came this afternoon were more ignorant than any I have seen. Their replies to some of our questions might surprise you. 'What kind of a being is God?' 'We don't know.' 'Did you never hear any thing about him?' 'No.' 'Who made you?' 'We don't know.' 'How came this earth, and all things that you see around you?' 'We don't know.' 'Do you go to the temples?' 'Yes.' 'For what?' 'To worship.' 'To worship what?' 'We don't know.' 'Did you ever see what you worship; what is its shape?' 'We don't know, we never saw it.' 'In what manner do you worship?' 'We hold up our hands.' 'Do you ever pray at the temple?' 'Sometimes when we want something.' 'Do you know that you will live again after your bodies are dead?' 'We don't know.' 'Did you ever hear of heaven and hell?' 'No.' 'What is sin?' 'We don't know.'

"*November* 5.—The ordinance of the Lord's supper was administered here to-day for the first time, and we were permitted to enjoy the privileges of a church at our own station. Mr. Poor was with us. I must tell you, my dear friends, that I seldom derived so much strength and animation from this ordinance at home, as I have done here. The Lord Jesus seems to make up for the loss of friends and privileges by his own more sensible presence.

"A small collection of women this morning gave me more pleasure than any I have before seen, because they listened with attention to what I said, and manifested no impatience to be going. One of them was quite talkative. It is common for one to speak in behalf of all. She seemed to have some notions, though very incorrect, about heaven. She said, 'It is a place of happiness, and the great God is there.' I inquired if people have sickness in heaven, if they are ever hungry, and if they will be obliged to work for their living, and carry burdens. She replied, 'They are sometimes hungry, they must work, they have pain and sickness, and I expect,' said she, 'to carry my load there!' pointing to one she had just taken from her head. 'How long do people who go to heaven remain?' 'Some longer, and others for a shorter time.' 'Do they come back to the earth?' 'Yes.' 'How do they come, and in what form?' 'They are born just as they were at first.' 'After the second birth what becomes of them?' 'They live awhile and then go again to heaven or to hell, according to their works.' 'And where do you all expect to go after death?' 'If our works are good, we shall go to heaven, if bad, to hell.' 'Well, are your works good?' 'Yes.' 'Have you done nothing wrong?' 'No, we have done nothing wrong.' I attempted in vain to show them the wickedness of the heart, and the insufficiency of all their sacrifices, bathing in the holy waters, and rubbing ashes on their bodies, to cleanse them from sin. How painful it is to see these poor creatures, on the borders of an awful eternity, disregarding our most solemn admonitions."

As implied above, the Hindoos all believe in the metempsychosis or transmigration of souls. They suppose that evil has come into the world in consequence of the union of spirit with matter, and is to be done away by suffering, or acts of charity, or religious observances. The soul, as it passes from one body to another, is preparing for a re-union with the divine spirit of which it is a part, as a drop of water with the ocean. It is the same in man and in the lower animals. After having obtained a human birth it may be doomed to be born a brute, or to exist as a tree or plant. According to the character formed in any birth will be the condition of that next succeeding. Good and evil, both natural and moral, are *entailed* from one birth to another; and the *fate* of each one is written in his *head* when he is born. This is indicated by the sutures of the skull. This fate is unalterable, and excludes the idea of blame or praise. It is a sufficient excuse for any course of evil conduct to say, "it is *fate* in my head—my forehead is bad."

They speak of heaven and hell, but in a different sense from christians. Each corporeal god has his own heaven, where he receives his worshippers, and grants them various sensual indulgences for a longer or shorter period, according to their merit, after which they become subject again to the vicissitudes of mortal birth. Even the gods must descend to this, if they would be released from matter, and obtain *Mookshum*, or *absorption* in the divine essence. If any die without sufficient merit to obtain *Mookshum*, or go to either of the heavens, or have another birth in this world, they must be sent to the *Yuma-loka*, or world of Yuma, the god of death, and tormented as in purgatory, until their sins are so far expiated as to allow of their being launched again on the sea of transmigration. They are allowed at first, perhaps, only an inferior birth, but gradually may rise to inhabit a human form, and eventually, like others, obtain absorption. This fatalism and belief that all will end well, almost destroys their sense of accountability and fear of the consequences of sin; and their apathy is increased by the ease with which sin is done away. The putting of a light in a temple, bathing in any of the holy waters, marking the forehead, breast, and arms with holy ashes, repeating the name of some god, though unintentionally, doing charity, or performing any of the various kinds of penance, to say nothing of many other methods, will effectually atone for sin, and secure happiness after death.* Of course, to alarm their fears, or

* Among the many examples of the efficacy of these observances, as related in their books and generally believed, are such as the following: A rat was one night in a temple,

awaken their consciences, is all but impossible. With them, emphatically, it is the work of the Spirit. The following letters will corroborate these views:

"OODOOVILLE, (JAFFNA,) February 28, 1821.

"MY DEAR MARIA,—Before this reaches America you will probably have heard that we are happily settled at Oodooville. We commenced our labors here in July, with Mr. and Mrs. Spaulding, under pleasant circumstances. At first we had many visiters, and flattered ourselves that we could easily exert a good influence. But we had

where the lamp before the idol had burned down so as to be dim. Being hungry, the rat went to the lamp for oil, and in attempting to get it, pulled up the wick so as to make it burn brightly. The god was so much pleased by the light being made before him, as to cause the rat to be born a king, to whom he gave the dominion of the three worlds—the sky, the earth, and the lower regions—for a thousand years.

We add another, and leave the reader to judge of the effect which a belief in such methods of expiation must have on the whole population of a country: A wicked boy was in the habit of abusing his mother, and calling her "*vaysee*," which is bad woman. She said, do not say *vaysee* only, but *vaysee-vah*, which means "come here, you bad woman." He then continued to say "*vaysee-vah*," "*vaysee-vah*," and in saying it, pronounced the name of Siva, that being in the vocative case *See-vah*. The god hearing his name called, appeared and took the boy to *Kylasu*, or the heaven of Siva.

not learned the duplicity of this idolatrous people. As soon as they found that they could obtain neither iches nor greatness by listening to us, they ceased coming. We must now go to their houses to find them. After many perplexing circumstances, we have a school of nine promising boys, to some of whom we have given names which are familiar to you. These are my more particular charge. I provide food and clothing for them, and instruct them in English. They have a Tamul teacher. Their religious instruction is principally at morning and evening prayers, and on the Sabbath.

"The people are more degraded, more ignorant, more stupid, and yet more attached to their idols than you can imagine. It is like talking to the wind, to tell them of the true God or the Saviour of sinners. Their religion is suited to their corrupt inclinations, and they desire no other. Oh, could our friends at home, who know something of the worth of the soul, and yet think it unnecessary to send the Gospel to the heathen, see this people living as though they had no souls; could they every night hear their yells and horrid music at some temple, while they are prostrating themselves before a huge car, on which is borne an idol of gold or brass, or perhaps three idols, a god with a wife on each side, or see hundreds at a time rolling for hours in the dust after the car, with hands and feet extended, until life is nearly extinct; could they see these, with many other ceremonies, at the idol festivals, their eyes would certainly affect their hearts.

"The heathen around us are poor, but most of them get something to eat, and they seek little else, unless it be to sleep. If we talk to them of an hereafter, they say, 'We know nothing about it. That is not for us to think of. Our fathers worshipped idols, and so we worship them.' If we ask, 'Would you hang yourselves if your fathers had done so?' 'Yes.' 'If they had burnt their houses, would you burn yours?' 'Yes.' 'And because they have gone to a place of misery, you wish to go there?' 'Yes.' Heaven and hell are to most of them unmeaning sounds.

"A friend said to me before I left home, We shall wish to know how you look, how you eat, &c. We look, I believe, much as when we left home. We do not yet eat like the natives, but sit at a small table just large enough for two persons, and use such furniture as we should at home; at least so far as we have it. I know not how much we may alter our habits in these things. In almost all respects you may expect us to deteriorate, for we are in a destructive atmosphere. I sometimes think that I should feel very awkward, even now, to be in the society to which I was once accustomed. I assure you it is no small disadvantage to our mental progress, to have the stimulus of refined social intercourse taken away, and to be shut up mostly to a strange language, so barren of useful thought as is the Tamul.

"You wish to know if the heathen are what I expected to find them, and if my work is pleasant. They are more wedded to their idols, more unwilling to hear of changing their religion, and more ignorant and stupid than I supposed. Their vices are what you would expect from people destitute of all restraint, except that of fear. Almost every one will lie, cheat, and steal, every opportunity. An honest domestic is not to be expected. We have no dependence upon them, and this adds greatly to the care of house-keeping. I have not as yet the pleasure of seeing the heathen come to inquire what they shall do to be saved; but it is pleasant to labor among them.

"MISS MARIA LEFFINGWELL."

"OODOOVILLE, February 17, 1821.

"MY DEAR BROTHER D——, I received your letter by Mr. Garrett, and read it with feelings which I cannot describe. How often have we wished that Providence might lead you to preach the Gospel, and sometimes almost said it must be so. There was never less reason to expect it than when we left home; but circumstances appear to have made your duty plain. If you carefully, and with much prayer, examined the subject, I am confident that you will always rejoice in your determination. Whatever may be the difficulties and sufferings connected with your work, the consciousness of doing the will of God cannot but support and comfort you.

"I suppose you will expect to hear that we are doing something for the heathen. I hope we are; but so little impression is made by preaching and conversation, that we are sometimes ready to say we labor in vain. All our encouragement is from the word of God. We have to contend not only with the carnal heart, but with a strong attachment to an alluring system of idolatry, and with an almost perfect and universal indifference to the future, joined, in most instances, to ignorance and stupidity. We sometimes labor in vain for hours to impress upon the mind of a native the most simple truth. He cannot comprehend it. We must 'walk by faith.' Christians at home must help us to do so.

"One year is gone since we landed in Jaffna. I look back upon the scenes through which I have passed, as I used to those at home: some sickness, some anxieties, and some enjoyment, with some *attempts* to serve God, have made up the variety. On the whole, I believe I never was more happy. We are united with the brother and sister at the station in the best bonds, and have much fellowship with them in spiritual things."

On the 7th May, 1821, the mission sustained a severe loss in the death of Mrs. Poor; but her end was joyful, even triumphant. It was a privilege to stand by her dying pillow and hear her say, "Even my beloved husband and children cease to be ties to bind me to earth. Every cord is now broken. This is a victory for which I scarcely dared to hope." And it was affecting when, near the closing scene, the little circle at her bed-side commenced singing,

"Jesus, with all thy saints above,"

to hear her trembling voice unexpectedly burst forth, and while her countenance reflected "glory begun," rise higher and clearer in its thrilling tones, until it subdued that of her weeping friends, and was heard alone in the song of praise. Almost her last words, while hardly conscious of any thing, were, "Glory be to God the Father—to God the Son—to God the Holy Ghost."

Mr. *Garrett*, whose arrival has been noticed, was sent out by the Board as a *printer* for the mission; but was not allowed by the government to remain on the island. The missionaries forwarded their petition that he might be permitted to join the mission, and also a remonstrance against his being sent away, founded on the encouragement given by the preceding governor to the establishment of the mission, with leave to have a press, as well as on the moral necessities of the natives. But the governor was so averse to any increase of the number of Americans on the island, that the order for his removal was enforced. Indeed, an injunction was subsequently obtained from his Majesty's Secretary for the colonies, against any future additions to the mission. This was in force *eleven* years, until after the arrival of Sir Robert Wilmot Horton as governor; by whose kind representation to the home-government the injunction was removed. During this whole period, contrary to the expectation of such as looked for the extinction of the mission, *none of the brethren previously in health, were removed by death or permanently disabled by sickness.*

CHAPTER V.

Second and Third years in Ceylon—the establishment of the Mission Seminary and Female Central School.

Progress of the mission—joy in God—Maternal Society—letter to Maternal Society, Portland, Maine—some girls obtained for the school—Mrs. Schrayder—letter to the Female Society for prayer—to a female associate—privilege of prayer—four received to the church—preaching at a school bungalow—anniversary observed by the "Indus fraternity"—meetings for prayer—death of Rev. Mr. Richards—his early devotion to missions—prayers of native children—beggars—employment of a day—religious privileges—heathen children—school for girls opened.

The *five* stations of which the mission was for many years composed, were now occupied; though at Manepy only *bungalows* of mud walls covered with leaves were then erected. The walls of the old dwelling-house having been entirely destroyed, a dwelling was after some time prepared by taking off a part of the old church. None of the churches, except that at Tillipally, which was only covered with leaves and had a floor of earth, were as yet repaired; but at all the other stations large *bungalows*, consisting of a slight roof covered with leaves, supported by two rows of taller and two of shorter posts, with a hard floor of earth, and surrounded by a half wall of unburnt brick, were soon built for public worship. The dilapidated houses at Oodooville and Panditeripo, as well as at Tillipally and Batticotta were gradually made comfortable dwelling-places. *Boarding-schools*, containing in all *eighty-seven* children, were in successful operation at the different stations, except Manepy, where one was soon commenced, and *native free-schools* were taught in bungalows in most of the villages near each station: the whole number of these schools in 1821 being twenty-four, in which were *one thousand one hundred and forty-nine* children.

On the evening of May 15, 1821, Dr. Scudder, who had attended to the study of theology on his way to India, as well as after his arrival, and had for about a year been licensed to preach, was ordained in the Wesleyan mission chapel in Jaffnapatam. A good audience was present. Mr. Chater, a Baptist, and Mr. Roberts, a Wesleyan missionary, assisted in the interesting services of the occasion.

On the 22d April, the Sabbath before Mrs. Poor was taken ill, *Nathaniel Niles* and *Jordan Lodge*, two lads of the boarding school at Tillipally, were received to the church. This was an interesting event, as they were the *first fruits* of the mission from among the *heathen;* those previously admitted having been educated either as Protestants or Roman Catholics.

After the two following extracts, in which Mrs. W. records the dealings of God with her own soul, she proceeds, in journal-letters to her friends, to notice such events connected with the mission as she thought might be of interest.

"*June* 3, 1821.—New light has broken in upon my soul. I think I can now understand the reason of God's dealings with me in leaving me so much to darkness and disquietude. I have felt greatly tried in being unable to employ myself more actively for God, while I have not done all the good that was within my reach. Besides this, instead of flying to Christ, I have listened to the suggestions of the adversary, in doubt and unbelief.

"24.—I have hesitated whether I ought to record what the Lord has done for me during the last week. On Tuesday, throughout the day, I seemed to have new views of the character and works of God. In the morning, after reading the first part of Genesis, with Scott's notes on the creation of man in the image of his Maker, and his disastrous fall, the wonderful love of God in the plan of salvation filled my soul with adoring thoughts, and I hope with gratitude and love. I do not remember ever spending a day in such a delightful frame. Compared with what is generally the case with me, God was in all my thoughts. I found it good to be at the throne of grace, and I spent much time there. I entreated the Lord to show me if this was his own work, or if it was Satan transformed into an angel of light. How I longed to open my heart, and to say, 'come, hear what the Lord has done for my soul.' I felt more love for all my brethren and sisters. At night I would have told my husband, but still feared that it was delusion.

"*July* 29.—Have been out with Mrs. S. this afternoon, and felt, more than usual, the superiority of the christian religion. A man of respectability said, 'The god Scanda, to whom sacrifices were offered at a temple near us this morning, can see and hear, but cannot speak.' 'Of what is he made?' 'Pure gold.' 'Who made you and all this people?' 'Another god, the father of Scanda.' 'Why then do you worship him; is not the greater god angry?' 'No, for we worship them both.'

"*August* 8.—Last Friday we had a most interesting day at Tillipally. George Koch, a young man of Dutch descent, who is studying medicine with Dr. Scudder, one of the boys belonging to the boarding-school, and a hired man of Mr. Poor's, were received as members of the church. All our little band were together, except Mr. and

Mrs. S. The occasion was truly animating. After the admission of these persons we sat down to tho table of the Lord, with *seven* native converts. The Sabbath after was likewise a good day. The new members appear already to be preachers of righteousness, and even others join them in speaking to many whom they meet concerning their souls.

"9.—Went out with Mrs. S. this evening, and found some women quite attentive. Others would not hear unless we would tell them how to get a living. We endeavored to persuade them that our message was far more important than if we could show them how to obtain food for their bodies. The ruins of a temple, burnt a few nights ago, were near. Finding a woman standing by, we said, 'Where do you expect to go after death?' 'If I frequent the temples, and worship the gods, I shall go to glory.' 'Was not your god burnt up the other night?' 'Yes, but the people can make another.' We tried to show her the folly of worshipping gods made by men's hands, and the necessity of worshipping the one living and true God; but she insisted that she could not leave her religion.

"After our walk we enjoyed an hour in the verandah with our husbands, while the moon shone pleasantly around us, speaking of the shortness of life, and especially of a missionary's life in this Eastern world. In one, two, or three years it may be said of us, they are dead. This is an incitement to activity, for our work is very great, and seems scarcely yet begun. Our weekly meeting was pleasant; our thoughts were carried to 'where Christ sitteth at the right hand of God.' I felt that to contemplate the happiness of heaven, though only 'through a glass darkly,' is a sweet consolation in this world of sorrow.

"14.—To-day all the sisters met at Batticotta to enjoy a little season of christian fellowship, and to make arrangements for forming *a maternal society*. We resolved to hold a quarterly meeting for our own benefit and that of our children. I have not promised myself so much from any thing of the kind since I came to India. It has been a day long to be remembered. I trust it will be remembered, even in eternity, with thanksgiving."

The interesting association here mentioned, was evidently made a blessing. Nearly all the older children connected with it have become hopefully pious. The responsibility of *mothers*—the power they have of moulding the plastic minds of their little ones—the effect on their character of the very expression of countenance, the tone of voice, and the whole moral atmosphere which a mother throws around her, with a silent but pervading influence, while the young and smiling infant is still in her arms—has probably never been sufficiently appreciated; and maternal associations are adapted to bring this responsibility to the mind and lay it on the heart of those to whom these treasures are committed. Though our Saviour said, "suffer little children to come unto me, and forbid them not," there is reason to fear that they have not been carried to Him in *faith*, while *young*. The soil of the human heart should not be left unoccupied. The enemy will sow tares. As far as possible he should be anticipated. Good seed should be sown in the spring-time of life: in early morning. It should be mingled carefully and prayerfully with the first elements of moral character. The *habits* of the infant should be formed for holiness, and the child be actually educated and trained for heaven. With the blessing of God it may be done; in some instances it has been done; it will be done more extensively. A new generation, early commencing the divine life, and growing up to the stature of perfect ones in Christ Jesus, shall yet arise to bless the world.

Mrs. W. was the secretary of the Maternal Association until her death. Soon after its formation she addressed the following communication to a similar society in Portland, Maine, almost the only one then existing, accompanied by a private letter to Mrs. Payson, the secretary.

"OODOOVILLE, October 8, 1821.

"DEAR FRIEND AND SISTER,—In view of the many difficulties which are connected with the education of children in India, and the high responsibility of christian parents, the female members of our mission have been induced to associate themselves for mutual aid, in adopting the best methods for training up their children for usefulness in the church of God; and we feel anxious to maintain a correspondence with similar societies, that we may be assisted and encouraged by them. We feel some embarrassment in proposing to be recognized by a society at home, because we are a little band, and at a great distance; but we trust that our necessities will make our excuse, and that the advantages to be derived from an interest in your prayers, and from your correspondence, will form a plea in our favor which will not be rejected.

"At the first meeting for consultation on the subject of forming a society, the Spirit of God appeared to be present. All were greatly refreshed and strengthened in the belief that much benefit would result to our own souls, as well as to those of our children. The season for special supplication, on Saturday evening, which has been observed a number of weeks, has likewise been peculiarly precious, so that we are enabled to say, 'hitherto hath the Lord helped us.'

"The society is but just formed, and is as yet confined to ourselves, with the exception of Mrs. Mooyart, a daughter of the late Dr. Johns, of Tranquebar, who is an active and intelligent christian. We expect, however, that some ladies of the Wesleyan and Church Missionary Societies will unite with us. The children of the present members are sixteen in number. Our *first* wish concerning them is that they may become children of God, and successful laborers in his service among the heathen. They are surrounded by temptations to which children in christian countries are not exposed, and we know that they can be preserved only by the power of God. Allow us therefore to request the frequent and fervent prayers of every member of your society, that the great and good Shepherd may gather them as lambs in his arms, and carry them in his bosom."

"My dear Mrs. Payson,—The slight acquaintance which I was permitted to have with you in New Haven might not warrant in me the liberty of addressing you; but the object for which I write will I trust be a sufficient apology.

"As I am writing, you may expect to hear something concerning our missionary work. We are just now particularly encouraged by seeing *females* more ready to come out, and by having more easy access to them at their own houses than before. Many who at first would run and hide themselves if a missionary was seen entering the yard, now not only permit us to sit down with them there, but some of them attend preaching at our stations. More or less come out every Sabbath, and on some special occasions congregations of from thirty to forty have been collected. A few days since, a woman of much influence, after listening to a plain and solemn address, said, 'What must I do, if I leave my religion, to obtain forgiveness of God for all my sins.' To have a female show that she understands any thing said to her on these subjects, is encouraging. They are generally too talkative to listen, or if to please us they give any attention, it is without trying to understand what we say. In the degraded condition of our sex here, we see much to call forth our commiseration, and much to turn from with abhorrence. We do believe, however, that the time is near when they will regard us as their friends, and, through the influences of the Holy Spirit, be induced to 'come with us that we may do them good.'

"The duty of visiting females at their own houses is so plain, that we cannot neglect it; but it is not that pleasant employment which we imagined at a distance. To have our message treated with derision by those whose eternal happiness is at stake; to hear them ridicule and blaspheme the name of Christ, ascribing all the blessings purchased by his blood, to beings whose lives were stained with every crime—and to see them worshipping lifeless images of wood, stone, gold, and silver, is too trying to be described. I believe I may say, in relation to all our number, as well as of myself, we have but one source of pleasure in our efforts with them, and that is, the reflection that they are made in the name of Him who has designs of mercy towards this people, and will yet show them his glory, and turn their hearts to himself.

"In obtaining female children to instruct, we have much reason for thankfulness that of late we have had some success. 'Females have no custom to learn,' is the universal excuse, and generally it has more weight than all we can urge in favor of what would prepare them for usefulness and happiness. We consider every female child added to our number as a great acquisition, on account of her subsequent influence, and of the strength of prejudice and custom against females being instructed.

"I cannot fail to speak of the great goodness of God in uniting all the members of our mission very closely in the bonds of christian love; and in giving us brethren and sisters of other denominations who hold up our hands and encourage our hearts. We have many seasons of precious intercourse, when I trust we know something of the communion of saints; particularly on the first Monday in every month, when we spend the day together in united prayer and mutual exhortation. Do we not, on these days especially, unite with all who love the Lord Jesus, in praying that He will hasten his coming in his kingdom. Can it be that there is a christian who does not every day inquire, 'Lord, how long?' In times of despondency we are often cheered by thinking of the great numbers in our native land who we believe pray for us, and who desire, above every thing else, the conversion of the world."

The mission family at Oodooville, which had been so happily united, was before this called to separate. Mr. and Mrs. Spaulding were removed in August to the station at Manepy, left vacant by the illness of Mr. Woodward. He had been obliged to take a voyage to Calcutta for his health; and on his return was appointed to supply the place of Mr. Richards at Batticotta, who, with Mrs. R., had gone to Tillipally after the death of Mrs. Poor. These changes, though trying to those concerned, were necessary, to make the best disposal of the strength of the mission. Before Mr. S. left Oodooville, a large *bungalow* for a chapel was nearly finished; and soon after, it was opened.

"*September* 23, 1821.—This has been an interesting day. Our new bungalow for preaching was dedicated. Mr. David preached on the occasion to about five hundred adults and children. Mr. Lambric, church missionary from Kandy, Mr. Knight, from Nellore, Mr. Layard, provincial judge of the district, and all our own brethren, with some of the sisters, were assembled. After the public services in Tamul, we had religious exercises among ourselves in English; when we felt that the Holy Spirit was in the midst of us. Oh that it may be the beginning of days to this people.

"24.—I have long been trying to obtain *girls* to attend school. Was much encouraged to-day, because one came whom we have often tried in vain to get. There were before two day-scholars who have attended pretty constantly for several months, besides the little one in the family, who is the daughter of a domestic. So a commencement is made.

"25.—Went out this evening and saw a considerable number of men and women, who promised to attend preaching to-morrow. Had a pleasant time at one place with a number of women, until, as I was about leaving, a very boisterous woman came up and almost drove me away.

"26.—None of the people who promised to come were at meeting to-day; but we had others, more than we expected, the weather being unfavorable. How animating the belief that this house shall be filled with humble worshippers. We *see* nothing to encourage this hope, but we believe that the purpose of God shall stand. All nations shall come and worship before him. I must tell you, my dear parents, for your comfort, and to magnify the grace of God, that I have some precious Sabbaths in this land of darkness. Not as once in the 'great congregation,' or in the social circle for prayer, or in the little school which was so delightful, but in retirement, in what I trust is *communion with God*. I think I never in America had such views of the character of God; never felt so sensibly that he is *good* as well as *great;* nor admired so much his vast designs. For a considerable time after leaving home, although I had many seasons of great enjoyment, yet on account, perhaps, of sickness and various changes of situation, some clouds rested over me which my weak faith could not penetrate; but of late I have been able to say that the Lord remembers his promise, 'Lo, I am with you alway,' in its fullest extent, except so far as immediate fruit of my labor is concerned, and in that he does not withhold his smiles. O, my dear parents, brothers, and sisters, how much do those who have an interest in the blood of the covenant owe to their Redeemer. What are time, talents and all that we can give? How much is committed to the care, the watchfulness, the prayers of christians. The weight of responsibility sometimes overwhelms me."

At this time she addressed the following letter of encouragement to the female praying-circle which she so highly valued in her native town; and also a kind communication to a female associate, whose salvation she greatly desired.

"OODOOVILLE, October 6, 1821.

"MY DEAR MISS T——, In addressing you as a member of the 'Society for prayer' with which I was once associated, I wish to be considered as addressing all the circle. I have often thought of writing, but at this time feel constrained to say that I rejoice with you. A letter lately received from America mentions the stately goings of the Lord in Connecticut, and that *Norwich* has shared in the showers of divine grace. I almost immediately thought of our little band, and felt that God had condescended to regard our cries.

"Now, my dear sisters, if the Lord has heard you in the thing which you greatly desired, will he not still listen to your requests, and does he not by this kindness call upon you to *extend your desires*, to 'open your mouths wide, that they may be filled.' They who surround you are but a small proportion of the great family for whom you live. Most of your brethren and sisters of this family are in 'darkness which may be felt.' In the season of refreshing which you have enjoyed it may seem to you that the day of promise dawns upon all nations, that the darkness is fleeing away, and the true light shines; but your eyes have not seen, and your ears have not heard the deplorable state of the heathen. I do not doubt that you pray for the salvation of all men, that the glory of the church is an object of ardent desire; but I may ask without fear of offence, do you exert every power of body and soul in this great cause? Is it your chief concern, disregarding selfish accommodations, and rising above a frowning world, to benefit those who are around you, and to see the salvation of God among all nations?

"I wish further to suggest that perhaps you cannot do more for the cause of Christ than to set apart stated and frequent seasons for *special supplication* in behalf of the heathen. It is not by the number or strength of missionaries that the great work is to be accomplished, but through the intercessions of the children of God the Holy Spirit must be given. This is a part of your appropriate work. Allow me to say, *a great part* —a talent put into your hands, for which you must render an account.

'Very affectionately, your HARRIET."

"My Dear ——, My soul is often in heaviness on account of those I have left, because I know that they who so long reject the truth, 'treasure up wrath against the day of wrath.' If the heathen be condemned before God, where will the enlightened unbeliever appear?

"From your first letter I infer that you are more established in your opinions and feelings, and may I not hope that you are decidedly on the Lord's side; that you have grown in grace, and that each successive day brings you forward in the divine life? If this be the case, accept my congratulations, accept the affectionate sympathy of one who hopes she knows how to share your joys and sorrows; of one who, having had some experience in the christian warfare before you, would admonish you to stand fast in the faith; and if you would obtain the victory over the world and be a growing christian, *keep near to your Redeemer*. There is no spiritual life at a distance from the cross, no devotion but that which is kindled upon the altar. I would say, let no human example be the standard to which you strive to bring yourself; keep the Lord Jesus Christ always in your eye, and feel that if you do not imitate him you come short of what God requires. You must *dwell* at the fountain; that is an unfailing source; yes, my friend, a source of joy unspeakable and full of glory

"If I could sit down by you a few hours I would tell you of some of the snares into which I have fallen, and show you how in some instances God has chastened me for backsliding. I would tell you how necessary it is to avoid the occasions of sin, and in intercourse with the world to gird on the whole armor of Christ. I would entreat you not to dishonor your Saviour in the house of his friends, but cheerfully be conformed to him in his humiliation and in his sufferings, that you may hereafter reign with him above. If you are devout, you will be persecuted; if you reprove sin, you will be reviled; but is it not enough that the disciple be as his Lord? I entreat you be not satisfied with barely securing your own salvation; seek to obtain an *abundant entrance* to the kingdom of heaven, and to bring many of your fellow-beings with you."

TO HER PARENTS.

"*October* 28.—Mrs. Schrayder, a pious woman of Dutch descent, from Jaffnapatam, came, by request, to spend the day with us, and address some women. More than *thirty*, most of them respectable, were collected in our dining-room. Mrs S. addressed them in a very interesting manner. She took her seat at one end of the room just behind a small table, on which lay a Tamul New Testament and a hymn-book. She was dressed in a neat but plain white short-gown, with a full calico petticoat. Her hair, grey with age, was carefully braided, and fastened up with a silver pin. Her form was tall and erect, and her countenance venerable and placid. Before her, upon mats spread on the floor, sat her female auditors in a half-circle, with their eyes fixed on her as she kindly told them why she had come, and bespoke their attention. She opened the hymn-book, sang a Tamul hymn, and then read a chapter from the Testament in an impressive manner; commenting very fully upon it, and closing with an address embracing the leading articles of the christian faith. Every eye was intent, and every ear was open. The eagerness with which her audience heard her was manifest by their bending forward, as though to catch her words. Her discourse was appropriate; her manner tender; her voice clear; and in uttering some of the finely sonorous sounds of the Tamul language, it was highly musical. Her 'speech dropped like the dew, and distilled like the rain.' It was the voice of instruction to the ignorant, of comfort to the unhappy. We were highly gratified.

"After our meeting I had some conversation with a man who has often promised to send his daughter to school. 'What wages will you give her?' said he. 'It will be great wages if I give instruction; but I will give more. If you will let her remain all the time, I will give a cloth and jacket, and her food.' 'No! she shall not eat with your girls.' 'Is she better than they?' 'Yes.' 'Well, I see that you never intended to send her, and I have nothing more to say.' 'If you will send somebody home with her every day, and give her fruit whenever she is hungry, I will bring her.' I did not believe he was in earnest; but this afternoon he brought the child, and immediately claimed the cloth and jacket. 'No, I will wait awhile to see if she is a good girl, and deserves one; and whether she is not taken away in a few days.' He left her rather reluctantly, having designed, probably, to secure the clothes and then take her home again."

Under the next date we again accompany Mrs. W. to her closet, and witness where she obtained her strength for the christian course.

"*November* 21.—This day has been a privileged one. I have, I trust, prayed for the assistance of the Spirit in trying the state of my heart. I would be searched as with candles. Have looked at the evidence I find of sincere love to God, and of being under the influence of the Spirit from day to day. I do hope that I can say, 'I love the Lord because he hath heard my voice and my supplications.' I have gained so little victory over some besetting sins of late, that I have greatly feared my hopes were delusive. The great change which I experience is in having more distinct views of God, of his holiness, majesty, and gracious designs; in seeing him in all respects so good, so full of every thing great and glorious, that I can find no language to express my feelings. I have more delight in prayer, as the means of quickening my affections, of guarding me from the assaults of the adversary, of bringing me nearer to the blood of Christ when I have sinned, of relieving my doubts, controlling my fears, supporting my despondency, and making the word more rich and precious. I cannot live without prayer. If it is omitted, I feel that I have lost my meat and my drink. In regard to others, I prize the privilege of drawing near to God for them. I never had such delight in contemplating the promises and resting in them with sweet assurance. Sometimes I believe that even my eyes shall see their fulfillment. I can plead them before God, even with groaning, when language fails. I cannot describe the feelings with which I think of a dying world, and especially of the heathen perishing around me."

"*November* 22.—Our congregation has been pretty good at the station to-day, and Mr. W. was much encouraged at Mallagum this morning, and at Santillapoy this afternoon. As our number of female scholars is now increased to six, and it will be long before they can read, I have thought best to attempt giving them religious instruction, systematically, without books. Made an encouraging commencement of this interesting exercise this afternoon, .and almost felt as though I had again a Sabbath-school.

"23.—Have been much animated this afternoon to find that a woman with whom I conversed last week remembered what I said. On seeing me to-day, she inquired what reason I had for saying it. I told her and some other women that God had promised to make all nations christians; to bring them to renounce their idols, and love and serve him alone; that he had lately done great things for some nations, and would yet show this people his power and glory; so that if those who are older do not regard the message sent them, their children or children's children will. I continued the subject, and think I had never before so much pleasure in talking to any of the women here. A number listened with much attention.

"On first going to another house, I inquired of a woman why she did not come to hear Mrs. S last Friday as she promised to do. Her answer was, 'I was fasting, and could not go from home.' 'Why do you fast?' 'Because I was once sick, and made a vow to God, that if he would restore me, I would fast every Friday so long as I live.' 'To what god did you make the vow?' 'To Swamy.' 'Where is Swamy?' 'I did not see Swamy; I went to the temple and worshipped the image there.' 'Did the image know that you worshipped it, or did Swamy know that you worshipped the image?' 'No.' 'Why not, then, worship an image any where else as well as in the temple?' 'Oh, we go to the temple to see the pictures.' 'If that is all, why are the people made to believe that God is there?' 'The Brahmins do that because it brings them much profit.'

"*December* 3.—My dear friends, I rejoice to tell you that since my last date we are encouraged by the prospect of soon receiving *four* members to the church at Oodooville; the wife of our interpreter, the teacher of our boarding children, whose name is Solomon, a hired man, named James, and a hired woman. They have for some time been convinced of the truth of christianity, but never until now have been made willing to bear the reproach, and perhaps entire desertion of their friends, for the sake of Christ. We feel that the Holy Spirit is with us.

"Within a few days the *cholera* has appeared at Oodooville. Many have died. All this day *tum-tums*, or drums, have been beating at a temple within a few rods of our house, on account of a sacrifice for a sick man who has been carried there. Word is gone out, through all parts of the district where this disease is raging, that the goddess who sends the cholera, and whose sport or play it is supposed to be, is angry because some people have applied to christians for relief. They are, therefore, afraid to apply to us, or do any thing for themselves. They go in succession to the grave, as the sheep in a flock follow one another down a precipice. Some have no friend left to lay them in their narrow house.

"*January* 10, 1822.—Antache and her husband, who had the cholera, were so affected by our kindness to them in their sickness, and that of our interpreter in assisting to bury their mother, when they were deserted by all their friends, as to be very favorably affected towards christianity. They are both apparently sincere inquirers, and of Antache in particular we have hope that the Holy Spirit has begun a good work in her heart. These make seven who have now for some time regularly attended an inquiry meeting once or twice a week."

The reception to the church of *four* inquirers, April 21, 1822, was a most pleasing event. *Eleven* native communicants now joined with *six* members of the mission in commemorating the Lord's death. It was the first communion at which so many had been received to the church, and the first in which there had been an accession, as in the case of Antache, of one in no way connected with the mission. It was the more interesting, too, as the one thus received was a respectable *woman*, and the converts were all adults of good standing in society. This accession made the number of natives added within a year, at all the stations, *fourteen ;* there having been five admitted at Tillipally, about the time of Mrs. Poor's death, and subsequently, in December, at the same station, two girls of the boarding-school and a hired man; and at Panditeripo, at different times, two lads of the boarding-school.

Another interesting event, prior to this, was the licensing of *three native preachers ;* Franciscus Malleappah, Gabriel Tissera, and Nicholas Paramander. They all passed a satisfactory examination at Oodooville, November 5, 1821, and were licensed to preach as candidates for a more full induction into the christian ministry.

The following *journal-letter* presents a very interesting sketch of the varied scenes in this portion of Mrs. W.'s missionary life.

"OODOOVILLE, May 29, 1822.

"MY DEAR PARENTS,—I wrote you yesterday, and now promise myself to keep a record of events occurring, more regularly than I have done for some time past.

"Another son of an Odigar came to-day, bringing a relative, a promising boy of good family to live with us. This is ground of encouragement and thanks to God. It is a wonder that so many children are brought to us, when their parents see that all those already here profess to renounce the religion of their fathers.

"*June* 2.—This morning two women who are not in the habit of coming to the house called at the door to see what they could, as many others do. Before I could say any thing to them they started to go. I urged their stopping; but no they must go and see a sick woman, and would then return to hear the preaching. I had heard such promises too often to give any credit to theirs, and therefore thought best to compel them by sending one of our girls with them. This effected the object. They returned, but may never come again. By coming once they have heard of a Saviour for such sinners as they are, and oh that they may be made to feel their need of Him. We have reason to fear that we are to many 'a savor of death unto death.' The thought is awful, but our duty plain.

"In the afternoon I accompanied Mr. W. a short distance to a school bungalow, where he had an appointment to preach, and, to induce the women to come out, had engaged that I should be there. We went through a pleasant winding foot-path, on each side of which was a thick hedge of ever-greens that opened into a plain. In the centre of the plain stands a large tree, very much resembling the largest elm before the house we occupied on the plain in Norwich. I was forcibly reminded of the many hours I have spent in building rooms and entertaining company between the roots of that tree, and in later days how many hours I have sat under its shade with those whose faces I must see no more on earth. We entered a little gate made of leaves, and found a number of men, women, and children assembled to receive the *padre* and his wife, and, from their appearance, I think, wondering at the unheard of custom of a female walking arm in arm with her husband. The ground floor of a small bungalow was covered with mats, and others spread around in front of it, but no one sitting on them till we had taken our seats and requested them to sit. The men were quite talkative; had many questions to ask, and remarks to make. One woman who had been very attentive to the preaching said, 'What do you tell us we must do to escape going to hell, and go to heaven?' Mr. W. explained the nature of sin, of which she professed entire ignorance, and the necessity of regeneration. Had a person manifested as much interest at home I should have hoped well for her, but here we are continually deceived. Every thing of the kind, however, gives us some encouragement.

"*Monday evening, June* 3.—The monthly prayer-meeting here to-day, and a sweet season I believe it has been to all. I think we have not before been more sensible of the presence of the Holy Spirit. I was greatly animated; it has been one of my happiest days. The subject of remark was introduced by examples from Scripture of that 'effectual, fervent prayer' which prevails with God. It seemed that God was speaking by his word, and deep solemnity settled upon every one. I think it has been a glorious day to Zion; that her children have come near to the mercy-seat, have wrestled and prevailed; and that God will soon stretch forth his arm to rescue the nations.

"8.—This third anniversary of our farewell to the land of our fathers has been spent by all the 'Indus fraternity' at Manepy. We met before breakfast, and after family prayers the exercises of the day were commenced, first, after singing and prayer, by mentioning the friends each one has lost since leaving home, who we hope are ready to welcome us to a better world. We then mentioned those who remain behind, and are still out of Christ, and those who are numbered among his children. This carried our feelings home to our kindred and friends, and interested us in each other's friends, so that we were in some measure prepared unitedly to plead with God in behalf of all as though they were our own. We then took a brief view of the goodness of God towards us since we left our native shores. We endeavored to recall the views with which we at first dedicated ourselves to the work of the mission, and to compare them with those we have had for a few months past, to see whether we have lost or gained. The result was, that we feel less ardor than we sometimes did at home; but that a knowledge of the true condition of the heathen has given us more deep and solemn feelings concerning them, so that on the whole we have reason for thanks and encouragement. For myself I can say that I never felt such agony of soul on account of those under my care as within the last year. All of us could say that we were never happier in our work than at the present moment. Here we feel at home, and here we wish to remain till our Father calls us to our final rest. After closing our meeting with prayer and singing, we took some refreshment and spent the remainder of the time in telling each other freely if we had observed any thing in our deportment that might injure the cause, or any deficiency in our labors among the people, and in praying that every thing offensive to God may be removed, and that our lives may be more simple and devoted. It was a time of love; we all found it refreshing, and it will, I trust, bring us forward in our work.

"13.—I went on Monday morning to Tillipally, and spent three days. The object of the visit was to benefit brother Richards' health. He has been in such a state for a few weeks, that the company of friends from abroad is quite necessary. I have been once before with Mr. W. but we cannot both leave the station for so long a time, as we thought it best for me to remain. Brother R. appeared each day to have more strength than on the preceding one, but we cannot expect that he will remain long with us. I have had a pleasant visit, notwithstanding some trying reflections which I always have when on the spot where our lamented sister Poor labored and died. Mr. W. has been to-day at Manepy to attend the Tamul meeting, and I have been alone. Studied a little besides attending to family affairs, and had a long conversation with a man from Batticotta. He was ignorant and wicked—insisted that there are many gods, that they live in the temples, and are worshipped by every body who knows the right way. I felt bold to declare the truth, and though he asked why I, 'a woman, talked to him in this manner,' I could not refrain from warning him of his danger.

"18.—To-day the quarterly meeting of the Maternal Society was held at Manepy. We had a very pleasant time. I believe I have told you that our society engage to meet each other at the throne of grace every Saturday evening to pray for ourselves and children. We have some of us found these among our most precious seasons. I do not forget the circle of sisters who used to meet on this evening. And where are we all? We have had fellowship together—have lived and loved, and soon shall meet, if we are children of God, where our happiness will be perfected. In that bright world we shall not mourn the absence of our Saviour, and long and wait for his return. There we shall have tongues to utter all that sanctified hearts can dictate of praise and adoration, and there these bodies shall never say 'I am weary.'

"24, *Monday.*—I went on Saturday to Batticotta with sister Spaulding to spend the Sabbath, as it was communion. It was a refreshing time. I can still speak of the great goodness of God in making these seasons more precious to me than they used to be in America. They are not, it is true, attended with the emotions one must feel in sitting down with hundreds at the same table; but in regard to myself, it seems true that when I had more fellowship with saints I had less communion with God.

"28, *Friday.*—I believe I have told you that the Friday before the first Monday in the month is set apart as a season of fasting and prayer by all our number. Since Mr. W. and I have been alone we have found it pleasant occasionally to spend the day with our Manepy friends either here or there. Sister S. came up this morning, and Brother S. this afternoon. We have been permitted, I trust, to get near to God, and are strengthened. We have likewise had opportunity to speak for Christ to those who are ignorant, and it is numbered among our good days.

"29.—This morning one of the first women in an adjoining village came to bring back her runaway boy. He has been gone nearly a week, and we thought best not to oblige him to return. I was much pleased with an opportunity to converse with the woman, and particularly to see her so attentive to all I said. She promised to come to the bungalow once or twice every month, though she resides two miles distant. This morning a little girl was *brought to us* to receive into our family. This is a wonderful circumstance, and we hardly know how to understand it.

"*July* 1.—An interesting day at Manepy. The monthly prayer-meeting. We have for some months been in the habit of saying, after every meeting of the kind, 'this is the best.' There has seemed a growth in the good feelings of the brethren who conduct the meetings, and we never fail of being refreshed.

"*July* 4.—This has been a great day in Jaffna as well as in America—the first anniversary of a Bible Society. The collector of the district is president, and the principal men officers of various kinds. Some *speeches* were made, but you will not probably see them over the waters.

"15.—I believe I have not mentioned that Mr. W. and I spend Monday evenings in social prayer, reading, and conversation, on account of our children and for the benefit of our own souls. They are most valuable seasons. We have much anxiety for our children, and it is good to commend them to God. They are both generally well, and as pleasant and promising as other children. I could spend many pleasant hours with these dear ones, but if they are well I do not feel justified in giving time to them which I can employ in something more important. While so young, with a little of my care, they are comfortable in the hands of others. I therefore give them up almost entirely.

"*August* 3, *Saturday.*—Our dear Brother Richards has, we trust, at length entered into that rest which he has so long and so ardently desired. This morning, at about eleven o'clock, he quietly fell asleep. He has been patient, and his rational and christian views, as he approached the eternal world, were such that I could say concerning him, more emphatically than of any individual I have known, 'Let my last end be like his.'"

The death of *Mr. Richards* was an event long expected. He never recovered his strength, and only partially his voice, after his return from the Cape of Good Hope, though he was able to take charge of the schools, and to manage many of the temporal concerns of the stations with which he was connected.

He frequently remarked that such were his views of the divine character, and so desirable did it appear to him to have God glorified, that he felt willing, if necessary, to have his sufferings continued and even increased. He said, "It is *good* to suffer. It gives me some faint idea of what the Saviour bore for me. Thanks, eternal thanks to that grace which snatched me from the jaws of the devourer. When I get home, how will I sing the praises of Him who has washed away all my sins—crown him. Oh, I'll crown him Lord of all."

In speaking of his forgetfulness of mercies, he said with emphasis, "In heaven I shall never forget, no *never*. There I shall remember all. There I shall sing; there I shall sing glory to God. I have sometimes had as much joy in singing the praises of God here as my body could bear, yes, as much as it could bear. What will it be in heaven? 'I now see through a glass darkly, but soon, very soon, *face to face.*'"

He was eminently a *good man.* A more humble, mild, consistent and happy christian is seldom found. He had the spirit of Christ. At the age of *thirteen* he devoted himself to the Lord, and while a student in Williams' College, in connection with Mills, Hall, and others, he consecrated himself to the missionary work. This little band in 1808, while the subject of missions was almost unknown in America, and little felt even in England, used to retire to a consecrated spot under a *hay-stack* in a meadow, to fast and pray for divine direction; and there they bound themselves together by a written agreement, each to attempt in his own person, and aid the others in attempting, a mission to the heathen. This compact was afterwards renewed at the Theological Seminary in Andover, and the band of *brethren* was gradually enlarged. In 1810, four of them laid a paper expressive of their views before the General Association of Massachusetts, which led ultimately to the formation of the American Board of Commissioners for Foreign Missions. Mr. Richards' name was at first on this paper, but was omitted when it was presented, because he had not finished his theological studies. As there seemed little prospect of aid from the churches in America, he resolved, should no other door open, to work his passage on board of some vessel to a heathen shore, and there support himself as he could while proclaiming the Gospel; and in one of the last letters which he wrote to America he says, "*I have never been sorry that I came to India.* Had I ten thousand lives to give, they should all be sacrificed in this blessed cause." "Blessed is that servant whom when his Lord cometh he shall find so doing."

"*October* 21.—We were awaked this morning by the very pleasant voice of a person in prayer. I have seldom heard one more fervent. It appeared to be a lad whom we employ in the family. You would be surprised to hear how fluent our boys and girls often are in this exercise. Most of them seem to feel nothing of that timidity by which almost every one in christian countries is at first embarrassed; and you would wonder, also at the propriety, and correctness and feeling, with which they often pray.

"30.—Went to Manepy, and returned this evening by the light of a clear and full moon. I have seldom seen the face of nature more mild and pleasant. Certainly the evenings in this country are more delightful than they are in America; the atmosphere is so transparent, the moon and stars so bright, and the earth so verdant. Besides we can expose ourselves to the evening air, at all times, without injury, except in the rainy season, and for a short time after, when there are heavy dews. But in these sweet moonlight evenings the natives are flocking to their idol temples, or to temporary play-houses, erected here and there in the villages, for the acting of dramas and comedies; to which, and to card-playing, cock-fighting, and other kinds of gambling, they are much addicted.

"*November* 1.—We have had an unusually interesting season with the communicants this afternoon. They never appeared better; at the same time they are not in all respects like new converts in America. Their want of social habits, which contribute so much to our enjoyment, deprives them of many important aids in their christian course, and inclines them to be suspicious of each other. We strive to bring them together more closely, and are gratified to observe a growing mutual confidence and affection. It must, however, be long before they can know much of social intercourse. Males and females are quite separated in all their ordinary transactions. Husband and wife must never eat together, and a man cannot even touch a woman's hand in public without disgrace. They sometimes remark upon our familiarity; but are, I believe, convinced that it is not improper for us, though they have not the least notion of it among themselves.

"7.—Since my last date we have had a joyful season. Saturday, the 2d instant, Mr. and Mrs. S. and Mrs. R. came to spend the Sabbath with us In the evening we had a meeting among ourselves, preparatory to the communion; on Sabbath morning a prayer-meeting, and then a meeting of the church at the station, consisting of ourselves and five native members, to examine Katheraman, the husband of Antache, for communion. He was received. The congregation of men and women at the bungalow was large, and among them were nearly all the head men at Oodooville. Every circumstance seemed favorable and such as we could wish. I had previously a great desire to have many people present when this man should come forward, and was gratified; but think I never felt more sensibly that all is vain without the influences of the Holy Spirit. The communion season was precious. On Monday was a prayer-meeting here. It was a happy day on account of its religious privileges; and rendered more so by the receipt of forty-seven letters from our dear native land, containing many interesting accounts of the work of God there; for which we unitedly praised him.

"*November* 24.—We have lately had almost incessant rain. The poor natives suffer exceedingly in this weather in their health, and for want of food. All the common people lay by nothing for the morrow, and when there is a long storm, so that there is no market for a number of days, it is not easy to conceive the extent of their sufferings. It is sometimes difficult to determine how much of our allowance should be appropriated to supplying the temporal wants of this people. We profess to have come hither to do them good, and they can conceive of no benefit so great as that of giving them food when they are hungry. On the Sabbath we have large numbers of *beggars* who attend preaching regularly, and then receive something in charity. Yesterday I gave each of them a measure of rice in addition to the common gratuity, which quite overcame them. They were so full of thanks that I was obliged almost to drive them away. I am sure you never saw such miserable looking objects. Imagine, if you can, a colored man or woman who is a mere skeleton, having a wrinkled withered face, expressive only of ignorance, vice, grief and poverty, with loose dishevelled gray hair, which would seem to have been uncombed for years; a naked, withered body, tottering on a staff, and only a strip of cloth round the middle, which for dirt and tatters you might think had been worn from youth up, and you have some idea of the beggars around us. Their moral and spiritual condition is not so easily described. I wish I could say that of the number who have long attended on the preaching of the word and heard much religious truth, I have hope of any that they are truly converted. No class of people appear to me so hopeless. It seems as though they literally *cannot* feel or understand. At the same time I know that the Gospel is sent to the poor, and therefore there is encouragement to labor with them.

"*December* 21.—We have had a good day. Our congregations for a long time have generally been large. This morning a number of leading men were present and attentive; and the meeting for those who wish to learn more of christianity, which Mr. W. has held for some time past, immediately after service in the bungalow, was attended by a number for the first time. The wife of Solomon was present. She has been thoughtful and inquiring ever since her husband joined the church. One of her children died about four months since, and from that time she has appeared to be much more earnest in seeking the salvation of her soul. We have some hope that she is born again."

The following, giving a history of *the employment of a day*, with other details, may serve to introduce the reader more fully to the interior of the mission, and throw some light on the character of the Hindoos.

"I will tell you a little about my common round of duties, that you may be able to make some allowance for my letters. I am not, as you suppose, '*wholly*' occupied with missionary work, although my time is mostly taken up in engagements connected with the mission. To begin with the time of rising in the morning. My rule is, to be up as long before breakfast as I have health to be profitably employed. Our breakfast hour is half-past seven, and I have not of late been often in bed after six. The first thing is a season of retirement, which I find more absolutely indispensable here than I used to do at home. After this, family prayers and a little attention to household matters occupy me till breakfast.

"Some one must then usually be sent to market for vegetables for the boarding children, and perhaps something for the family. Every penny given for this purpose must be counted, the sum to be appropriated to each article specified, and the article particularly described. It must be ascertained that the hired man is at his post drawing water or cutting wood; and the low-caste woman must be attended to, for she is never trusted a moment in the house without watching. The native children have, by this time, attended prayers, and are ready to receive their directions about study. The domestics must be told what to do, for the best of them scarcely ever think of continuing even their customary employments without direction. When the market-man returns, I must go to the store-room. If he has bought rice, it must be measured, if vegetables, they must be counted. The children's cook and my own come to receive the allowance for the day. They must be carefully watched. If for a moment my eyes are turned from them, they will perhaps heap their measure of salt, or of rice, so as to make much more than the proper quantity, or slip a lime or some curry seeds into their clothes.

"When they are gone, somê stores commonly want attention. The rice may be damp and require to be spread in the sun. The curry seeds have insects in them and require drying. It may be the *white ants** are getting on the shelves, or

* These white ants are very troublesome. In many parts of Jaffna the ground seems almost filled with them. If any thing is laid on it which they can eat—and only something as hard as iron or stone will long resist them—it is very soon attacked. They come up bringing a sort of mortar of dirt, wet with something moist from their bodies, with which they form a covered way as fast as they make their approaches to any point, to shelter them from the large black ants and their other enemies. They will carry such lines up a wall or a post to the top of a building, and ascend in sufficient numbers to destroy the whole in time, if not interfered with. They must be attended to, and brushed down every few days, where any wood-work is exposed.

on the boxes and mats, and eating them so that they will soon be destroyed. Sometimes I thus spend two hours of the morning in the store-room; generally, however, half an hour is sufficient. I am but just seated in the house, perhaps, when the cook comes and says, 'there is no wood,' or 'no water.' A milk-man comes, or ironing-man, or washer-man, or some other wages-man, and wants a little money. Another is sick, and wants medicine. Just then a note comes in which must be answered. Work must be prepared for the girls; and the boys must be called at half past eleven to recite their lessons. I am generally occupied with them until *one*, at which time is our concert of prayer.

"I sometimes find a few minutes before this to bring my mind a little from its wanderings. After this is sleeping time for almost every body in India; but I believe not for most of our missionaries. I never sleep in the day, unless quite too

The lower floors, if of plank, would soon be destroyed. They are, therefore, of brick or cement. If a trunk of clothes, books, or any similar article, is placed on the floor at night, it may in the morning be found full of these depredators; which, unless disturbed, would go on quietly and devour all the contents inside, without giving any notice, by their appearance outside, what they were doing. You would find at length only a shell crumbling under your hand, and almost filled with earth brought up by them as a covering and defence.

unwell to be up, or after a sleepless night. I often bathe at this time, write a letter, or talk with some native who may call. Occasionally a difficulty among the boarding children or the domestics is to be settled. One day in the week they all bathe and wash their mats. I must go to the store-room and give them limes and oil for their heads; and perhaps when they are all ready, the well-rope breaks, or the water-basket is stolen, and others must be supplied. After they have bathed and oiled their heads, they must have clean cloths. Dinner then comes, but is soon dispatched. If able to go out among the people, I now go, and return at evening. If not, I occupy myself in mending my husband's clothes, or in other household affairs. By evening I am generally very much fatigued, and obliged to retire as early at least as eleven, but my writing, thinking, and reading must be principally at this time.

"In relation to our *evenings*, I might say that Sabbath evening we have a meeting with the children and servants; Monday evening a season of social prayer for ourselves and our dear Charles; Wednesday evening, with all the missionaries, we devote to prayer for a blessing on our work, in connection with the missionaries at Bombay; and Saturday evening, from *eight to nine*, is a concert of prayer by the members of the Maternal Society, for our children. We have, until the last two weeks, had a meeting for inquirers one or two evenings in the week, which we now have on Tuesday afternoon, and sometimes again on Friday.

"In my employments for the day I might have mentioned, too, that one morning every week I am occupied an hour in giving my clothes to the washer-man, and in receiving the clean ones that he brings. Here, probably, my patience is tried. Very likely he has torn the towels in two, so that he may count the right number, and keep one himself. The sheets he has kept back for his wife or somebody to wear. The cloths of the boarding children have been lent for his friends to wear, or perhaps are still at home unwashed. One day in the week I must go through much the same course with an ironing-man. You can have no idea of the dishonesty of this people. They very generally, from the richest to the poorest, think it no disgrace, but rather creditable, to steal from Europeans—as we are all considered—though it be the most trifling thing. If you leave a room for a few minutes with any thing in it that can be pilfered and sold, such as a spoon, a knife, a pair of scissors, or a piece of cloth, you must not expect to see it again if any idler is about.

"You may perhaps think that these employments are very different from what you expected me to be engaged in. They are not exactly what

I anticipated, but are absolutely necessary in a missionary establishment like ours. A family of boarding children cannot be supported without all this attention to minute concerns; and if a missionary has no boarding children, and lives alone, without a wife, a good deal of his time must be occupied in providing for himself; he also must suffer much inconvenience from the negligence of his domestics, and his patrons much loss of property by their dishonesty. That females are needed in all missionary establishments in India, no judicious person who ever saw them can question, and others have not the means of judging.

"A female need not, however, imagine that all her talents must be wasted on petty things. Her husband is to find all his society in her. He is to be encouraged and strengthened by her prayers, sometimes aided by her counsels, and always relieved as much as possible from worldly cares, from the trials of temper and patience, which would hinder him in his appropriate work, by her considerate attention to all the family concerns. I could readily tell you what a missionary female *should* be, but a reflection on what I am so rebukes me that I stop; only adding, that, with this multiplicity of cares, there is time to do much for the female sex, which all find must be done almost exclusively by females."

The following gives a view of the religious privileges of the mission, which few could prize more highly than did the subject of this memoir. They were to her emphatically "springs of water in a dry place." She always *longed* for communion with God's people, and to see his glory as she had seen it "in the *sanctuary*."

"MY DEAR L.—You inquire about our religious opportunities. Among the first are our monthly prayer-meetings, when we trust that we unite with the thousands of Israel in supplications for the world. We have also a quarterly meeting of the members of our mission, to unite in partaking of the Lord's supper, and to become more acquainted with each other, that we may the better 'bear one another's burdens, and so fulfill the law of Christ.' These are peculiarly refreshing seasons. We have this ordinance administered also at some one of our stations every month. At all the stations are regular congregations every Sabbath; and though preaching is in Tamul, we are most of us able to understand it enough to gain some benefit. It is not like going 'with the multitude to the house of God with the voice of joy and praise, with a multitude that keep holy day,' but it is a privilege which calls for much gratitude.

"Our religious meetings are more valuable to us, probably, because we have little intercourse with the world, and because they are so rare in heathen countries. We have more social enjoyment than most missionaries, as we are near each other, and have very much one heart. We have had some reason to fear, that being situated so near together, with tempers and habits very dissimilar, we should be in danger of contentions, but I rejoice to say that it is far otherwise. We have some intercourse with Europeans, of whom there are a few in Jaffna, but only enough to make us retire with greater relish to our domestic quietude, and the still round of our humble, but we hope to some extent, successful labors.

"You ask if I do not wonder that 'among those who are privileged with a knowledge of christianity, so few count it worthy of their regard.' Not only so, but I wonder that so many of those who profess to regard it as their chief good, neglect its precepts in respect to *seeking the salvation of sinners;* not merely that so few go to the heathen, but that so few do what their hands find to do, whether at home or abroad.

"Mrs. Laura E. Hyde."

"OODOOVILLE, January 16, 1823.

"MY DEAR MRS. C.—I should like to make you acquainted with my little family of heathen children, and some of the trials I have with them. These children are comforts in prospect. Now they require so much patience, forbearance, and self-denial, that I sometimes think myself altogether inadequate to the proper management of them. Indeed I feel more need of being furnished from above to discharge my duties towards these children, than for almost any thing else. They are *heathen children*, from the first moment of life accustomed to witness scenes of vice which scarcely ever enter the minds of children in christian countries, and as soon as they can speak and go alone, to imitate the example of their parents, and often to obey their *commands*, in lying, stealing, and swearing. It is impossible at once to make them feel that these things are sinful, or in any way to break up their bad habits. It seems to be a part of their very nature to tell a lie if it will serve their purpose any better than the truth, and to lay their hands on any thing which they wish to possess. In these trials, however, we have the happiness of seeing that they fear and love us, and become more and more conformed to our precepts. We have, besides, a rational and sure prospect that it will eventually be better with these children than with their fathers. Some in the mission are already numbered among those who are born of God.

"Mrs. William Cleaveland."

"*February* 11.—In conversing with the girls to-night, I reminded them of their obligations to their patrons in America, and that nothing would repay them for their kindness but to have the children whom they support become children ot God. They were deeply affected. Fanny Hall wept a great deal. I have not before known her so much overcome. The thought that her patrons, having no child of their own, had taken her, a poor heathen child, to be trained up for Christ, was quite too much.

"Since my last date I have been variously occupied. A part of Monday and Tuesday was very busy in copying the prospectus of a college, and sat up until one o'clock at night to finish it. Wednesday went to Manepy to the meeting of the Maternal Society. Mrs. Poor (late Miss Knight) was admitted as a member. We have increasing evidence that this small Society is one among the many means for the advancement of Christ's kingdom. On the Sabbath was communion at Manepy, and a man from among the heathen, in no way connected with the mission, was received into the church. I am again, since my return, copying the prospectus. You may wonder at my doing what others might do as well. There are no others here to do it, and I find it necessary to assist Mr. W. in this way, as he has much writing to do, and it wears upon his health.

"14.—On asking the girls this evening some questions about their souls, one of them misunderstanding me, replied, 'I have prayed five times.' I have noticed an increasing disposition in them to pray alone, and once to-day I distinctly heard this one praying earnestly for a long time.

"I have commenced a meeting of such women as we can get out to our house, once a week, to hear the Scriptures and unite in prayer. Have long waited for our interpreter's wife to return from Colombo, that I might do this; and now very much rejoice that a beginning is made. I cannot but hope that God will bless the reading of his word in this way.

"15.—Last night about twelve o'clock we were alarmed by voices in the street. Mr. W. going out, found a large number of people, who had brought a woman with a limb very badly broken. She was from a neighboring village. The natives seldom attempt to do any thing with a broken bone. Indeed they know little or nothing of surgery, and have no means for dressing wounds. Mr. W. found what is called a compound fracture, or a bad flesh wound, in addition to the broken bone. He dressed the limb, and the woman will remain here until she is better, should she live, which is doubtful. I could not but feel very sensibly how much we might do for the relief of this poor people, if we could devote more time to their bodily wants. They often suffer a long time and then die from the effects of very slight wounds

"I have never seen more to encourage the hope that the Holy Spirit is striving with some of our girls than this evening. I was sitting by the door just at sun-set, when Fanny came and stood by me, as the girls generally do at this hour, expecting me to say something. I found her very tender. She wept almost immediately on my speaking to her, and more and more as I proceeded. When I had done, she left me, and instead of joining the other girls, retired to pray. I heard her voice in very fervent prayer, accompanied by much sobbing, for a long time. Soon after the other girls came in, and one of them said of her own accord, 'I think of my sins all day, and Elizabeth too thinks a little about her soul.' This girl I have considered uncommonly thoughtless, though she is amiable and pleasant.

"22.—The native members of our church are beginning to hold quarterly meetings, and have had their first at Oodooville to-day. Malleappah preached in the morning, and in the afternoon they had a meeting for free conversation. I asked James, our hired man, if he had a good day. He replied, in broken English, 'It was very good. I never saw so good. My soul never feel so; because I could tell all I had in my heart—all I think.' We have much comfort in seeing those immediately connected with us grow in grace. I told James, when the sick woman was brought that he must improve the opportunities he might have to talk and read to her and her friends; for perhaps the Lord had sent her here that some of them might be saved. He replied, 'I think so, and I did talk to them last night. I waked up at four o'clock, and the woman was crying with pain; then I told her what master said when he was dressing her leg, how that pain comes because we are sinners, and if she did not repent, she would have pain after she die too.' Then the man asked some questions, and we talked a long time. I mentioned some parts of Scripture suitable for him to read. We have since repeatedly heard him reading and talking to them late in the evening, when all around were asleep. These native members are helpers, and they will, I trust, greatly promote the glory of God."

"April 1, 1823.

DEAR PARENTS, BROTHER AND SISTER.—In most respects our affairs are much as they were when we last wrote. The word goes forth from time to time, and multitudes hear it; some of them with attention, and others with much contempt and derision. On the whole, there is manifest progress, though we do not see 'a nation born in a day.' No, dear friends, we must not only sow the seed, but wait for the early and latter rain. In our boarding-school at this station, are seventeen boys and six girls, most of them too young to know, as yet, much of religion. Several *schools for girls only* have lately been established in the mission, which shows a great change in the feelings of the people. Heretofore they have strongly opposed every thing like learning in females. It was much more rare here to find a female who could read, than it would be to find a person in New England who cannot. I have lately commenced a *Sabbath-school of girls*, and three have attended. This we consider an important step, and have no doubt that others will soon come. Mr. W. commences his school for boys next Sabbath. I am sure you would be delighted, could you come into our bungalow on the Sabbath, to see *two hundred and forty boys* from the heathen families, seated in regular rows on large mats, listening to a christian sermon, and to hear them repeat their catechism and Scripture lessons which they have learnt during the week. You would say, 'If the *parents* of these children will not renounce their idols, surely their children will; and grow up a " generation to the praise of the living and true God." '

" Mr. Nathaniel Winslow, and R. Morton, Esq."

CHAPTER VI.

Fourth and Fifth Years in Ceylon—embracing the general revival of religion in 1824.

Mission Seminary—Female Central School—burial of the dead—car-festival at Nellore—*General Revival at all the stations*—wrestling prayer—meeting of youth—meetings at the several stations—access to God—meeting of children of the boarding-schools—the work revived—blessing of social prayer—new year reflections—character of the work—reception of forty-nine to the church.

The prospectus or plan of a College,* which has been mentioned, proposed the establishment, on a liberal scale, of a christian institution for the instruction of Tamul and other youth in the literature of the country, and also in the English language and the elements of European science.

The great object was to prepare catechists, schoolmasters, and other assistants in the missionary work, especially *native preachers*, without whom the progress of the Gospel among the millions of the East must be very slow. Foreign laborers are too few, supported at too great ex-

* See Missionary Herald, 1824.

pense, and have too little knowledge of the customs, language, and religion of the people, to give christianity a dominant and pervading influence They are also but poorly able to bear the heat of the climate, and mingle, under all circumstances, with the population of the country. Native energies of body and mind, and native feelings must be enlisted in the work. The extended provinces of Satan's empire must furnish materials to aid in their own subjection to Christ, as India has been subdued to a foreign power principally by native troops—but such is the indolence, and such the moral weakness of the natives, that they need much early discipline as well as piety to give them generally any efficiency. Their own course of instruction forms in them no strength of character, and a thorough christian education, both mental and moral, is necessary to furnish them properly for the native ministry.

It was also an object to qualify and employ translators and writers who should be able to transfer some of the treasures of *European literature and science* into the native languages, as well as enrich them from the stores of christian devotion in English, and it was designed to teach true science as a means of exploding false philosophy and superstition. As the whole fabric of idolatry rests on the same foundation with the most absurd systems of geography and astronomy, and the most stupid fictions in natural science, which could be overthrown at once by demonstration and experiment, it was seen that to extend true science would be to undermine this fortress of Satan and prepare the way to build the temple of God on its ruins.

* A single instance may be given. They believe that the earth is *flat*, having in the centre a mountain, around which the sun goes, causing the succession of day and night. Encircling the part on which we live, is a sea of salt water, and beyond this an annular continent surrounded on the outside by a sea of milk. Then another similar continent and a sea of buttermilk; and thus seven continents and seven seas in concentric circles—the *first* sea being of salt water, the *second* of milk, the *third* of buttermilk or curds, the *fourth* of ghee, or melted butter, the *fifth* of molasses, or sugar-cane juice, the *sixth* of honey, and the *seventh* of fresh water; beyond which is a mountainous barrier, and then "outer darkness." In past ages there was a deluge, which swept almost every thing valuable into the sea of milk. To recover what was lost, and particularly the ambrosia—which is the food of the gods, and gives immortality—the gods and asooras (a species of demons) agreed to churn the sea. For this purpose they took mount Mandra for a churning-stick, and the great five-headed serpent called Vaysookee for a rope, and winding the serpent round the mountain, they rolled it back and forth and agitated the sea so as to bring up the lost articles. When the ambrosia appeared, the gods were afraid the asooras would eat it and become immortal. To prevent this, Vishnu assumed the form of a most beautiful female, who taking the ambrosia in a golden pot, stood before the gods and asooras, offering them their choice of the ambrosia or herself. The

These and other advantages connected with raising the standard of education in the country were proposed by the college; the way for which had been prepared by the boarding-school establishments. Indeed the state of these establishments was such as to make a higher institution necessary. There were more than one hundred lads at the five different stations of the mission, of whom many were so far advanced in their studies as to require more attention in carrying them forward to higher branches than could be given by each missionary. It was indispensable to have the more forward of them brought together under one teacher, and furnished with suitable apparatus and other helps. This was

asoc ras being fascinated, left the ambrosia to the gods and began to quarrel with each other for the enchanting beauty. Some were slain. Two of them seeing the folly of the contest, left the affray, and joining the gods in disguise, began with them to eat the ambrosia. They were soon discovered and informed against by the sun and moon, who are supposed to be animated beings. Vishnu, who had again assumed his own form, immediately cut off their heads with the spoon with which he was lading the ambrosia. Their bodies perished, but as the ambrosia had descended as low as their necks, their heads could not die. They were immortal; and having ascended into the heavens, they remain there as two serpents. They are called Rahu and Keetu, and represent the moon's nodes. By occasionally attempting to swallow or devour the sun and moon—against whom they seem to bear a grudge—they occasion eclipses!

accordingly done, and the school made the *germ* of the intended college.

It was commenced at Batticotta in 1823, under the care of Mr. Poor. *Forty-eight* lads were received the first year, who passed a satisfactory examination in the Tamul and English Testament, and the ground rules of Arithmetic. This school has gradually increased, until it has become, in a good measure, what was first designed, a *college*, though known by the name of the *Mission Seminary*. The reason for this is, that the government interposed obstacles to carrying the whole plan into effect, after it had been approved by the Board, and funds had been conditionally pledged in America, and instructors engaged, for its successful commencement.

Soon after commencing the Seminary for boys, it was thought advisable to form also a *Central School for Girls*; as it was inconvenient to have them at all the different stations of the mission, and especially to have boys and girls at the same station. An establishment was accordingly made at Oodooville. The boys there were removed to other stations, and such of the girls at those stations as were willing to remove, and were thought suitable to be received, were transferred to Oodooville. The school commenced with twenty-two girls, but was soon increased to *twenty-nine*, who were generally children of good promise. In reference to this school, Mrs. W. writes in September,

"It is agreed to have the Female Central School here. I feel that it is a great object; but how can I undertake it while so unfaithful to my present charge? Yet I wish to do all I can; and perhaps this is in answer to the prayer, 'Lord, what wilt thou have me to do?' I have used this petition more frequently of late than formerly. If it is the will of God that the school should come here, may we be prepared by his Spirit to enter on the work with right hearts, feeling our helplessness and entire dependence on him. As little children, may we look to our Father for his direction and assistance in humility and faith; and may the beginnings of the school be marked with his especial blessing."

The desire thus expressed led to faithful exertion and prayer, and the blessing was not withheld. All the girls who had passed through a regular course in the school, or were far advanced in it previous to Mrs. W.'s death, had then become hopefully pious, and were members of the church; and what was very pleasing, no one of them, *twenty-four* in number, had dishonored her profession.

"*September* 3, 1823.—Mr. W. has to-day visited the temple at Nellore, it being the closing ceremony there for this season. He saw about ten thousand people, and with Mr. Knight and Mr. S. distributed fifteen hundred Tracts. *More than four hundred people rolled after the car.* One of them, an old man from our neighborhood, who has heard much of the truth, died at the temple in consequence of fatigue and fasting. He was brought home and buried near our door, after the common method of burial in this country.*

* All the more respectable people, and generally those who are able to afford it, *burn* the dead with many ceremonies. At a "dead-house," as the place where the body lies is called, there is often much mourning, but not always much real grief; and in the funeral processions to the grave, or to the place of burning, which are attended only by men—the women remaining behind at the dead-house until their return—there is generally the utmost levity and unconcern. It is affecting, however, to witness their mourning, especially that of the women. Their funeral cry, which is a most dismal howl, is heard the moment a friend is dead. This calls together other relations and friends. The principal mourner receives them as they come. She is seated probably on the ground in the yard, with her hair dishevelled, her clothes loose or torn, and her head covered with ashes or dust. She sings a sort of dirge in a most plaintive and piercing tone, describing, perhaps, the excellencies of the deceased, or blaming him for dying, or expostulating with the gods for taking him away. As she chants and varies this at intervals, swinging her body back and forth, she tears her hair and beats her breast with

A small hole was dug, not long enough for the body without a coffin, and not deep enough to prevent it from being dug up by the dogs. It would make you shudder to see the unfeeling manner in which they treat their dead. About fifteen men stood around. Only one looked even sober, and that was the girls' schoolmaster at this station, who has been somewhat serious. He uttered an ejaculation of surprise and feeling, when, finding the grave too short, one man stepped on the limbs, and another on the head of the corpse, to crowd it down.

"I saw in the girls a few nights since a striking contrast to this conduct; and was comforted in the belief that if they gain nothing else by being with us, they will learn that it is an awful thing to die. Three of them were standing in the verandah just at twilight, and looking at the distant smoke rising from the burning of a dead

both hands, bringing them up so violently with the fists clenched, as almost to drive the breath from her body. Occasionally she throws herself prostrate in the dust. As one friend after another comes in, she rises to meet them, throws her arms around their necks, and utters her mournful howls, in which all the friends join in sad concert. They hang on each other's necks, forming sometimes a large circle, and raise their cries so as to be heard at a great distance. In the silence of the night these cries are peculiarly dismal, especially when you are awakened by them out of sleep.

body. Betsey said, 'Another soul is gone before God to-day.' 'Yes,' said Elizabeth, 'and where is it, in heaven or hell?' One replied, 'We don't know, but we think it is in hell!' 'Yes,' said another, 'and this is three since last night; and perhaps one of us may be there before to-morrow morning.' 'And many of this people too,' said E. 'for a great many die in a day.' They sighed, and said, 'All this people are going to hell.' In this strain they continued their conversation for some time, without knowing that I overheard them."

The temple at Nellore, mentioned above, is devoted to Scanda, the second son of Siva, and is more frequented, perhaps, than any other in the district. There is a high wall of masonry enclosing an area of an acre or more, within which, besides rooms built against the wall inside, for the residence of the brahmins and others connected with the temple, are various small buildings and domes for the idols. The principal one is, like most other Hindoo temples, in three parts. There is an open court in front, in which the people occasionally assemble to hear their puranas, or the mythological fables of their gods; an inner court, enclosed on three sides and open in front, where is an altar for the offering of fruits and flowers, on which is the image of some god or animal; and a more secluded court, or sanctuary, where the idol is enshrined. This sanctuary is small and dark. It has no window, and receives no light but through a narrow door. The roof is arched, and surmounted by a heavy cupola, ornamented with hideous and grotesque figures in sculpture. Here the idol sits in darkness. No one enters its sanctuary but the officiating brahmin or priest. In performing the daily worship, he takes a light in one hand and a bell in the other, and as he enters waves the light before the idol, that the people without may perhaps catch some glimpse of it, and prostrate themselves; or raise their hands to their foreheads with the palms joined. He then bathes the idol, anoints it, offers it food and incense, and throws over it garlands of sweet-scented flowers; at the same time ringing the bell in his hand, that the people around may perform the necessary prostrations, or other acts of worship.

On the festival days the idol is brought out in public procession for about twenty successive nights, and then the festival ends with what is called the *tair*, or drawing the principal car by day. This is the grand ceremony; but it is not so imposing as the processions by night; for then there are innumerable flambeaus and torches, perhaps also fire-works, which produce a splendid effect. Whether by night or day, at a given signal the idol is brought out with the sound of music and many ceremonies. It is crowned with gold, wears a breast-plate of precious stones, and is covered with the richest jewels. Being placed on a throne, and under a canopy loaded with garlands of flowers, it is elevated on a high *car*. This is of a pyramidal form, in galleries lessening to the top, and is supported and borne along on three or four pairs of heavy wheels. The whole *car* is covered with figures in sculpture and painting, and adorned with the most gaudy wreaths, tassels, and drapery. The lower galleries are filled with brahmins, and in the upper, around the god, are some to fan it, hold umbrellas over it, and to offer it incense. There are strong cables attached to the car, by which the people, in immense numbers, draw it slowly round the precincts of the temple. On either side, as it proceeds, are banners, and flags, and ensigns displayed all along the dense lines of people, while in front are bands of music playing and numerous temple-girls dancing; and behind it hundreds of poor devotees rolling over and over in the dust, with their feet and hands extended, accomplishing in this way the whole circuit of the procession. As the car stops occasionally, the ground behind it seems paved with their bodies lying close to each other. They are nearly naked, and generally a profuse perspiration mingles with the dust, so as to coat their skins with mud, while their eyes, mouth, and hair are almost filled with dirt. This sight is painful; that of the dancing girls is offensive. They are among the handsomest native females; are very gaudily, and often richly dressed, with a great profusion of jewelry Their dress is commonly a blue or scarlet silk robe, covering the body, and girt round them with a variety of bands of different colored silks and chains of gold. On their feet are a kind of greaves, surrounded at the ancle by small bells. Their dance is a stepping to the sound of music, so as to keep time by jingling and striking these bells together, attended with a swinging and indecent motion of their bodies, and waving with their hands towards the idol. The whole procession, which commonly occupies two or three hours, is very alluring and fascinating to those so much affected as the natives are by pomp and display. Attachment to these festivals is also interwoven with their earliest associations, as the child and even the infant is carried and made to hold up its little hands to the idol, and with its first accents to say, swamy, or god; and the older children of all classes flock to them as their principal holydays. They are scenes of great wickedness, especially of licentiousness; and the whole system is most polluting and degrading.

We now approach the period when God displayed his abounding mercy in visiting *all the stations by the special influences of the Holy Spirit.* The following extracts from the private diary of Mrs. W. show how she humbled herself before Him, and wrestled in prayer for the blessing:

"*August* 27, 1823.—Yesterday morning I felt much cast down. I did not get relief, and after breakfast went to God. My mind was turned from myself to the heathen, by reading a hymn concerning the coming of Christ's kingdom to all nations; and during prayer I seemed to feel a new desire, or rather to ask with new earnestness for *the abundant outpouring of the Spirit* at this station, so that every heart should feel, and every one coming to the house should say, 'How awful is this place!' The more I thought of it and prayed for it, the more hopeful it appeared I could see no reason why it should not be so, and every reason why it should.

"*September* 7.—I have to-day been with Jesus in his last interviews with his disciples, his agony in the garden and on the cross, and his appearance again after his resurrection; scenes which never before seemed so full of every thing encouraging, strengthening, and comforting. Oh what displays of love, of tenderness, of glorious majesty! In view of all this I feel that, even for me, there is a way of access to God *in behalf of this poor people.* If my prayers are heard for my self and my husband, surely I may have hope of their being heard for others. I hesitate to say there is a connection between my prayers and the blessings we receive; but of this I am sure, that what I desire and ask is given in very many instances. Would that I had a heart to continue instant in prayer. Lord, take away my sloth, my unbelief, my hardness of heart, my distrust of thee; and grant me humility, activity, tenderness of heart, and strong faith. Can I not say, Lord, thou knowest that I desire above every thing to be like my Redeemer; to have his spirit, to be filled with his fullness, that I may glorify thee among this people?

"20.—I have been feeble in body and feeble in spirit, but trust I have had some earnest desires and some delight in reading God's word. *That* is to me more and more the Book of books. I relish very little besides on the Sabbath. What can men say like the language of God? Oh that I loved and understood it more.

"*January* 31, 1824.—Some weeks ago, as I was partly recovered from my sickness, and could command my time, I resolved to observe my old season of prayer at noon, and to pray for similar objects. The individual first selected was Betsey, partly because I thought her conversion would be a great blessing to the school, and partly because she has repeatedly been serious. For a few days I bore her on my heart, but with more or less variation of feeling.

"On Charles' birth-day, January 12, we were at Manepy. He told me, as I thought, a lie; the first I ever knew him tell. From that time I regarded him in a new light. I before knew that he was a sinner, but now it was a reality; and the thought took complete possession of my soul. That I had borne a child who was an enemy to God, a rebel, an heir of hell, was humbling, overwhelming. I could not endure the reflection. Immediately I resolved to give the Lord no rest, if he would permit me to plead with him, until this brand should be plucked from the burning. He became then my burden almost to the exclusion of every thing. Betsey was almost forgotten, and I thought I could neither eat nor sleep till the desire of my heart was granted. We were called to Tillipally, and I earnestly hoped that his being where the Holy Spirit was operating on the hearts of sinners would be blessed to his soul. My two great petitions were, that he might share in the influences of the Spirit, and that Mr. W. might be prepared to see a work at home. Here I cannot help saying, what appears to me a just tribute of gratitude to God, that in nothing of late have I thought my prayers were heard so evidently as when I pray perseveringly for my husband."

JOURNAL LETTER TO HER FRIENDS.

"*January* 28, 1824.—I cannot delay telling you what the Lord is doing among us. Last Monday a messenger came from Tillipally, saying that a number of the boys were under serious impressions, and that Mr. Woodward needed some assistance. Mr. W. immediately went there, and I accompanied him. We found the boys in meeting, and from their appearance, and that of others around, were at once impressed with the conviction that the Holy Spirit was indeed present. Nothing unusual had appeared until the day before, near the close of the morning sermon, when some special interest was manifested by a few. The afternoon service was more marked, and in the evening, at a special meeting, ten or twelve attended. We remained till Wednesday evening, and saw much to encourage the hope that a work of grace was commenced in a number of hearts. There were frequent meetings, and solemnity reigned around.

" Yesterday, at this station, Mr. W. had scarcely begun his sermon when it was evident that the Holy Spirit was near. He had some overwhelming views, which for a time rendered him unable to speak. Many of the congregation were affected. It was a solemn place. All the exercises were impressive beyond any thing I have known here. It was manifest that the truth took effect. The services at noon and in the afternoon were of a similar character; and this evening a number of the girls stopped after prayers to speak about their souls. Betsey, the most forward girl in school, and two or three others, appear very tender. We are greatly encouraged, and yet have a degree of anxiety which cannot be described.

"31.—We have had repeated inquiry-meetings during the week, and from five to eight girls have attended. Mr. W. has to-day had a very interesting time with the schoolmasters. One who has been a little anxious, is now convinced fully of the truth. A hired man also appears serious. We hear of nothing new at the other stations; but begin strongly to hope that the time is near when we shall see a great work.

"*February* 3.—The prayer-meeting yesterday was at Batticotta. All came together with the hope, apparently, that it would be an uncommon day; and it was so. The morning exercises were conducted as usual, but with more feeling; and in the afternoon the Holy Spirit came down with power, such as probably none of us ever felt or witnessed before, and filled all the house where we were sitting. The brother who first led in prayer was so much overcome as to be unable to proceed. For some time he had scarcely strength to rise from his knees. The afternoon was spent in prayer, interrupted only by singing, and occasionally reading or repeating a verse from the Bible. It was not *common* prayer, but wrestling with the angel of the covenant, with strong crying and tears. Every thing was awfully solemn; such as language cannot describe. The worth of souls and the love of Christ pressed upon the conscience and the heart almost too strongly to be endured. We came home exceedingly exhausted. To-day the girls are more serious, and every thing around seems to say that God is here. Oh that we may stand aside while the Lord passes by, as Elijah did, when he wrapped his face in his mantle and stood in the entrance of the cave. I feel afraid to do or say any thing, lest I should in some way hinder the work. May God direct.

"9.—Yesterday we were at Manepy. It was a most interesting day. A number of the serious boys from Tillipally, and all the girls from Oodooville were there. The Lord's supper was administered. A native man was admitted to the communion. In the afternoon there was a meeting of the youth, which was attended by the manifest influences of the Spirit. One who was sometime since awakened, rose and confessed his sin of backsliding, and with many tears admonished his companions not to grieve the blessed Spirit as he had done. A number of others spoke of their feelings in an affecting manner. At the close, a lad of the seminary, who joined the church at Batticotta last Sabbath, prayed with an overflowing heart. In thanking God that Satan's kingdom is declining, and the kingdom of Christ advancing, he seemed to rise with his subject, until the room was full of solemnity. We had another meeting in the evening, and this morning it appears that five or six hope they were yesterday born again.

" 11.—Some of the brethren and sisters came to Oodooville for a prayer-meeting last evening. It was a time of wrestling prayer until two o'clock. The principal subject of intercession was the seminary at Batticotta. If our interviews may hereafter be like this, we shall indeed be most favored.

" 13.—Last evening there was another prayer-meeting here. Mr. Woodward and Mr. Knight came. It was again a precious time. The Lord has certainly given us a new spirit in our approaches to him; and will, I believe, answer the prayers which he himself inspires, though we are utterly unworthy. We have just received a note from Dr. S. saying that a work is commenced at Panditeripo. Mr. W. has gone to his aid. There is progress at Oodooville. All the older girls, the woman who has the care of them, a hired man, and several others are affected. We have scarcely hoped to see so much, and now it seems but the beginning of days. How ungrateful and unbelieving we have been, but blessed be God that he can work by the weakest instruments.

" 14.—Most animating accounts from Panditeripo. Dr. and Mrs. S. went the day before yesterday, at evening, to Batticotta. As they were stepping into the gig, Amy, the colored woman, said, 'Now, Lord, send down thy Spirit while thy servant is absent.' The boys had a meeting, conducted by two of their number, who are members of the church. After it was over, and all were preparing to lie down on their mats, Amy said to one of them, 'You must go out and talk to those boys again, for how do you know but they will die to-night.' He went to them, and some listened to the warning. They left their mats one after another and resorted to different places in the garden, under the cocoa-nut trees, to call upon God. Some were alone, and others in little companies, crying, 'Come, Holy Spirit,' 'Lord have mercy,' &c. Dr. and Mrs. S. returning home, heard them on entering the yard. He immediately rung the bell, and they came in with streaming eyes, confessing their guilt and danger. Mr. W. says that to-day many appear under deep conviction.

" 17.—Last evening a prayer-meeting was held

at Panditeripo, and another at Batticotta, in reference to the seminary. There was thus a union of prayer by all the mission until midnight. It was a time of deep solemnity—of feelings which cannot be uttered. The walls were compassed by prayer *seven* times. This morning all met at Panditeripo. The brethren who came from Batticotta are full of confidence that the Lord has at length appeared there. All but Mr. Woodward afterwards went to that station, and had a most solemn meeting with the members of the seminary.

" 18.—We have had a meeting in our verandah this evening of some of the head-men and boys from Tillipally and Manepy. It was handsomely lighted up. Mr. and Mrs. Mooyart and the brethren, Knight, Spaulding, and Woodward, were present. It was a most interesting season. Our friends stay over night, as to-morrow is our quarterly meeting here.

" 19.—Another great day. We have never sat down to the table of our Lord under such interesting circumstances. Mr. W. preached from the text, 'Bring ye all the tithes into the storehouse,' &c. Oh that we may indeed do this, and prove the Lord therewith. It was a time of weeping for joy, and breaking of heart for sin.

" 24.—We went yesterday afternoon to Nellore, and with Mr. and Mrs. S. accompanied Mr. K. to two evening meetings at the houses of natives in Jaffnapatam. They were the first of the kind there, but full and solemn.

"25.—A meeting at Oodooville for all the schoolmasters and the more serious boys. The brethren, and some of the sisters, were here. About seventy adult natives were present, of whom thirty rose and testified their belief in christianity. Sixty or seventy children did the same. It is not to be supposed that many have as yet much knowledge of their own hearts.

"*March* 12.—Evening before last we went to a school bungalow, about two miles distant, to attend a meeting with Mr. and Mrs. S. and Dr. S. The bungalow was well filled, and the people gave good attention. It was cheering. Our humble chapel was surrounded by tall palmyras pointing to the bright skies, through which the moon was pursuing her majestic way among the stars. All around spoke of the glory of God; and there was in some breasts, it may be hoped, a brighter scene than even that which met the eye from without. The next morning was spent at Panditeripo in prayer, and the afternoon and evening at Batticotta. There was a precious meeting with the lads in the Seminary. The Spirit of God seemed to come down anew.

"18.—This morning we went to Jaffna to take leave of Mr. and Mrs. Mooyart, who are about removing to the south of the island. All the missionaries of the district were there, and we had a day of prayer long to be remembered. Mr. M. took his leave of us in a very affectionate manner, and with special thanksgiving to God for permitting him to depart with such high hopes for the wretched inhabitants of Jaffna. In the evening we attended an interesting meeting at the house of a native christian, and returned home."

"*March* 20, *Private Journal.*—Last Sabbath I had unusual nearness to God, and a feeling that I could ask any thing I would, without fear of a denial. He appeared *my friend*, to whom I could come very near, so as to talk face to face and order my cause before him. This feeling continues, and I would say with deep humility, that I never felt so much that it is a time to call upon God, to get near and to wait before him, and plead with him, as during the last week. It has been an unusual week; I have had some seasons which cannot be forgotten. I enjoy our social-meetings very much, but they are not to be compared with coming near to God in secret. To-day I have wrestled principally for the children here; have felt as I never did previously for them; have wondered that I have before felt so little. Perhaps God will now permit me to call, and not hear. It would be right, but still it is my privilege to pray."

"*March* 28.—We have had a very solemn day at Batticotta. I went with Mr. W. and found the brethren all there, but none of the sisters from the other stations. In the morning the brethren had a meeting for prayer and counsel concerning the exercises of the day. Sister P. and myself at the same time had a season of prayer. All then assembled for a general meeting with the boys, who were afterwards divided into classes, that each brother might take some of them to separate rooms. All the forenoon they thus conversed and prayed with them collectively and individually. In the meantime sister P. and myself called in some females attached to the family. I had also a meeting with the children. In the afternoon there was a united meeting with the youth of the Seminary, which continued till dark. I have seldom felt so sensibly the force of the expression, 'the Lord is in this place.'

"29.—We have new evidence that the Spirit is among us, by the opposition excited. Some who have heretofore been very civil, and have heard patiently, and some who have professed to be anxious about their souls, now take a decided stand on the side of the adversary. Betsey's father forbids her embracing the christian religion. He keeps a temple dedicated to a female devil, and is said to have devoted a sister of hers to its service. Probably he wants her for the same object; but I trust the Lord has better things in store for her. Her feelings are very tender, and her concern for her friends is great.

"30.—To-day there was a meeting at Manepy of all the children of our boarding-schools. About ninety stood up to express their belief in Christ. Some who did not rise, however, give more evidence of a change of heart than some who did. It has been a solemn day, full of interest. What would the patrons of these children have felt, could they have witnessed it? What would many christian friends feel, could they be present with us in such seasons of rejoicing and trembling. They would no doubt find an abundant reward for all they have done for these children, and encouragement to do more, as well as to plead with God for the outpouring of the Spirit on all heathen nations.

"*May* 21.—I may again record a precious day. Yesterday was our quarterly meeting at Manepy. The morning was spent much as usual. The afternoon was devoted to thanksgiving. Some of the more prominent objects for praise, connected with the present state of things, were, that God has so manifestly answered prayer, and that he has so carried on his work here as to leave no room for boasting—in fact, to pour contempt on human wisdom. A view was taken of the magnitude of the work, in its various bearings on ourselves, on the heathen around, on future generations; and the encouragement it may afford to missionaries in other parts of the world, and to the christian public. The subject grew and warmed our hearts. The second quarterly meeting of the schoolmasters is to be next week, and it was agreed to have special seasons of fasting and prayer for them.

"*June* 9.—The anniversary of our leaving America was observed yesterday at Panditeripo. We occupied the morning in contemplating the great goodness of God towards us, and in attempting to praise him. Never have we had so much cause for praise. Never have we assembled with so much love towards each other, and with such great mercies to recount. We are all alive after a five years' separation from our native country, and in as good health as on the day we sailed—have received *nine children* who are still spared to us, and above all, have seen the goings of God in our midst."

For a time the special influences of the Spirit were less apparent; but before the close of the year there was renewed evidence that he was present of a truth.

"*November* 5.—The Lord has come near us again, and surprised us when we had almost ceased talking about another refreshing. Our monthly meeting before the last was unusually solemn; the quarterly meeting, a fortnight after, still more so; and last Monday, at Oodooville, the prayer-meeting was peculiarly marked. Some of the native members appear more awake, and on the minds of the brethren and sisters generally there is a deep conviction that the Lord is ready to pour us out a blessing.

" 13.—Appearances of a revival continue. We have this evening had a prayer-meeting here. Yesterday was communion at Manepy. A precious time, though I felt more for the people than for myself. All was still and solemn, and I believe that the Holy Spirit accompanied the word and ordinances. I have for some time had unusual delight in prayer; but have thought too much of some hinderances to a work of grace. Have had a good season to-night, but felt too little my exceeding sinfulness. I have at all times too little feeling for the people.

" 25.—I have been deterred from writing since the last date, through fear of saying more than I ought concerning what we now term a *revival.* It is so great a thing that *our eyes* should again see the stately goings of God in this way, that I know not how to speak of it. There is an unusual seriousness at all our stations. The children who give evidence of conversion are much engaged. Some who were careless are awakened; and we hope two or three are born again. One of the first boys in *the Seminary*, named Dwight, for whom, more than almost any other, prayer has been made without ceasing, is of the number. This school is, as it was before, the principal burden of our hearts. Nearly all in it now profess to be under some concern of mind. In the *Female Central School* eight or ten profess to be again awakened, and by their prayers and tears manifest that they feel something. The older ones, who give evidence of a change of heart, every day call one or more of the others aside, and pray and converse with them; a means which has been blessed.

"*December* 8.—The goodness of God is still manifested among us. The members of the seminary are all somewhat affected. A young man, superintendent of schools at Tillipally, and one schoolmaster, hope they are born again. Yesterday was our prayer-meeting at Jaffnapatam, and a very solemn day. In the evening we remained to attend a meeting in the Wesleyan chapel. The house was full of English, Dutch, Portuguese, and Tamulians; and addresses were made in English, Portuguese, and Tamul. We returned late by a fine moon. This morning the collector of the district and his lady came out to breakfast, and remained with us till twelve o'clock, conversing freely on religious subjects.

"11.—We had last evening another season of social prayer at Oodooville—a time of wrestling with the angel of the covenant. I think I never knew until lately the blessings of social prayer. We had the communion yesterday at Manepy—a good day. Two domestics there, who have long been exceedingly hardened, and during the previous outpouring of the Spirit felt nothing, are bowed down under a sense of sin. It was very affecting to see the cook, an old Portuguese man, stand up, with more than thirty native children, to signify that he felt he was a great sinner, and hoped to give himself no rest until he found it in Jesus. You cannot understand the import of this without considering that 'Jesus Christ' is here a despised name. The girls' schoolmaster at Oodooville is grandson of an Odigar, and of a high family. He has perhaps excited as much feeling in our hearts as any one. In the time of the last attention to religion he was awakened, but his friends were too strong for him. Now he is in great distress.

"16.—We have had a meeting of the schoolmasters at this station. It was a time of deep emotion and of triumph. To our surprise and great joy the girls' schoolmaster addressed them, and then led in prayer. His utterance was several times checked by weeping.

"*January* 1, 1825.—I feel disposed this evening to wish you a 'happy new year,' and to tell you something of our enjoyments. We did not 'dance out the old year,' but we prayed and sang praises to the Lord; and blessed be his name for having given us such occasion. I hope you know that at the commencement of the last year we were blest with a revival of religion. We again witness the influences of the Spirit on many hearts, and are permitted to rejoice over several young men of talents and influence as apparently born again. Some others, particularly in the boarding-schools, are in a very encouraging state. Many are more or less affected. Several domestics who have seemed harder than the 'nether millstone,' are now very solemn. The young men, if they prove to be children of God, will be a great acquisition. Prayers have long been offered on their account, and much labor bestowed on them. We may and do hope that the Lord has graciously answered prayer.

"These visitations of the Spirit have, I believe, been marked with similar features to revivals at home. They were preceeded by a deep sense of deficiency in the missionaries, which led them to humble themselves before God; and were accompanied throughout with a spirit of prayer; a pleading—a wrestling for souls—something I think of what our Saviour expressed when he said, 'I have a baptism to be baptized with, and how am I straitened till it be accomplished.' Social prayer-meetings have been peculiarly blest. Even while we have been speaking, our prayers have seemed to be answered. In a number of instances the missionaries have set apart one hour in the day to unite in prayer for the same object, for five days in succession. On the sixth a part of the day has been spent in fasting and prayer, and on the seventh, all have met together for united supplication. One of these was in behalf of the young men whom I have mentioned. They were called together for a meeting by themselves on the seventh day, while several of the brethren and sisters were praying for them. After a very solemn meeting they were called in and addressed with much feeling. The concern felt for them while the Spirit of God is so near, was mentioned with weeping. They have all since seemed to tremble for their salvation; and of some we hope that they have found peace in believing.

"After looking back upon the past year, we closed it with overflowing hearts, and entered upon the new one with such expectations for the church as we never had before. What may we not look for in the year to come? How many precious souls will begin to live? How may the Saviour be honored, and the adversary confounded? Are we sufficiently thankful that we live in these glorious days?

"14.—The candidates for admission to the church were examined to-day, and *forty-one* accepted to be received next week. Who could have expected that we should ever see such a day? I have many times of late been ready to inquire, is it so? or is it a dream, that I see such things among the heathen? Do you not rejoice more than you can express? How then must we feel, who see and know far more than you can, the indifference and the wants of this poor people. Just now the cholera is raging in some parts of the district to a dreadful extent; so that whole families are swept off in a few hours. In one house, where were twelve persons, only one child remained in a few days. It is an awful scourge. After it abated a little, the people made an idolatrous ceremony at great expense, as a token of gratitude to the gods; but the epidemic immediately raged again with more violence than ever. Still they do not learn righteousness. On the contrary, they seem more than ever mad upon their idols.

"23.—The great and joyful day is past. I thought we could not well feel more, while in these bodies of clay. Mr. W. wrote to D. and gave an account of the scene, the evening of the same day," as follows:

"The large temporary building erected for the

occasion, was in a scattered grove of palm-trees, in the village of Santillepay, which is central to all our stations. It was about one hundred feet long and nearly seventy in width. At one end was placed a decent pulpit, brought from one of our stations, and towards the other the floor of earth was made a little ascending, to bring the audience into view, as they sat upon it on neat mats, with which the whole was spread. The top and sides of the building, which were covered with the braided leaves of the cocoa-nut tree, were lined with white cotton cloth, giving the whole a light and neat appearance. In front were two or three fine spreading trees, like large branching elms. On one side open rice fields were in sight, and on the other thick gardens filled with large fruit trees, shading the low mud-walled and leaf-covered houses of the natives. In the rear was a school *bungalow*, where many heathen children had been taught the first principles of christianity, and the word of God had been often preached, and prayer frequently offered; but neither the place where the temporary church stood, nor the adjacent habitations, had ever resounded with the voice of prayer or praise.

"In front of the pulpit was the communion table, before which, in the form of a half-moon, were the candidates, forty-one in number, and native members. Back of these, through the centre of the building, were the head men and other more respectable natives, while the common people occupied either side. In all, from twelve to fifteen hundred were present. There would probably have been twice that number, but for the prevalence of the cholera in the village at the time, and a heavy fall of rain the preceding night.

"The exercises were appropriate and well received. At the close of the sermon the candidates—from a small girl of *twelve*, to a gray-headed man of *seventy*—presented themselves, publicly renounced idolatry, and consecrated themselves to the love and service of the one only living and true God. The old man, whose head was nearly as white as the cloth round his body, as he vowed to be the Lord's, seemed to say, 'Now lettest thou thy servant depart in peace.' This Andrew is a fisher. All these and the members of the church rose together, and entered into covenant with the Lord and with each other, to walk as christians. The affecting ordinance of the Lord's supper was administered to *seventy native members* and sixteen of our own number, including three brethren of other denominations. As the congregation were dispersing, we united in singing, 'Come, let us anew our journey pursue.' It has been indeed a day of joyful solemnity."

In regard to the subjects of this work, there was a previous preparation. The greater part of them were members of the boarding-schools, or schoolmasters, domestics, and other assistants, who had been formed into Bible classes and diligently instructed. The remainder were such as lived in the vicinity of the stations, and had often attended preaching. There were few cases of permanent conviction where there was not some previous knowledge of the truth, and few in which religious impressions were not cherished by much patient labor of the missionaries or their assistants, in conversing and praying with the individuals alone. It was this *repeated and personal application of the truth* to those able in some measure to comprehend it, which principally took effect. At the same time the nearness of the stations to each other enabled the missionaries to give mutual aid in these and similar labors, and to make their public meetings more animating and impressive. Their own souls also were quickened by their seasons of social devotion. Seldom perhaps has the promise to two or three *met together* been more strikingly fulfilled. The revival commenced after a special season of fasting and prayer, and its progress was marked by a spirit of fervent intercession, and sometimes a travailing in birth for souls, of which the journal and letters of Mrs. W. give such delightful evidence.

"23, *Sabbath.*—On Friday evening some of our number met at Oodooville for a *thanksgiving season*, and it was a precious time. To-day has been full of interest. Mr. W. preached from the words, 'I thank thee, O Father, Lord of heaven and earth, that thou hast hid these things,' &c. A thanksgiving sermon. Some who, but a short time since, had no ears to hear, and no hearts to feel, and no minds to understand, were evidently fed by the word, and united in thanksgiving to God for his great mercy. After service, Mr. W. proposed that those who, from a full sense of the importance of the subject, wished to be considered candidates for admission to the church six months hence, should come to the house and give in their names—and hereafter meet him once a week for instruction with reference to such an event. Twelve, besides girls of the school, gave in their names."

A similar meeting to that in January was held at the same place in July, when eight were added to the church. Some, who gave pleasing evidence of being truly converted, were still kept back by their friends from making a profession of their faith in Christ. A young man who was then received, was obliged to leave his relations privately two or three days before the meeting, and go to one of the stations at a distance from them.

They then waylaid him on the road to meeting, but he escaped them and reached the temporary chapel. A native constable was there to prevent disturbance, who protected him against his relatives, or they would have dragged him away even from the communion-table.

CHAPTER VII.

Sixth to Tenth Years in Ceylon—including Journey to Madras and Calcutta.

Failure of health—dangerous passage to Madras and Calcutta—death of a daughter—brief description of Madras—letters to Miss Bird at Gorruckpore—Roman and Pagan ceremonies compared—communion with God—appeal to an early associate—diaries—admissions to the church—robbers—conversion of a schoolmaster—death of an infant son—conversion of sisters—sense of responsibility—Sunday-school at Oodooville—influence of the climate—sufferings of the natives—prayers of the churches.

In the summer of 1825 the health of Mrs. W. was so much impaired that her life was seriously threatened. A change of air was tried for some weeks, by a removal to a small fort on a rock surrounded by the sea, a few miles west of Batticotta. This proving insufficient, late in the season a voyage was determined on. As the north-east monsoon was about to set in, during which the native boats do not venture along the coast, it was with difficulty that a dhonie* was engaged, and when engaged, it was dangerous to attempt the passage to Madras as proposed. A few particulars of this passage were afterwards given by Mrs. W. in a letter to her friends.

"On the 7th November we left our home, and went forth, not knowing the things which should befall us. I had not sat up at all for some days, and was unable to make any arrangements for our voyage. I was carried to Manepy, and there we parted from our two dear little ones. Harriet was delighted with being at M. and gave me the last kiss with a smiling face. Joanna I left on the floor with her toys. Charles accompanied us. Many people from Oodooville came to take leave, but I could only cast my eye around upon the circle without saying a word. The least indulgence of my feelings would have overcome me.

* The native boats, called dhonies, have no decks, and are very sharp both fore and aft. Over the greater part of the vessel is a roof of sticks and braided cocoa-nut leaves, to keep off the sun and rain; under which, in what may be called the *hold*, the passengers, if any, must accommodate themselves.

Do you ask what were my expectations, and how I felt? I did not expect to see again the faces of those whom I left; but I believed I was going with the approbation and direction of God, and that I should have his presence and support in all that was before me. I was exceedingly borne down under a sense of my unfaithfulness to the people, and my ingratitude to my Saviour, in not having exhibited before them more of the purity of his blessed Gospel.

"We were accompanied to Kaits, ten or twelve miles, by Mr. S. At the sea-shore where we were to take a boat for that place, we found the brethren M. and P. from Batticotta. Took leave of them, and went into the boat just after sunset. A cloud soon came up. It was dark, and threatened rain. The boatmen being ignorant of the channel, soon got out of it into shoal water, and the boat run aground. The danger of my being in an open boat through the night, and probably in the rain, was so great, that Mr. S. and Mr. W. jumped into the water, and after much urging and bribing induced the boatmen to follow their example, and with great difficulty shoved the boat off. Soon, however, it was again in the mud. After several attempts and working long in the water, they succeeded in getting under way, and we arrived at Kaits about midnight. I was much fatigued, but was put on a couch in the magistrate's verandah, and after a cup of tea which his lady kindly provided, had a little rest.

"The next day there was no wind. I was very ill, and our prospect was dark. Not a ripple appeared on the surface of the water. The boatmen said they would not go after the 9th, as it would then be new moon and they expected the setting in of the monsoon with a storm. We felt that it was the last moment, and the necessity of our going was urgent. A light breeze sprung up the next morning about 7 o'clock. We were soon at sea. It carried us across the straits before 5 o'clock, and to Negapatam by midnight. Here the boatmen anchored, and nothing would induce them to proceed any farther till daylight. As they have no compass, they are exceedingly careful to keep near the shore, and will not usually sail in the night. We came on by short distances, and should have done by much shorter, had not Mr. W. sat up with the men every night till 12 o'clock, and encouraged them to keep their sails spread till that time. Afterwards we lay at anchor, rolling with the waves in a very uncomfortable manner, till morning. The weather was rainy. Heavy clouds were on all sides of us, with at times much lightning and thunder. The season was so far advanced that almost every thing was threatening. We however reached Madras safely on the fifth day, in the morning.

I had gained a little at sea, though our situation was so uncomfortable. The surf being high, we had some difficulty in getting on shore, and the exertion occasioned my fainting as soon as I reached the custom-house. We proceeded to the Wesleyan mission-house, and were received most kindly by Messrs. Carver and Hoole, and by Mr. and Mrs. Williamson.

"Our first step was to consult a physician. Dr. L. visited me, and at once made himself so well acquainted with my case that I felt much confidence in him. He did not encourage any hope that I should soon be well; and advised us to proceed to Calcutta, or try a land journey. We waited some days, and no passage by ship could be secured. The rains had fully commenced. How then could we undertake a land journey? There was however no alternative, and we made arrangements to go to Bangalore, two hundred miles distant, in palankeens. The rains continued so violent that we were detained a few days. When they abated, we prepared to leave. Our palankeens and bearers were at the door. Food for a day or two was cooked, and every thing packed. Suddenly a heavy rain came on, and we found it impossible to go that evening. The next morning a note came in, saying that a ship was approaching the town. This induced us to turn our faces again towards the sea. Some friends advised us not to venture out, as storms and a long passage were to be expected. We however sought, and believe found direction; and, November 8th, embarked on the 'Sir Edward Paget.' We reached Calcutta Sabbath morning, the 27th, the same day on which, as we afterwards learned, our darling Harriet died at Jaffna. We did not go on shore till next morning."

A residence in Calcutta for about three months of the cold season, when the climate is comparatively fine, produced a good effect on the health of Mrs. W.; and her husband improved the opportunity to solicit funds for the Seminary at Batticotta, as well as in other ways to promote the objects of the mission. In his applications for aid he was in a good degree successful, being favored with the countenance of Bishop Heber, Archdeacon Corrie, and the Rev. Mr. Thomason, names connected with those of Carey, Martyn, and Buchanan, in the religious improvement of India; and of some gentleman high in office in the government, as well as missionaries of different denominations.

"Calcutta, January 18, 1826.

"My beloved Parents,—Mr. W. has written to you a number of times since we arrived at this place, and I have constantly intended to do so, but have been unable. Before this you will know of our having been called from our work to Madras, and thence to this place, by my ill health; and that a change of medical treatment, the voyage, and the cold air of Calcutta, have, by the blessing of God, produced a favorable change. A few lines sent last week by Mr. W. will have informed you, also, of the dealings of God with our mission since we left home. Our dear sister Woodward sweetly closed her eyes upon the world on the 24th November. We left her quite feeble. She became gradually more so, and at length sunk before her friends were aware of her danger. On the 27th of the same month our dear Harriet Maria, and Jane Spaulding, were both cut down in the midst of health by the cholera. A day or two after, two native adult members of the church, and one candidate for admission, died of the same dreadful disease.

"Mr. Spaulding, in writing us, gives the particulars of Harriet's sickness, which lasted only nine hours, and then says, 'The closing scene I need not describe. She fell asleep, we trust, in Jesus, at half past ten on Sabbath morning. Jane was attacked at half past one, and died at half past six, after just five hours' illness. Our dear Harriet and Jane both cut down in one day! Oh, it was a shock which seemed to break our hold on earth. Just as Jane left us, I read the 226th

Select Hymn, 'Ye mourning saints,' &c. which expresses our feelings and consolations better than I can myself. The dear children were always kind and affectionate to their little sisters, and exceedingly attached to each other. In death they were not divided, and to us they are more lovely than ever. They used to pray for you all, and in many ways were great comforts to us. But they are gone. The Lord is as kind in taking as in giving, and as brother Richards said under a similar trial, they 'exactly fill the place which God from all eternity designed they should fill.' Is not this enough? We pity and mourn for dear sister H. We think it must be more trying to her, and to you to hear the sad intelligence alone, and in a strange land, than it would have been to see and know all as it passed; and then after the scene had closed, to sit down with those whose hearts and whose souls could have flowed and felt with your own. We long more than ever to see you. Oh! how it would fill a sad vacancy.

"Now, my dear parents, what shall I say of our feelings when letters containing all this intelligence were brought us at once? It was a stroke which I knew not at first how to bear; but the Lord soon comforted me. In regard to dear H. it is a wise and kind providence to her and to me—to her, because she is, I trust, where she often prayed to be, 'with God in heaven,' and to me, because I needed something to wean me from my cares and attachments, and to humble me before God. I have long felt myself exceedingly unfit either to live or to die. It is now my great desire that this affliction may be the means of preparing me for the whole will of God. You know we have thought that Harriet had an uncommon sense of sin, and dread of offending God. She has often affected me so much by talking on this subject, that I have been obliged to get away from her and give vent to my feelings in tears. But whether she is saved or lost, the will of the Lord is done. Let him be glorified."

The return of Mrs. W. to Ceylon was by way of Madras. Her better health enabled her now to enjoy the prospect in approaching this place on a fine morning in April. The air was clear, the atmosphere perfectly transparent, and the bright sun gave full effect to the grouping of the various objects presented in an Indian city. There were to be seen burning sands and green groves; low and dirty houses along narrow streets, and splendid mansions surrounded by extensive and luxuriant gardens; the low domes of many dingy heathen pagodas, and three or four tall white spires of christian churches. Fort St. George is an immense fortification, enclosing many large edifices, among which is a church. South of it is the Nabob's palace, a large irregular pile, and also a little back from the water the Governor's residence and hall of audience, two spacious buildings with porticoes and marble-like colonnades, surrounded by extensive pleasure-grounds. Northward of the fort is Black Town, inhabited principally by the native Hindoos, Armenians, and descendants of Europeans. The English usually reside in country-seats scattered in the midst of beautiful gardens, in all parts of the vicinity. The town is walled on two sides; the side next the sea is not walled, and the remaining one only in part, ending with a battery, which, with a fort, commands the open space. There are but few good houses within the walls. On the beach, however, are long rows of high buildings with upper and lower *verandahs*, which appear to good advantage from the water. These and other large buildings are *stuccoed* with white cement, which at Madras is made in such perfection as to have the smoothness and almost the durability of polished marble. It gives the smaller houses a neat, and the larger edifices a splendid appearance.

This, as well as the general brightness of the scene, always strikes a stranger from a temperate climate, as does also the dirty appearance of the almost naked and dark-colored natives who throng the streets and the beach. Among these are, however, many in flowing robes of white muslin, with rich turbans on their heads. Some are *doobashes*, or interpreters, of whom several usually resort to a ship to offer their services the moment it comes to anchor. One at least, if possible, attaches himself to each passenger, whose eyes and every motion he will watch, to meet or anticipate his wishes, as though born to wait upon him. Indeed, in landing, the services of some one are needed. The surf rises so high that the ship boats cannot pass it. Every thing is landed in *surf-boats*. These are wide and high, formed without timbers, of boards sewed together, and stopped with *coir*, so as to yield to the waves and sand as they take the shore. As soon as the boatmen get into the surf with a passenger unacquainted with the language, the man in the stern drops the oar with which he was guiding the boat and begins to ask for presents. If then the passenger has no one with him who can speak the language, he must probably choose between giving a dollar or two, or getting wet in the surf. When on shore, if he has no one to look after his luggage, he will find himself surrounded by *coolies*, one of whom snatches a trunk, another a box, and a third a cloak or umbrella, and there will be as many helping him as there are articles to be carried, and all perhaps going different ways. One may thus very soon find no desirable evidence that he is in a heathen country.

While at Calcutta Mrs. W. became acquainted with Miss Bird, a pious English lady, who left her native country to devote herself and her property to the good of India. She was a niece of the celebrated Mr. Wilberforce, and a cousin of the two Bishops Sumner. For many years she resided at Gorruckpore, in one of the upper provinces, laboring principally with adult females and superintending a few schools for girls. Afterwards she took up her residence at Calcutta, continuing her exertions for the instruction of ignorant females and preparing elementary books for the use of the natives. In these labors her health failed. She was then urged by her friends to try the air of her native country. But she was unwilling to leave her work, and remained in it until called recently to her gracious reward. Two letters of Mrs. W. to this lady give valuable intelligence as to the mission in Ceylon, and contain important hints respecting the work of missions generally.

"Oodooville, June 28, 1826.

"My dear Miss Bird,—You have perhaps heard of our safe arrival at home, and may have expected to receive a letter from me. We left Calcutta with mingled emotions of pain and pleasure; pain at the thought that we should no more see the faces of those we left, and that we had done and received so little good, but pleasure, and I trust gratitude, in view of the mercies experienced there, and in the hope of soon meeting our Jaffna friends, and engaging in our delightful work among the heathen. We had a tedious and somewhat dangerous time, of seven days, in getting down the river; but the weather after we got to sea was very mild, and our passage, though long, was pleasant and conducive to my health. We arrived at Madras on the 1st April, and having spent two weeks there very pleasantly, except that I suffered from the excessive heat, embarked for Jaffna in a small brig. We had rough and threatening weather; and the vessel being light, we were much tossed about and exceedingly uncomfortable, but after eleven days' beating against the monsoon, we reached Jaffna, and were welcomed by our dear friends and associates with great joy. Our first visit was to Manepy, where we left two darling children seven months before. One of them was not. The other remained, but was unwell. My health seemed declining, and I thought that I had returned only to take a final leave of my friends, and of all earthly scenes. Mr. W. too, was quite ill. After visiting the different stations, and enjoying some seasons of prayer and thanksgiving with our brethren and sisters, we came to our own home—the spot, more than all others, dear to us, where our health has been improving. Our brethren and sisters were not alone in giving us a welcome. Many of the people around expressed much joy to see us once more. The members of the church, especially, evinced their feelings by many tears; and when I learnt how much they felt on our account when we were absent, and how much they prayed for us, I thought it might be in answer to their prayers that we were preserved in sickness and danger, and brought back to them in safety.

"Little has occurred in the mission since our return likely to interest one so far away. About three weeks since, a pleasant evening was spent at Batticotta in dedicating several small *houses for prayer*. The youth in the seminary have complained that they had not convenient places for religious retirement. Twelve low houses or rooms about eight feet square, were consequently erected for their accommodation on one side of the *academic grove*, which is a grove of coçoanut trees, covering more than an acre, and having on the three sides the buildings of the Institution. That the students might consider these rooms as sacredly appropriated to their proper object, the missionaries, with their wives, were, invited to spend an evening in religious exercises suitable to the occasion. Mats were spread for the company along the front of the neat white houses, between two rows of young cocoa-nut trees, whose broad-spreading and drooping leaves met and formed over our heads a most luxuriant and beautiful canopy, scarcely concealing the mild but bright moon-beams, that gave to night almost the cheerfulness of day. The enchanting beauty of the scenery, together with the reflection that these houses were erected at the request of youth, there seated with us, who were recently enveloped in heathen darkness, added not a little to the interest of the exercises; and had no doubt some influence in prompting the earnest petition, that, in the great day, it may be said of many, 'This and that man was born there.'

"There are no special religious impressions manifest in our schools or among the people just now, but one poor old man daily comes bending upon his staff into our verandah to receive instruction. His tall form and white locks would attract your attention, and his emaciated body induce the inquiry whether he wanted food or medicine. He was formerly an Odigar, or head man of a village. He can read understandingly the New Testament and Tracts. His relatives are dead, except a grandson about twelve years old, who accompanies him at all times. While tottering over the grave, the old man's eyes appear to be opened to see his danger, and he listens to instruction like one really hungering for the bread of life. He is an affecting object; none can know how much so, who have never seen an aged heathen convinced of his long delusion, and looking to Jesus for forgiveness of sin, and for preparation of heart to die in peace.

"The death of Bishop Heber must have occasioned much mourning in your circle. Pray how was Mrs. Heber supported under the heavy stroke? When will his loss be made up to the natives and christians of India? Some one told us that the Rev. Mr. Sumner, a relative of yours, and chaplain to his majesty, is a candidate for the place."

"MY DEAR FRIEND,—Your kind letter of September 29th came to hand three weeks since. We were very glad to hear of your safe arrival at Gorruckpore, and that you had again entered on your interesting labors. The difficulties you experience in prosecuting your work as you wish, are, I think, such as we well understand in Jaffna. Nothing you can say of the 'deceit and unchastity' of the natives there, will be too much to apply here, and we have many trials even with those who are separated from the multitude, and of whom we hope well. Christianity, instead of effecting a greater change in those who are hopefully converted, than it does in converts in a christian country, seems to effect less; and it is long before they appear to see a beauty in holiness, so as to pant after it. Most of our members have generally 'run well,' and they seem to grow in grace. A few have been under discipline for a time, and then have been restored; the discipline having been attended with much apparent benefit. There may be more chaff with the wheat than we suppose, but the sifting-time will come.

"I am happy to answer your inquiries concerning our *girls' school.* This school, as you are aware, was commenced with girls from each of the different stations. An account of the manner in which we began to collect them *here*, will, I think, give you a correct view of the course pursued at the other places.

"Soon after we came to Oodooville, two little girls were often seen about the house, and sometimes looking in at a door or window. If we spoke to them, they appeared alarmed, and ran away. After a while, as we noticed them a little, they became more familiar, ventured to stop and listen to us, then to sit down on the door-steps a few minutes, afterwards to receive a little fruit when offered; and at length, by the promise of a jacket when they should be able to make one, they were induced to take a needle and learn to sew. They were much pleased, and every day came and sat in the door two or three hours. We then told them of the advantages of being able to read, and persuaded them to try to learn. After about six months they felt quite at home, and were on the premises nearly the whole day. After this we spoke to their parents about allowing them to remain all the time. They however could not think of having their children 'lose caste' by eating on our premises, and there was 'no custom' for girls to be instructed. The father of one of them was the keeper of a devil's temple next door to us; a very bad man. The mother was little better.

"About this time we had a native woman in the family to take charge of my infant, and she requested to have her daughter, a girl about eight years of age, with her. Soon after a member of our church brought his sister, and another her daughter. Thus we had three who took their food on the mission premises; but nothing could induce either of the parents of the two day-scholars to leave them with us, until these three had been nearly one year in the school. One night a hard storm prevented their going home. They staid with the girls, and one of them was persuaded to partake of their supper. The other would eat nothing. Some weeks after this the father of the girl who had eaten on the premises brought her to us and said, 'You have been like a father and mother to her, so you may now take her; but tell me what you will do for her; you must find her a husband.' We told him that if she continued a good girl we should take care of her, and he must not come in a few months and take her away. The man was evidently induced to give up the child by her own entreaties. After this we had less difficulty in inducing others to come to us, or their parents to give them up.

"An old Portuguese woman is with them night and day, to watch over them, and they are wholly excluded from intercourse with the other sex, except what is unavoidable with the domestics of the family. No stranger, male or female, is allowed to go to their *bungalow*, and if friends come to see them, they meet in the verandah of the house.

"'How many assistants are employed for them, and for what are they training?' Their washing is done by a man, and they have a girl to assist them in cooking. They have a Tamul teacher half the day, the other half is spent in sewing under my direction. We are training them up to be christian teachers, and wives for our native assistants. Three of those who are hopefully pious are now teaching girls' schools, and they do much better with them than men. Four have married native assistants. The benefits visible to the people are already such that we have now *many more girls brought to us than we can re-*

ceive, and we could obtain almost any number, though many still think that females are only the worse for any kind of learning.

"'Do you allow them to visit their friends, &c.?' They spend two days and one night at home every month; and do not go at other times, except in case of sickness, death, or weddings. They marry as soon as marriageable, when they have an eligible offer; though, if it were not for the very loose habits of the people, we should prefer having them wait longer.

"You inquire about the adult population, our labors among them, and hopes and expectations concerning them. We are surrounded exclusively by heathen and Roman Catholics. Our hopes do rest *principally* on the youth in our schools, but by no means, as Bishop Turner thought, *exclusively*. Our church consists of about *one hundred and sixty-five* native members, of whom a majority are over twenty, and several are over fifty years of age. Of all of these we have more or less satisfactory evidence that they are truly converted from sin to holiness, and that from being idolaters and the slaves of Satan they have become 'the sons and daughters of the Lord Almighty.' You will perceive, therefore, that our labors are by no means confined to children, and that we could not without great ingratitude limit our hopes to them. '*Bazar-preaching*' is practised to some extent at the two principal market-places within our limits. The missionary near each has a stated season once or twice in the week, when he goes to distribute Tracts and converse with the people. At both a bungalow is erected, in which those who choose can assemble and listen to regular instruction.

"The native helpers at these stations also visit the *bazars* in the same way, but a method more practised and more successful is to visit the people at their own dwellings, and hold meetings for preaching at the *school-bungalows*, and at private houses. A respectable man will invite his neighbors to come to his house to a meeting, telling them that the missionary is coming and he wishes to see them all. Thus fifty or more adults are frequently collected, who sit down quietly and listen to the Gospel. After preaching they are usually allowed to ask any questions they wish concerning what they have heard. On these occasions a few women also come and sit in some retired part of the house where they can hear without being seen. At some seasons, when the people are at leisure and there is moon-light, large congregations of adults will assemble in the evening at a *school-bungalow*, being invited by the master and native assistants. I have seen one or two hundred, including nearly all the principal men of a village, thus assembled at a common evening-meeting; and perhaps no opportunities are more favorable for producing an impression by the preaching of the word than those offered at such meetings. The experience of our missionaries is not much in favor of *debates* with the heathen. Preaching to them Jesus, and him crucified, seems the most direct way to affect their hearts. Debates, both private and public, have been held with the brahmins and Roman Catholics, but it is not considered desirable to have them frequent. Tracts are circulated extensively, combating prejudice and error, and some are replied to both by the heathen and Romanists. These have done much to enlighten the dark minds of the people. Preaching on the Sabbath at our five churches, and in the distant school-bungalows, is another very important and perhaps the most encouraging method of making known the Gospel. In each of the churches, on Sabbath mornings, from fifty to one hundred adults are usually present, and occasionally three or four times that number, besides three or four hundred children. More general meetings are also held of the whole mission with the native church members, children of the schools, schoolmasters and domestics.

"In regard to there being no 'absolute promises that a blessing shall attend the Gospel wherever it is preached,' I think there are many plainly implied, if not plainly expressed, and am far from thinking you altogether in the wrong, when you do not like to hear that text too often quoted, 'one soweth and another reapeth.' We should however, no doubt, cheerfully acquiesce, if it be the divine will to give us no immediate and apparent success in our labors. Our work, if of the Lord, cannot be in vain. I have increasing delight in the belief that the word of God never returns to him void, that it does take effect, and will bring forth fruit to his praise and glory; though, as to many, it will only increase their condemnation."

The Roman Catholics, with whom some debates were held, and some discussions by means of Tracts, as mentioned in this letter, had their attention somewhat excited by a *comparison of their doctrines and ceremonies with those of the heathen.*

Their use of *images* is similar to that of the heathen; and the same reasons are urged for it; that they represent beings who ought to be reverenced, and that it is necessary for the people, generally, to have some object to worship which may address itself to their senses.

Placing *lights* before these images, or idols, is a practice alike of the Papists and Pagans. To keep a light burning in a temple is a great act of merit among the Hindoos.

The offering of *incense* and the sprinkling with *holy water* are the same in Catholic churches and heathen temples.

The church festivals, when the images and the host are carried about in procession, are similar to the *idol feasts*, when the idols are drawn on cars round the temple yards.

The use of the *rosary* by the Romanists is the same with that of the *suppah-mahly*, or *prayer-garland* of the Hindoos; and the *pater-nosters* and *ave-marias* of the former are recited and re-iterated in the same manner as the *mantras* of the latter, an account being kept of the number of repetitions by means of the beads.

The doctrine of *penance*, insisted on so much in the papal church, is altogether a heathen doctrine, and also that of *purgatory*, and the necessity of *ceremonies for the souls of the dead*; all which are seen among the Hindoos.

The fast-days and feast-days, the ringing of bells, their idolatrous reverence for the priests, who are the keepers of their disciples' consciences, the repetition of prayers in a dead language—in the Latin by one and in Sanscrit by the other—and all the attention to outward show and parade, are the same among Roman and heathen idolaters. The exposing of this relationship between the two forms of superstition caused no small stir among the Roman priests, and induced them to prohibit or modify some of their public processions which were too obviously of heathen origin.

"*November* 19, 1826.—*Private Journal.*—I will record for my future encouragement, and for the glory of God, that after seeking assistance of the Holy Spirit, I have tried myself by Baxter's rule, and feel peculiar delight in the conviction that I *do* 'take God for my chief good, and heartily accept of Christ as my only Saviour and Lord.'—I have not previously, I think, seen these two evidences so clearly, nor ever before rested so sweetly on the Lord as all my salvation and all my desire.

"*Evening.*—This has been a precious day. I have enjoyed communion with my God and Father. Had unusual desires in behalf of some individuals in church this afternoon. I think that the influences of the Holy Spirit attended the word preached. Some neglected duties came to my mind; one of which is, not employing the piety of some native converts around me in exhorting the heathen to turn to the Lord.

"27.—One year since our darling H—— was committed to the dust, and the same day we landed at Calcutta in pursuit of health, which I little expected to obtain. Our dear brother and sister, who were afflicted with us, have been to spend the day here, in meditating on the past and looking forward to the future. Concerning the beloved ones who are gone, the will of God is done. As to those who remain, what are our duties and what our obligations to God who gave them? But for the constant effort necessary to control my feelings, I should have enjoyed the day very much. Yesterday was a solemn time. I think our Saviour was with us, and that his own word was accompanied by the influence of his Spirit. Oh how I long to get near to God. Is he my Father? Endearing title! I believe he is. I have of late had unusual delight in calling him my Father, my Redeemer, my Sanctifier. O Lord, search me, and try me, and see if there be any wicked way in me, and lead me in the way everlasting."

"Oodooville, Feb. 3, 1827.

"My dear E——, I have been out this afternoon with Mr. Winslow to a school-bungalow nearly three miles distant, where the people have not often heard the word of God. We left home at 3 o'clock. The sun was very powerful, and we rode some of the way through heavy sands. The people who had assembled came out into the road to meet us. We found more than 100 boys seated around the sides of the bungalow, and mats spread in the centre for men. Not expecting that 'the lady' would come, they had provided but one chair. Soon, however, a large mortar was brought, on which Mr. W. sat. The first class of boys then read while we waited for more people to come in, and receiving the approbation of the *padre*, they were much delighted. Mr. W. addressed the people on the certainty of the resurrection and future judgment. They were very attentive, and begged that he would come again in a month, and stay longer. There is much benefit in preaching in this way; many come to these bungalows who would not come to our churches, and they are much more attentive when seated quietly, than when addressed in the bazars and roads, or even at their own homes.

"On Monday next we hope to meet you in the concert of prayer. And how, dear friend, is your heart affected by an increase of worldly cares? And, dear Mr——, do you love to pray for the heathen, and for missionaries, *and for the world*, as much as you once did?"

At this time she addressed another solemn appeal to the female associate to whom she wrote May, 1818, who, it is gratifying to add, has since publicly consecrated herself to the service of Christ.

"OODOOVILLE, Feb. 28, 1827.

"MY DEAR ——, I have often felt a desire to write to you since I left America, but have been in doubt whether a letter would afford you any pleasure. Your very kind remembrance of me, expressed in a letter from my dear mother, has awakened new desires to write, and determined me to delay it no longer.

"I have not any thing to tell you concerning the mission, or the state of the people and country around us that is new or particularly interesting; nor have I taken my pen with a view to describe my family circle, and tell you of many enjoyments that I have in this *far distant heathen land*, and that I never, for a moment, regret coming hither, but rejoice that I am permitted to do a little for the welfare of the miserable people among whom we dwell—no, my dear friend, not for any nor all these do I write; but to tell you *once more*, that I long to hear that you are as happy as the 'peace of God which passeth all understanding' can make you; to know that you have a portion with the people of God, and that your treasure is in heaven. If this is the case, do permit me to know it from your pen.

"You have been afflicted since I saw you. I loved and respected your departed mother, and felt that her death was a loss to me—to you how much greater. Did you consider that by this bereavement the Lord in great tenderness said to you, 'Daughter, give me thine heart;' and have you done so? Have you consecrated to him, with love and gratitude, the talents which he committed to you that they might be employed for him? If you have, accept my congratulations; but if not, permit me to say, dear ——, 'To-day, if you will hear his voice, harden not your heart!' 'Without holiness no man shall see the Lord.' You wish to be happy—you hope to be happy; but—be not deceived. The language of God is plain, 'Except ye be converted ye cannot see the kingdom of God.' It is a small thing to lose the world with all its honors and pleasures; but how immense the loss to be shut out of heaven—to be for ever excluded from the society of God and of all holy beings, and to have our portion with his enemies Be entreated to inquire with yourself whether it be not wise to look away from the few fleeting days which constitute the longest life upon earth, to that life which will never end. Heaven and hell are set before you by Him who desires not the death of the sinner, but would have men every where to repent. Be entreated to accept of mercy as it is freely offered; to be happy in this life, and happy for ever. Dear ——, forgive me if I grieve or offend you. If I did not love you more than the world love you, I could not write thus. To the sovereign mercy of God I commend you, praying that you may not cast aside this my affectionate and earnest entreaty, without beseeching the Lord to give you repentance unto eternal life.

"Believe me your sincere friend,

"HARRIET."

"OODOOVILLE, March 14, 1827.

"MY DEAR FATHER WINSLOW,—I am induced to address you at this time, by having read some letters which you wrote my dear husband when he concluded to leave his business and commence study. I admire the cheerful submission which you manifested in the disappointment of your plans for him, as also the plain and candid manner in which you placed before his mind the difficulties to be anticipated in the path which he was about entering. Could you know how plain his way has been marked out before him, and how much enjoyment he has had in pursuing it, and especially the reason we have to hope that the blessing of God has rested on his labors among these poor deluded heathen, you would, I am sure, (as I believe you now do,) rejoice that he was brought to the decision to come out hither instead of remaining in the bosom of his friends and country.

"When I think of the severe trial you must have had in relinquishing your long-cherished expectations concerning him, so soon after the death of his beloved mother, I almost exclaim, can it be right thus to grieve a widowed parent—is it not unnatural, unchristian? I however fully believe it to be sometimes proper and necessary; and that such sacrifices on the part of the parent and child are followed by the special blessing of heaven! Can you not say, dear father, at this advanced period of life, and after so long experience, that you never gave up any thing to your Saviour, not even the companion of your youth, the object of your earliest, tenderest love, or your children, the precious pledges of that love, but he awarded you a hundred fold? How much pleasure I should have in hearing you relate some of your trials, and the consolations which you have experienced from your covenant Father. Has he not always been as kind as your fondest hopes? Has he not wiped away your tears, healed your wounds, and enabled you always to speak of mercy more than judgment? Should I be so happy as to see you in a better world, I hope I may know more of all this; may be better acquainted with one to whom I am indebted for the greatest temporal blessing of my life.

"Sister C. could wish this dear brother 'God speed' when she first heard of his plans. Her heart seemed full of joy at the thought that God had called him to preach the Gospel. Dear sister,

I am sure you have not since mourned on this account, even though it has removed him far from you. Does not the hope of meeting him at the last day, surrounded by souls redeemed from among these heathen by his instrumentality, more than compensate for all that any of you have suffered in the loss of his society here? At that great day how differently will all earthly things appear to us, from what they now do. How little shall we then think of our changes and sufferings in this world, when we find that they have prepared us for the pure and perfect enjoyments of heaven.

"MR. NATHANIEL WINSLOW."

TO HER PARENTS.

"OODOOVILLE, March 16, 1827.

"I had this evening an interesting conversation with Charles. It seemed a new thought to him that those who go to hell have never after an opportunity to repent; and it was difficult to convince him that they cannot put an end to their sufferings by killing themselves. He said, 'But if Jesus should come to them and call them, would they not love him and go to him?' Oh that I knew how to give him *right thoughts* in a *right manner*, and that God would send his Spirit upon him. It will indeed be strange if I see *my children* converted before I have 'travailed in birth' for them many, many times. I cannot expect it, though I do hope, with some degree of confidence, that they will in the end be saved, and also that they may have the privilege of doing something for the cause of Christ on earth. I have never thought so much of the happiness which christian parents must feel in having their children all born of God, as of late. And what joy it would give me to hear that you, my beloved parents, were thus made happy; to hear that the *three* dear ones whom we fear are still '*without God in the world,*' had consecrated themselves, their all, for time and eternity, to the Lord, who has a right to and demands their *best service—the vigor of their days*—and who offers no encouragement that he will hereafter receive what is now denied or withheld from him."

How would her heart have rejoiced, could she have known that all the "three dear ones" for whom she here pleads, would so soon enter into her labors among the heathen.

"*April* 1, 1827, *Sabbath.*—Private Journal.—I have again sat at the table of the Lord. Oh how unworthy. Our lecture on Friday was pleasant. This morning we had a season of social prayer, which I enjoyed. Went to church in a quiet frame of mind. Katheraman and the old woman

Seethavy publicly professed their faith. I was affected to see them, and particularly when I stood up with the church to promise my part of the duty in watching over them. The thought of adding to my obligations, now so poorly performed, for a few moments overwhelmed me. Had some enjoyment at the table; something like lying in the hands of God as a little child, helpless and hopeless unless he should condescend to make me his own. Retained much the same feelings afterward, but my body was exceedingly exhausted.

"*June* 15.—Our little George commenced his immortal existence on the 12th of May. Goodness and mercy have followed me ever since. How great a debtor. I am feeble, and have had few seasons of retirement, but in some have found it good to wait upon the Lord. With all my coldness and worldly-mindedness, what could I do without the privilege of going to the throne of grace. Have had a refreshing season this morning in preparation for the duties of the Sabbath, when we hope to sit at the table of our Redeemer. Oh that he would meet with us. I think I do long to live nearer to him, to be hidden with him. Have been trying to see if I have any right spirit, and think I can say, 'whom have I in heaven but Thee, and there is none upon earth that I desire besides Thee.' I think I do place my chief happiness in God, and that I would not have any other portion; but my life, Oh how unlike that of the blessed Jesus! I have no other refuge than his blood, which can cleanse from all sin. Yes, precious thought, he 'came not to call the righteous, but sinners to repentance.' He will save all who trust in him. May I trust in him alone for myself and my children. Especially do I desire to consecrate this dear child, by faith, to him. Oh my God, receive our little one; receive him as thine *own*. Oh let him have no other portion in time or in eternity.

"*September* 23.—There are some signs of new life amongst us. I think this has been a great day to some souls; that some congregations have been visited by the saving influences of the Spirit. I have of late more prevailing desires to see the heathen converted, and more reluctance to secular employments and thoughts in myself and others; but I do not see my sins as I have done, or so pant after a pure heart and an unblameable life. Of late, too, it has seemed to me that I have not such an interest at the throne of grace as formerly.

"*October* 20.—Some remarks made about *diaries*, that they are seldom written without the expectation of other eyes seeing them besides those of the writer, accompanied by my own reflections, have made me almost resolve to burn all that I have ever written, now while I am in health, lest sickness and death, by suddenly over taking me, should prevent it; but I am deterred by the recollection that I once burned a journal of the kind, which I ever afterwards regretted; and also that what I have written has often been useful to warn, quicken and encourage me, as well as to make me humble. I have sometimes tried to clothe my sins and sorrows in language, but have never succeeded so as to show *me as I am;* and oh how thankful should I be that only a Divine eye can see my heart, especially that it is the eye of Him who pities and forgives."

TO HER PARENTS.

"*October* 20, 1827.—Yesterday, by urgent request, we went to Jaffna, to be present at the formation of a Wesleyan Missionary Society. There were present English, Dutch, Portuguese, Tamulians, and Americans, besides some grades and gradations of country and color not easily defined or described. It is trying to leave our families and go out for a day several miles, and my principles as well as feelings would forbid it, if I did not see that it is useful, and even necessary. For a society like ours, composed of Episcopalians, Wesleyans, and Presbyterians, from different countries, to act in concert in our great work, there must be occasional intercourse, and we must be ready especially to assist each other's operations.

"This is a dark and stormy evening. Mr. W. is in his study—a room taken off from the end of the church. The rain falls plentifully in large drops upon the leaves and tiles of the house, sounding like small hail-stones. The children are in bed, and I am just so much *alone* as I still love sometimes to be. I have not forgotten with what feelings I used to enter my little closet, in the house under the hill, and shut the door to all the world on such an evening as this. I could then turn from the unsatisfying scenes of earth, and with deep feeling contemplate that heavenly city where is no tempest or darkness; where all is serene; 'for the glory of God doth lighten it, and the Lamb is the light thereof.' Then, as now, I felt that I was *not alone.* I know not how many of my formerly much loved friends and companions may be hovering around me. Many of them certainly have no longer a body like my own, and if they know my heart, they may rejoice that with many of its feelings they can now have no sympathy.

"*February* 19, 1828.—We were, at our last dates, anticipating a very pleasant season at our quarterly meeting in January. The number of candidates for admission to the church was twenty-five; but of these only seventeen were propounded. The remaining eight were kept back by sickness, the opposition of friends, and the opinion of the missionaries that they ought to have a longer trial.

"The enemy was never before so fully on the watch, or so much alarmed, as now. Among the candidates were a number of whom the opposers could not say either that they were 'low-caste,' or dependent on us for support. We were disappointed and grieved at the instability of some, but the Lord knoweth them that are his, and will eventually give them grace to stand against any opposition.

"*May* 28.—Mr. W. left home on the 1st inst. for a missionary tour on the continent, in company with Mr. Woodward, who is going to the Neilgherry Hills for his health, and I have been for four long weeks alone. When I last heard from him he had visited the missionary stations at Tanjore and Trichinopoly, also many heathen temples and villages, and found Tracts in so great demand that he had given away nearly all he had, and would return home sooner than he had at first intended.

"To show you a little of the state of society here, in one respect, I will mention the trouble that thieves have occasioned me. Just before Mr. W. left, some of our neighbors being afraid of thieves, requested to have their most valuable articles deposited in two boxes in our *go-down.* As soon as he was gone, thieves began to come every night to their houses, and throw stones at them to ascertain if the people were asleep. They were thus kept watching till they could bear it no longer, and complained to the magistrate. He ordered all the suspected persons in the vicinity to be brought before him. There was no difficulty in doing this, because those who are engaged in robberies are well known to many of the people.

"In this instance more than sixty were brought up; of whom some are considered respectable, as a Maniagar, and Odigar. They were reprimanded and charged to keep the peace, and not to disturb *the Ammah* while her husband was absent.

"Some of the accused said that I had entered the complaint because they had not become christians when exhorted to do so by Mr. W. The disturbance has been so near us as to keep those in our yard in constant alarm; especially as it was supposed that the object was to draw the domestics from the house, by a cry of thieves elsewhere, and then come and attack our premises.

"I have felt little apprehension of them myself, though I knew that they might with ease have stripped the house of every thing valuable. They sometimes come in such numbers to commit robberies that all efforts to resist them would be vain. The poor natives, though their most valuable goods are stolen, seldom attempt any resistance, but sliding into a corner, are glad to escape without having their ears cut off for the jewels in them, or some other serious injury done to their persons. It is said that there has been much less thieving in this neighborhood since we came than before, and probably there would have been no disturbance now if Mr. W. had been at home.

"*June* 25.—Two days after the last date Mr W. arrived. I had been quite anxious, as the weather was tempestuous. He had been six days in an open boat, when, with a favorable wind, he could have come in half a day. You will rejoice to hear that the *schoolmaster*, whom we have often mentioned with peculiar interest as serious and desirous to join the church, but kept back by persecution, has at length come forward and professed his faith in Christ. As it was believed that his relations would use force to keep him back, he was not propounded publicly, but only to the members of the church, and was received at Manepy. On his return home his wife told him that he should not come into the house, and as he did so, she left it and went to that of her mother. A great number of the relatives collected together the next morning, and remained through the whole day, ridiculing him and expressing their indignation. His mother has gone on a pilgrimage to the continent to make offerings at a temple there, to prevent her son from becoming a christian. She has for a long time been trying to cheat him out of his property, though her only son, and she a widow, by causing forged deeds to be made, because she found that she could not keep him in the shackles of heathenism. I think no one has joined us before, possessing talents, learning, and family influence so great as this man. He has long been Mr. W.'s assistant in Tamul, and is, I believe, considered the best qualified in the language of any in the mission. He has, however, too much diffidence and timidity. We can only plead with God, who knows how much we need such helpers, to make him a bold and successful champion of the faith—a burning and a shining light in the midst of darkness. In his own neighborhood and family is Satan's seat; for his grandfather has a temple and is a prime mover in heathenism."

This "schoolmaster," then employed as a superintendent of schools and assistant in Tamul, continued steadfast in his profession. His grandfather had threatened him; his mother had told him she could not live if he became a christian; and his wife, to whom he was then recently married, had given sufficient assurance of her intention to leave him, should he thus disgrace himself.

After he was received to the church, his mother returned from her pilgrimage, which had been performed to prevent this consummation. Her soul was filled with grief and anger when she found that her son had partaken of the Lord's supper with christians. She was resolved if possible to prevent a recurrence of this calamity, and when the next season of communion arrived, called the family friends to aid in keeping him from attending. They surrounded him in the yard, but he insisted on going, until his mother threw herself in the gate-way and said, "My son, you shall not go out of this yard without treading on the body of the mother that bore you." He yielded for the time, but on the next occasion went away previous to the day of communion, and enjoyed the ordinance. His wife left him for a time, but afterwards returned, and the opposition of his friends gradually abated.

The custom of thieves to go in large companies, as mentioned above, is very common. They sometimes enter a village with lights and fire a gun. The natives are too much alarmed to think of defending themselves, and the robbers take what they please, and go off unmolested. There is not usually sufficient public virtue to bring them to justice, even when their crimes are known to many. The head men, whose duty it is to detect the thieves, are often in league with them. A large robbery was committed in one of the villages near Oodooville. The police *vedan*, or native constable, was ordered to make thorough search for the stolen goods. He made diligent and extensive search, but without any success—and for good reason, as it was afterwards discovered that they were concealed in his own house.

Few christians, perhaps, make great advances in piety without passing through trials. It usually requires many heavy strokes to break us off from our too strong attachment to earth. It was under the mellowing influence of grief, as well as the exhilaration of joy, that the subject of this memoir was prepared for heaven. The fruits of the Spirit were ripened by an alternation of rain and sunshine. At this time she was called to mourn the loss of a lovely babe at the age of fifteen months.

"*September* 26, 1828.—We have been greatly afflicted in the removal of our darling George. He was a precious treasure, and we flattered ourselves that his sweet smile would cheer us many years, and that he would add one to the number of the heralds of the cross, to proclaim Christ to the heathen after our work should be done and our bodies be laid in the grave. But he has been taken from us, and his spirit is, we fully believe, engaged in a more glorious work above than it could be here below. I never followed a loved spirit to the heavenly world with such feelings of entire *satisfaction* that it was in a place more suited to it than any could be here, and I have since delighted to think of this precious one as freed from all earthly hinderances to a pure and perfect worship 'before the throne of God and the Lamb.' We have deeply felt this stroke; and I hope are benefited by it. We feel that it is from our Father, who has not only a right to his own, but who afflicts his children to bring them back from their wanderings, and to draw them nearer to himself."

TO HER SISTER ELIZABETH.

"OODOOVILLE, ——, 1828.

"MY DEAR E——, I need not tell you that we greatly rejoice in the hope that you have become one of those whose 'names are written in heaven.' Be not deceived. I am glad to see that you are not over-confident of your good estate. It well becomes such poor wretched sinners as we are to walk softly and to speak tremblingly; yet whatever we are, the grace of God is the same; and if we have tasted it, we ought to magnify it, by our actions especially. I hope you will; I hope indeed that you have given yourself and your all to Him whose service you will delight in, and whose name you will honor.

"I would advise you in many particulars, for I think young converts need advice; but you have those near at hand much better able, those who, in a 20 years' professed service, have not so often and so grievously wandered from the fountain of all good, and been satisfied with forbidden streams. Listen to them, and especially seek *constantly* the guidance of the Saviour; *keep very near to him, and let your first, your unceasing effort, be to drink deeply of his Spirit.* He will tell you 'what to do for the heathen' far better than I can; and he will tell you what to do *for those around you.* Be a consistent christian where you are and in what you are, and you will be prepared for any work that may be in reserve for you.

"You would be gratified to see what we have at Oodooville to-day. Notice having been given; not generally, but to some extent, at all our stations that girls would be received to the Female Boarding-school—*thirty-seven* were brought, and after we had selected 12, the remaining ones were urged upon us by every plea that their parents could use. In contrast with this, seven years ago we could not by any arguments induce more than three or four to live on our premises. My charge now consists of 38, and I assure you I feel it to be no light thing; partly because I think I never did and never shall do my duty towards them.

How much my dear sister E. could help me, or either of my sisters; but I can never invite you to come alone as some ladies come to the heathen."

"OODOOVILLE, July, 1828.

"MY DEAR SISTER F——, I have for some time thought of asking you if you continue to think of us on the hour appointed—on Saturday evening; and since the Lord has so graciously granted what we asked for in reference to our sisters, (though it may not be in answer to our prayers,) may we not be encouraged to extend our subjects, and enlarge our requests. I have thought my own dear children, with D——'s, may come up before you with much propriety, if you think so. I feel, dear sister, as though *the one thing* is so important for these dear ones, that I scarcely ask for them any thing else. I can, I hope, cheerfully leave every thing else concerning them. Oh that we may have a spirit of grace and supplication for them, and not forget continually to thank the Lord for what he has done for us and ours."

"*August* 15.—This is an interesting, solemn anniversary, such an one as I hope you may not know. I have felt not as I wished, though I believe no murmuring nor desire to recall the precious child. Life is a blessing, and it is pleasant to hope that those to whom we have given birth may be useful in the world; but there is much to comfort us when they are removed, as we hope, to a better world; and if there were nothing else, the fact that the Lord has done his own pleasure with them is, I hope, enough to make me lay my hand upon my mouth.

"As to the publishing of a part of my letter, I only hope it will do no hurt. I am more content with being *harmless* than I once was, for I find it easier to *do injury*, and less easy to *do much good* than I once thought. But it would embarrass me too much in my familiar letters, to think it even *possible* that my name would find place in a public paper."

"*Nov.* 23.—*Private Journal.*—We have twelve girls added to the school. I feel for them as I think I never did for any before; I view them as more promising subjects to aid in the conversion of this people, and have more hope of doing something for them myself, though, alas, it may be very little. My own dear children I feel to be the Lord's. Ever since a short time after George's death I have had an assurance that has greatly comforted me. Charles had hurt himself, and I feared lock-jaw for a week. It was a week of unusual prayer. Before it closed I felt that I could say with confidence, *he is the Lord's;* and, oh blessed be God who has not turned away my prayer, nor his mercy from me, I have not yet lost this sweet confidence. I praise God for it, while I hope it may be made the means of increasing my fidelity in training up these precious ones for his service. For our poor domestics my cold heart sometimes mourns and weeps.

"*February* 23, 1829.—Some pleasing prospects of a revival of religion among us have disappeared. I fear it is said, He could not do 'many mighty works there, because of their unbelief.' I trust, however, that God has been glorified in the conversion of some, and in convincing others of the truth. I do love still to pray that he will arise and plead his own cause.

"*March* 29.—My sins are a heavy burden; nothing is half so heavy. Yet, in one respect, I can praise the Lord that he has heard my voice and my supplications. What I mourned over for years after coming to Jaffna, and even long before, has not, I believe, troubled me at all for two years past. Other things, however, cleave to me. Oh that I had grace to arise and say, 'Through Christ, I can do all things.' I have had many comforts of late, and much peace of mind. My hopes for the heathen are not fully realized, but the Lord hath remembered me and mine in great mercy.

"*April* 12.—This will probably be my last Sabbath of health at present. Lord, I commit myself and my all to thee. Thou art my refuge and strength, be thou my 'very present help in time of trouble.' Be the stay of my husband and children. If I have never again opportunity to say it, I would here testify some sense of gratitude for a husband who has been so much my comfort in this life of variety and change. If I am permitted to live, may I be far more useful to him than I have ever been; and if I am taken away, wilt thou, Lord, be his support. Oh be better to him than his unworthy wife, and better than all earthly comforts. The dear children I have given to thee—whatever may befall them in this life, prepare them for a better; living or dying, may they be only thine. Help me, gracious God, to leave my all with thee."

"OODOOVILLE, November 15, 1829.

"MY DEAR SISTER F.—Our *Sunday-school* this morning was unusually pleasant. I have told you that there are sometimes more than *one hundred girls*. These belong to my part of the school. They are divided into twelve classes, over each of which is one of the girls of the boarding-school. They meet in the verandah of the girls' bungalow. When the bell rings at 8 o'clock, I go out and give tickets for attendance to all present, and see that the teachers are in their places. At 9 o'clock I go again to hear their lessons, and reward those who deserve it with another ticket. This morning, on going a second time, I found nearly all the teachers exhorting the girls to repent and believe on the Lord Jesus Christ. Old Mareal, the low caste woman, who is a member of the church, was seated by one class, while the girls in it and the teachers were alike listening to the exhortations of this poor and ignorant, but I hope sincere follower of the Saviour. As I passed on from one class to another nearly round the school, without venturing to interrupt what I thought was better for the time than their catechisms and other lessons, I thought, how would dear F. enjoy this scene. Oh for that Spirit which can save these souls, as well as those on whom the Gospel shines in all its splendor. Sometimes I am almost discouraged. Every thing connected with the school is such up-hill work, that I am ready to think nothing is done, and nothing can be done.

"23.—As I have begun to tell you about our Sunday-school, perhaps you will be interested to see another side of the picture. Yesterday I found, on going out the second time, that most of the classes were engaged as the week before —the teachers explaining the lessons and talking to the children. I joined myself to the first class, which consists of five who are able to read well. They have committed to memory all the catechisms, a Scripture-history used in the schools, and some prayers. They have read nearly through the second Gospel, and of late have given some account of the sermon heard the preceding Sabbath. On asking them some questions, as I often do, but such as were a little new, I was surprised at their ignorance. Very simple questions, which I should have thought they could answer at once, and which I am sure they have heard many times, they could not answer. It seemed as though words conveyed no ideas to their minds, and it is a fact, that they hear and repeat them many times without knowing what they mean. They do not *think*.

"I never felt so deeply that there is a thick veil spread over their minds, which nothing but the Holy Spirit can remove. They are in gross darkness; and not these little ones only, but children of a larger growth—all are in Egyptian darkness. Some part of what is committed to memory will no doubt be remembered, and by continued explanation a little truth will be understood; but the process is very slow. Does this look like the conversion of India in a day? Would that those who report progress, and those who hear their reports, did not so often confound the preparatory work with the work itself.

"The prospect for females is, it is true, much darker than that for the other sex. The prejudices against their learning any thing are very strong; and after they are instructed, there are many hinderances to their exerting any but a feeble influence. Still I hope I can say, with sincere thankfulness to Him whose work it is, that something has been done and is doing to prepare the way of the Lord. But what are human wisdom and human efforts without his life-giving Spirit? If he breathe upon us, we shall be revived, and these dry bones will live and become an exceeding great army. Do not cease to offer your prayers for us, because we have been favored heretofore, and have still many mercies.

"Your affectionate

"HARRIET.

"MRS. FANNY L. HALLOCK."

"December 2, 1829.

"MY DEAR SUSAN,—As to my health, since our journey to Calcutta I have been most of the time able to perform the common duties of housekeeping, and take the necessary care of my children and of the boarding-school. But the best health in this country is very far from what it is in America. Those who call themselves well, can still bear but little fatigue compared with what they could there. Mr. W. could preach three times on the Sabbath at home with more ease than he can twice here. When he now preaches three times he is quite exhausted. As to myself, half an hour in Sunday-school in the morning, attending church twice, instructing my own children, and hearing the lessons of the girls in the boarding-school, is all that I can accomplish. We have, however, much to be thankful for in this respect. The climate of Jaffna we think more favorable to health than most parts of India where missionaries are, and, with occasional exceptions, we all enjoy it. I would add, that my own experience leads me to advise females who are feeble, or *who have not generally good health*, to remain at home, rather than to enter a missionary field; or at least I would advise missionaries to seek companions who have health. Do not understand me as discontented. Nothing tends more to make us satisfied with any circumstances than to feel assured that they are ordered by Providence, and of this, in regard to my life being spent here, I know not that I have a single doubt."

"MRS. SUSAN C. KELLOGG."

"OODOOVILLE, (Jaffna,) Dec. 9, 1829.

"MY DEAR AUNT LEFFINGWELL,—In the want of something new in our mission to write about, I thought of giving you a particular account of the prayer-meeting which was to be held on Monday last; but instead of a meeting, we had a severe storm, and were not only confined at home, but almost driven out of our house by the rain. The poor natives suffered in various ways, as indeed they always do in storms of this kind. Those connected with our family came to us, one for a cloth, another for a piece of flannel, and all for food. With their utmost endeavors to protect their defenceless bodies, they were drenched with water like the trees of the garden. At such times the mud-walled cottages of the poor creatures, to which they and their cattle promiscuously crowd for shelter, often fall down, the walls being soaked with water; or the covering of leaves is blown off by the wind. Their cattle also die, and if the storm continues two or three days, they have nothing to eat. The habit of obtaining supplies day by day is so universal, that even the wealthy have nothing 'laid by in store,' except grain not in a state of preparation for food. They have no wood, no fruit, and no vegetables, unless their own garden happens to furnish them. Perhaps all the members of a family huddle into a corner, and, sitting upon their heels, take their cloths from their waist, put them round their shoulders, and wait for the storm to abate, till a sense of hunger prompts some of them to look about for food. The mother probably, (though in times of general distress the father is ready to do something not ordinarily his employment,) putting a basket on her head for an umbrella, creeps out to pick up a few sticks, if she can find them near, or breaks them off the hedge, to make a little fire and prepare any thing they may have to eat.

"In sickness, also, this people feel the bitterness of poverty, ignorance, and heathenism. They have no *comforts.* It is not uncommon to see a man with a fever (for fevers are frequent and severe, though not often malignant,) stretched for weeks upon a mat on the ground-floor of a verandah, with a stone or board for his pillow, having no change of clothing, no savory drink to allay his distressing thirst, nothing to bathe his burning limbs, and almost no medicine, because his purse does not allow him to pay the doctor, whose charges are in proportion to his pretensions rather than his skill. If the poor man is willing to give his little all to attempt securing a few more days of uncertain and low enjoyment in this world, his wife's jewels, perhaps, must be pawned to pay for the doctor's attendance, and his friends must make their daily offerings at the temple to appease the idol, who is angry at him for having failed, it may be, in performing some ceremony, or to induce the goddess, who sends disease as an amusement to herself, to withdraw her hand and cease her sport. If he recovers, some new offering, or some penance, or a pilgrimage in honor of this same senseless idol, is the only return of gratitude which his religion enjoins; and when he has performed it, he feels under no further obligation. How unlike this the sick-bed of a christian, in a place where there are numberless alleviations of suffering, and where the mind is stayed upon that God who does not afflict willingly,—upon that Saviour who pities and forgives, and has himself taken away the sting of death!

"There are times, my dear aunt, when the view of such scenes makes it easy to endure trials—easy to count not our lives dear to us, if souls may be converted to Christ; but can you believe that in this corner of the world there are many hinderances to a cheerful consecration of every thing to this glorious service? Yes, I am sure you know enough of the human heart, and perhaps I should say of mine in particular, to believe it is even so. We have a *world* here, though it is a very small one, and it has power to draw our hearts aside too much. We have had no revival of religion the last year, but there has been an addition to the church of eight or ten individuals at our several stations. Many children have been instructed,—the Gospel has been preached to very many in various places,—Tracts have been more generally distributed, and, I believe, much more extensively read, than in any previous year. I hope, also, that much prayer has been offered that darkness may flee away, both here and in christian lands, and the true light shine upon all people."

"*December* 25.—This is a day of riotous mirth to many poor creatures in this district. The Roman catholics, and the native protestants at Jaffnapatam, after some religious exercises, make it a season of continued dissipation from this time until the new year; and practice excesses which I should be sorry to name.

"Yesterday the native free schools connected with this station were examined. Mr. W. attended to their lessons in the church, while I redeemed the children's tickets and gave cloths to the girls. I am sure it would have given you, and any other of our friends, pleasure to see this group of *five hundred* children. More than one hundred of them were *girls*, who, by their regular attendance and progress in learning, were most of them entitled to receive cloths. They made quite a neat appearance after getting them, compared with what they did before, and were very happy. We were both of us busily employed for more than five hours, and I assure you it was an agreeable occupation.

"Oodooville, January 9, 1830.

"Dear E——, Good Mrs. Lanman has gone,

and how great her joy now, who can tell? Who are now your leaders in all that is good?

"Mr. Winslow's theological class has done well, and my school better, perhaps, than any preceding year. The schools generally prosper; many hear the Gospel, read Tracts, &c. but they do not 'come bending unto Jesus.' What hindereth I know not; but the Holy Spirit is not given. Perhaps those who used to hold up our hands are dead, and none stand in their places. We certainly need what we have not, before we can see the conversion of this people. A few inquire, and some make professions; but what are they compared with the multitude. The girls in the boarding school have been more awake of late; and the members of the church seem to desire to do something for others. For a time they went out two afternoons in each week with my Ache, of whom you have heard, and read and conversed with such women as would hear them; but of late they have told me of such treatment from some that I dare not send them, except occasionally.

"I wish you would think more of the degraded condition of females here, and bear them on your heart more, and try to induce your friends to do so also. Prayer will, I believe, be the principal instrument by which they will be brought into the family of Christ, and thus elevated above the dust. You cannot conceive how low they are, and yet they have minds and hearts; they have souls which must live for ever. Oh how delightful if we could together, with one voice, plead in their behalf."

CHAPTER VIII.

Qualifications of Missionaries—Revival of 1831—Governmental Restrictions removed.

Qualifications of missionaries—house and furniture—manners and customs—singular fishing-boat—letter to her sisters—to her parents—native marriages—female influence—*revival of religion*—sixty-one received to the church—fire at Manepy—death of her father—son sent to America—reasons for return of children—letters to her son—governmental restrictions removed—conversion of a Court Moodeliar.

The following suggestions in reference to *missionary qualifications*, with the annexed facts, throwing additional light on the manners and customs of the natives of India, and the circumstances of a missionary among them, will be read, at least by some, with interest.

"Oodooville, January 13, 1830.

"My dear Sister Elizabeth,—Very many thanks for your long kind letter, which we received a few weeks since. I can sympathize with you, from experience, in some of your darkness of mind; and I rejoice that you are now so happily free from it. May your faith henceforth be strong and uniform, and then you will have sweet and uniform peace. It is said that you think much of missions. I should rejoice if you are qualified, which I trust you are, to have you 'even as I am,' except these infirmities and sins. Perhaps you will not take it amiss if I attempt to tell you what I think *a missionary's wife* should be. She should have *sincere and humble piety—a good temper—common sense—a cultivated mind—a thorough knowledge of household economy—and affable manners.*

"By the first, I mean something more than such a degree of piety as secures the safety of the individual. With clear and distinguishing views of what christianity is, and what it requires, and with a well-grounded hope of an interest in the Saviour, there should be a heart glowing with love to him, a lively and abiding sense of his fullness and sufficiency, of the excellence and truth of the promises of his word, and deep views of the utter helplessness of sinners and their dependence on him. There should also exist a strong and impelling desire to do whatever the Lord requires; a willingness to give up comforts and submit to privations, to forsake ease and endure toil, to change the society of friends for that of enemies, to assemble no more with the 'great congregation,' but seek the Lord in the wilderness, or in the desert, with one friend or with none; in short, to make every sacrifice of personal ease and gratification for the one great object of making known a crucified Saviour to those who are perishing in ignorance and sin. If your hands would be soiled by performing acts of kindness and charity to the poor and wretched—if your mind would necessarily be contaminated by intercourse with the moral depravity and degradation of the heathen—if your habits are such that you shrink from all acquaintance with what is uncourteous and unpolished—if you love refined society so much that you cannot cheerfully relinquish it—if the pursuit of literature is so charming that it cannot be abandoned—if you cannot 'spend and be spent' for others, and those, too, such as are degraded almost to the level of the brutes—you would better not think of the missionary work.

"By *good temper*, I mean not merely equanimity and mildness, but a readiness to please and be pleased, a desire to make others happy, and patience and forbearance towards all, even those who are the least agreeable—a willingness to submit one's own opinion to that of others, and cheerfully to bear contradiction; indeed, all that the apostle includes in his definition of charity in the thirteenth chapter of 1st Corinthians.

"By *common sense*, I mean that sense which enables a person to understand the common use of common things, the result of observation, of experience, and of sound judgment in the every-day affairs of common life; and be assured that, with all the learning to be acquired in ordinary circumstances, without this qualification you would do but little good in the missionary service.

"The *cultivation of mind* which is needful, may consist in a good acquaintance with grammar, arithmetic, geography, and history; some familiarity with polite literature, and a chaste and easy style of writing. Other acquirements, such as some knowledge of botany, chemistry, painting and music, would also be very useful. It is indispensable that the wife of a missionary be able to keep all her family and other accounts. She should also be able and apt to teach—should have studied human nature in various situations, so as to have some acquaintance with men and manners, and especially should be able to make a correct estimate of her own powers and attainments, and know how to make the best use of her time.

"A *thorough knowledge of household economy* is almost a *sine qua non* in the qualifications of the wife of a poor man, as a missionary is of course supposed to be. It is necessary to her own comfort in a heathen land, as well as to a proper provision for her household. All is confusion and waste if a woman at the head of a family here is not familiar with every kind of family business. She must know how to provide for its various wants, and how to take care of what is provided. She must know how to *cut*, and *make*, and *mend* every kind of garment, and be willing to do it also. I do not say it is in every case necessary for her to do this with her own hands, but in many it will be important.

"*Kind and conciliating manners* are very desirable, that she may be beloved by her brethren and sisters, if she have any in the same field, and that she may win the heathen around her to embrace the Gospel. This is of more importance than is often supposed. The heathen are governed by appearances, at least at first, and an unkind manner towards them shuts their ears and hardens their hearts.

"Now, dear E. do not say, 'This is too much, I can never think of engaging in the missionary work.' Does what I have said imply so much as the command, 'Be ye perfect, as your Father in heaven is perfect;' and is it not true, that 'if any man lack wisdom, he may ask of God, who giveth liberally and upbraideth not?'"

The hints contained in this letter, though brief, are thought to be valuable. Too much cannot be said or felt on the importance of the first-named requisite for missionaries. Apostolic holiness is wanted to insure apostolic success. A cheerful temper, or a sunshine of the soul, is scarcely less important, and is at the same time very difficult to be maintained by the mistress of a family who has to manage perverse, unprincipled, and indolent domestics, who will try her patience, as of set purpose, in almost every conceivable way. Good common sense is desirable in all situations, but is less necessary to those who are surrounded by friends able to make up their deficiencies, or help them in emergencies, than those who have only themselves to depend on, and are surrounded by a people quick-sighted to detect any mistake in judgment or practice. The employment of a female missionary, if married, will centre very much in her family and the care of the temporal concerns of the station, that she may relieve her husband, and enable him with less interruption to pursue his appropriate work; but she will also have opportunity for making known the Gospel, especially to those of her own sex, and superintending female schools, or perhaps making useful books for the natives. Her education should be practical and solid rather than theoretical and showy, and whatever may be her situation, habits of great industry, economy, and self-denial are of the utmost importance. It is well that they should be previously formed, and established by practice. However good may be the intentions of one brought up in indolence and self-indulgence, they cannot usually be depended on without previous trial. It is always easier to design than to execute, to resolve than to fulfil our resolutions; and this is especially the case where not a single act, requiring one great exertion of the will, is concerned, but a steady succession of self-denying duties. As great trials, which rouse the mind to special exertions and special applications for aid to Him who is able to grant it, are more easily borne than the unexpected annoyances of every day, so great sacrifices which are made once for all, are more easy than those which require the offerer to "die daily."

The following short extract is on a subject connected with the preceding, and may be interesting to some, as containing an opinion formed after long observation:

"There used to be much said before we left home, about missionaries going to the heathen *alone;* but I suppose the views of many are now altered. From a remark or two recently dropped to some of us, it appears, however, that when missionaries talk of sending their children home, the question returns, Would they not better have gone alone? Now it is too late for this question to affect us; but it may affect others, and I will, therefore, just say that we see more reasons why missionaries should take wives with them to India, than we did before we came ourselves. If a few young men could come to missionary stations already formed and in operation as ours are, and find a pleasant home, and have health to spend most of their time in itinerary labor among the natives, no doubt they would do much good. But it must be understood that they could thus perform but one part of the work. No boarding-schools nor seminaries for boys or girls could be conducted by them, and I suppose the number is very small of those who could be wholly devoted to this kind of work, and retain their cheerfulness of mind and health to prosecute it for any length of time, amidst the peculiar difficulties and trials of a life in India. It does not depend altogether upon their wishes or resolutions. These may be the best and the strongest. They may enter upon the work with every right feeling, but before many months elapse their health begins to fail, their cheerfulness is gone, and they must have a change of scene, or attentions which natives cannot give them. Their brethren and sisters are overwhelmed with cares and labors, and with every kindness which these can show, the invalid does not in all respects find a *home.* Various wants are multiplied, the mind becomes diseased, and soon perhaps a valuable life is lost to the church. While, then, it may be well for some to make such a sacrifice of comfort or even of life, it cannot be required as a general thing, nor are those who do not make it to be considered as of course less useful in their Master's service."

The following description of her dwelling, furniture, and mode of living, was written to correct misapprehensions, by which some had excused themselves from contributing to the cause of missions.

"As to our *house*, you have heard that there are four rooms, all on the same floor, one of which is a dining or sitting-room, having a table in the middle, very plain,—generally twelve chairs of jackwood, the cheapest and strongest to be obtained here, with rattan bottoms,—two couches, with mattresses, covered with dark, strong chintz,—a small work-table, which I brought from home, having on it an English and Tamul Bible, and some hymn-books,—two stands, on which are a pair of globes for the use of the school,—and two book-cases, containing our library, with a cupboard under each, containing medicine and work for the school. Another is a bed-room, containing a bed brought from Boston, without curtains, and covered by a coarse counterpane,—a bureau from Boston, with a large old looking-glass, a table, at which I now write, and two presses in which is our clothing,—a wash-stand, and a couch. In the children's room is a small table, two presses, a clothes' basket, and three small beds with grass mats, and very coarse muslin curtains to keep out musquetoes. In the remaining room is a long side-board full of drawers, where crockery, table-cloths and towels are kept, and two stands for jars, &c. In this room work is done as in a kitchen, except that there is no fire in it, and of course no cooking. The rooms are not very large, but high, as they reach to the roof. The walls are all white-washed, and the floors are covered with mats. One object of this is to keep the floors, which are of cement, from wearing out, as it is expensive repairing them. I do not know that we have an article of furniture not useful or needed, or which is not as plain as could well be, except that if we did not occasionally need couches for a friend to sleep on, we could have them without mattresses.

"Our food is principally *rice* and *curry*, though I use *bread* a good deal, as riee is too cold for me. What animal food we have is mostly fowls, which are poor, but we sometimes have kid, and tolerable mutton. We usually take coffee morning and evening, with a coarse country sweetening, called *jaggery*, inferior to molasses. We endeavor to eat what is necessary to keep up our health, and instead of thinking that it should be poorer, we regret sometimes that it is not better.

"As to our dress, it is generally light and not expensive. Our children wear country cloths principally; the girls, pantalettes and frocks, and the boys trowsers and jackets. They do not wear under garments or stockings until eight or ten years of age. They are when young dressed clean every day, and we are all obliged to change and bathe frequently on account of the heat and dust. The washerman keeps our clothes a week, and they are then a day or more in being ironed. You will, of course, see that we need a good many changes. For my children's sake, and for the sake of the school under my care, as well as for my own comfort, I hope to dress no less than I now do when at home; and when I go out, no less for the sake of those whom I meet. I have no time to put extra-work on any thing, being obliged to cut and prepare all my own and my children's clothes, and some of Mr. W.'s. My bonnet, bought in Boston in 1819, has served me until this time as my best.

"As to 'doing nothing,' I am certainly not idle. All day I am driven, and at night am often obliged to leave my work half done, because I can sit up no longer. I would gladly do the work of a kitchen at home, to be exempt from the responsibility, and even labor, of such an establishment as this. We have a cook, who does nothing out of the cook-house; a low caste woman, who does what no one else would do, and a man and boy in and about the house. All these do less than one woman would do in America. We have sometimes two women to take care of the children, who together do about one-third of a good nurse's work with you. While I have these helpers, I am teaching my children, writing for Mr. W. preparing little Tracts to be put into Tamul, or arranging lessons in geography or arithmetic for the girls to study. I must also give out daily every article of food for my own family and for the school, make all purchases, keep family and other accounts; besides running twenty times a day to get something for the people as they come ill or hungry. All the work done in the school is also to be prepared and superintended. Now, I would not make you think that I do very much, but I wish, when you hear it said, 'We will give no money to support missionaries who have so many domestics, and do nothing themselves,' you may be able to say, 'If they do not wash and bake, they do something else.' "

In a warm climate, and among a people like

the Hindoos, many things must of *necessity* be very different from what is common in America. A missionary might do much for which he employs a domestic, though not all—as for instance, he cannot go daily two or three miles to a market frequented only by natives, or spend several hours each day in cutting up roots of grass for his horse or cow—but while doing the work of a domestic he must leave undone his missionary work, and defeat the object for which he left his native country. He may hire that done for one shilling, which, reckoning the value of his own time, it would cost him ten to do himself! If a missionary is to " labor, working with his hands," to provide for his sustenance, he would better go where his labor may be more productive and less prejudicial to health than in India. It is an idle dream to talk of his going forth to that country " without purse and scrip;" for he could not there support himself by manual labor; and, though our Saviour sent out the apostles in this manner among their own countrymen, when they went in haste as his forerunners, he afterwards said to them, "He that hath a purse, let him take it."

The time is coming, it may be hoped, when numbers, having a purse, will " take it," and, like Paul, not " be chargeable to any;" and if christians remaining at home desire the *privilege* of aiding in the conversion of the heathen, they will feel that missionaries, generally, cannot preach "except they be sent," and will gladly send them forth at any necessary expense, furnished, not grudgingly, with every possible facility for their work. It is to be regarded as a favorable circumstance rather than otherwise, that the system of modern missions in the establishment of schools, the extensive use of the press, the employment of native agents, and other expensive operations, calls for liberal contributions; for this creates a community of interest, and a sympathy between those at home and those abroad, exciting them to earnest prayer for each other, while it opens one of those channels of benevolence whose running waters prevent the accumulating wealth of the church from stagnation.

The following extracts may give some additional light as to the manners and customs of the natives:

"The native christians do not change their dress on joining us, nor do we by any means wish it. It is altogether better for them than ours would be. You may be slow to believe, what is nevertheless true, that a female with a cloth round her waist and thrown over her shoulders, as she has when she attends meetings, appears quite as modestly dressed as ladies generally are in America. She is entirely covered, except her feet and hands, and in such a manner that the wind may almost take her off her feet without subjecting her person to observation.

"The children in our schools dress decently, as we think, though you might judge otherwise. Boys wear a cloth round the waist coming down nearly to their feet, the upper part of the body being left naked. Girls, unless very small, wear a cloth and jacket, which make them perfectly decent. This is only in our schools. Those living at home very seldom know what a jacket is, and women, except the higher castes, and those connected with us, or under our influence, seldom wear any thing above the waist. Children generally wear nothing until they are five or six years old, except a string or a silver chain around their middle, to which is often attached a bell or two in front, making a 'tinkling as they go.' You may easily conceive, therefore, that their minds are soon filled with all manner of impure thoughts. It is often disgusting to see them, and distressing to know their habits from their earliest years. A door to sin is thus thrown open which no man can shut; and nothing can do it but Almighty power."

"You might have learnt something of the native character, had you been here this morning. A *Maniagar*, who comes occasionally to borrow a dollar, and who, while owing it, generally attends church, called to sell some straw. He is the only native who does not pay some respect to me. He seems to hold me in perfect contempt, because I am a female. I was at the table as he came in, and afterwards I entered the room several times. I noticed him, of course, but he re garded me with his usual dignified stiffness. After Mr. W. left, however, he followed me to my bed-room door, which the natives are not allowed to enter, and then scraped on the floor, and made other noises, to attract attention. When I looked up, he raised both his hands to his head with the palms joined, after the manner practised in idol-worship, and at the same time bowing nearly to the floor, begged I would give him a little sugar. The highest and greatest will bow down to the dust, and flatter with the tongue of a ready flatterer, for a slight favor, and often to obtain what they are abundantly able to procure for themselves.

"The poor are frequently driven to beg for their living when they have health and could labor; if sick, there are no alms-houses or hospitals to receive them. Women of good caste may usually make a sort of living by pounding rice, though the lower castes have not this opportunity, as any thing prepared by them, where water is used, may not be eaten by the higher castes. They buy in the bazar one morning, say twenty-four quarts of paddy, that is rice in the husk, carry it home, and get from it, by nearly a day's labor, thirteen quarts of cleán rice, which to-morrow they may sell for two or three cents more than they paid. With this they can furnish themselves, and sometimes their children, with food for the time. They provide only for the passing day, literally 'taking no thought for the morrow.' Indeed this is remarkably the case in all their concerns. If a day-laborer, who receives his wages of about thirty cents a week, knows that after a month or two he shall be called upon for his yearly tax of the same sum, he never thinks of laying by a little every week till he saves the amount needed, but spends all as he receives it, and when the tax is called for he runs about from place to place to borrow of his neighbors, offering perhaps to pawn his wife's jewels. They not only are careless about laying up what they earn, but are always wanting their wages in advance. They frequently borrow, and avoid paying as long as possible, in hopes that the person to whom they are indebted will die, or lose the evidence of his claim, or in some way be unable to prosecute it, so that they shall escape the necessity of making payment."

"OODOOVILLE, January 30, 1830.

"MY DEAR BROTHER L.—I have returned this evening from a visit at Tillipally, where you know Mr. and Mrs. Spaulding reside. My health has been poor for some time, and we thought a few days' absence from the cares of home, and bathing in the sea would be beneficial. So it has proved, and I am again at home, much better than when I left. The sea is about two and a half miles from that station. Mrs. S. rode there with me, and bathed twice each day. We have seen, in a few minutes, a number of vessels built, rigged, manned, and launched into the sea; and have also seen them brought into port, unrigged, and after being taken to pieces, laid up 'high and dry' on the sand. All along the shore were timbers lying, which at first sight seemed to be old, rough, and good for nothing, but on further examination were found to be cut and prepared to lash together, two or more of them, in a few minutes. The first morning we went, a man was standing by some of these timbers. We requested him to go off a little distance, as we were wishing to bathe. He replied, 'I am going directly to fish.' We despaired of getting rid of him, but to our surprise, with the help of a lad, he lashed four of the timbers together, took his sail, oars and fish-net, and was out of sight within half an hour. In his haste, however, he did not neglect a form of devotion used by the native sailors when they set sail, and I could not but ask myself, 'Are all christians as careful to commend themselves to the protection of God, when they commence any new undertaking, as this poor man was to repeat the name of his senseless idol, and put up his hands in adoration to one who can neither see nor save?'

"The Preparatory School is at Tillipally, and I should like to introduce you to *one hundred black boys* almost naked, seated in a large school-room, some writing, some reading, some cyphering, &c. You would soon see that though their skin is less fair, their minds are no less capable of improvement than those of white boys in America; and the hope that they are preparing for usefulness in this life, and for eternal happiness in the life to come, would, I am sure, affect your heart."

The "*fishing-craft*" here mentioned, is certainly a curiosity. It is composed of mere logs, shaped a little like a canoe, and lashed together. As this, however, cannot sink, and is capable of being managed by an oar or sail, the natives venture out on it in almost any weather, attaching themselves, if necessary, by a rope, so as not to be washed off. They thus carry the mail across the straits between Ceylon and the continent when other boats could not venture, and accompany the surf-boats at Madras and other places to pick up passengers if upset, and go off to ships when on the coast.

"March 15, 1830.

"MY DEAR SISTERS,—I have thought much of my dear younger sisters of late, and if I had opportunity to tell them sometimes *what* I think, should it do them no good, it would at least show them how deeply concerned I am that they should be all that is estimable and useful. Do, my beloved sisters, strive to be *thorough* christians. Walk softly before God, and cautiously before your fellow-men. I hope you look to heaven for your motives and gracious reward, that you are crucified to the world and live with constant reference to eternity. I remember too well how it was with me at your age; and it is certain, however unacceptable the truth may be, that young christians know but little of their own hearts, and but little of the world around them. They are tempted when they know it not, and they are led astray by what appears perfectly harmless. Hence the necessity of being humble, prayerful, teachable. Were I to live my life over again, how would I strive 'to live, and move, and have my being' in Him who is all-wise to direct, all-powerful to preserve, and all-merciful to pity and forgive. How would I strive to live for others, and not for myself: to esteem my own ease and comfort of little consequence; but the influence I might exert on those around me worth living for, even while enduring every form of crosses and trials. I would strive to consider myself of no importance, except as I fulfilled the purposes of my existence.

"It is easy to be an 'active christian;' but to control the tongue, to bring the temper into subjection, to fulfil all relative duties, even if they cross our plans, to esteem others better than ourselves, and to live above the world, is hard work. It is easy to endure pain and fatigue, but how hard to 'subdue sin within us.' We shall not become eminent in piety by a miracle. It is a long, a patient, and a persevering work. None are ever successful without making it the business of every day as much as they do to live. I have lately more than ever derived assistance from Flavel and Baxter. The biographies of Martyn and Scott are also valuable: they instruct the heart. I am glad that you take a stand against the temptations of the world; but let all see that your religion makes you happy and consistent. They will not wonder if you sometimes say in relation to their large parties, 'I am doing a great work and cannot come down.' Love all for Christ's sake, and strive to do good to all. The christian need not say to the world, 'I am better than you,' but should always say, 'I am a follower of Christ —a pilgrim and a stranger, I must be *consistent*.' May the Lord give you grace even in the smallest things to do his will."

"*August* 30, 1830.—Dearly belôved parents, are you still on the earth, still subject to its cares and trials, or are you before the throne of the Eternal, arrayed in white robes, with palms in your hands? I should be glad to know where and how you are. But why? I could do nothing, not even sit by your side and strive, by my attention to all your wants, to discharge a small part of my great debt to you. Sometimes it looks unnatural thus to be separated from father and mother; but I fully believe you *have received already a hundred fold* for all the sacrifices you have made that your children might go to the gentiles. As to us, I am sure that not one thing has failed of all the good things which the Lord our God spake concerning us! It will not be long that we shall feel a separation now so painful. But oh! if I should not meet you in a better world! Many, many are my doubts—great is my unbelief, and great are my fears. It is not coming to the heathen, it is not being called a christian, that can enable one to say, 'I *know* that my Redeemer liveth.' Oh! for an overcoming faith. I did not mean, however, to talk of myself, but of you; for I have thought of you more than usual to-day—and of the churches of our native land—the 'great congregation'—the Sabbath-school,—the morning prayers, and the sacred stillness which rests on every thing where the

Lord is honored by those who fear him and keep his commandments.

"*September* 14.—We have married one of our native children, or I might say two of them, since I last wrote—Mary Sweetzer and J. W. Lawrence—the former from the female school, the latter from the Seminary, but now a catechist here. It was a pleasant occasion. Mary, however, felt sadly at leaving her home and companions. Her tears for two weeks previous evinced that her heart was heavy; and after all was over, except taking leave of us, she could hardly get away, though going only two and a half miles. They were married in the morning, in the church, by Mr. W. after the forms of the church of England."

The marriage here noticed was one of several within a year or two of this time, in accordance with a leading object of the school, to furnish suitable partners for the native preachers and other assistants in the mission. It was considered of great importance that they should marry educated and especially christian wives. If not, they would probably form unscriptural connections with the heathen, which would injure their usefulness and perhaps destroy their souls. This has, indeed, been one of the greatest temptations of the native converts, and more have fallen in this way than any other. It was, therefore, matter of gratitude that previous to the decease of Mrs. W. no less than *twelve* well instructed young women from the school, who gave pleasing evidence of being "born again," were married to christian husbands. They were settled among idolaters, where they had opportunity, as christian wives and christian mothers, to exhibit a pleasing contrast with heathen families, and to show the loveliness of domestic virtue in the midst of abounding vice. One such example in a dark heathen neighborhood is like a star on the thick brow of night.

"Oodooville, (Jaffna,) Sept. 30, 1830.

"My dear Friend,—We have been constantly hoping, and I wish I could add, expecting, to see a work of grace on some hearts around us; but as yet we have not this privilege to any extent. We have still many difficulties in the way of communicating truth to the females. My principal hope is from the Female Central School. When christian women are settled in the villages among the heathen, they will, we trust, prove that a little leaven leaveneth the whole lump. I have therefore been particularly gratified, recently, by the marriage of one such to a young man of respectable attainments and christian character; and in two others being now published, who will be married soon.

"Perhaps I may interest you a little by telling you something of the proceedings from the time a young man proposes to marry one of these girls, or rather from the time he consents to do so,—for he is usually solicited by her friends,—until the event is consummated. Previous acquaintance of the parties, or personal attachment, is almost out of the question. The first object of the young man is to satisfy himself as to the family, caste, and dowry of the proposed bride. These being to his mind, a marriage contract is drawn up, in presence of certain government officers, specifying the amount of the dowry, which is, however, settled on the wife and her children, the husband having only the use of it. The parties are then published three successive Sabbaths, and their names, caste, &c. are entered in a registry. If Christians, the law requires that they be soon after married by a christian minister. In preparation for this interesting occasion, a profusion of cakes, made principally of rice-flour and boiled in oil, aro provided, as also a varicty of fruits. The parties then invite their friends.

"At the wedding above alluded to, between fifty and sixty were present. The bride was dressed by her friends, and the groom by his, and without seeing each other, entered the church at different times, and took their seats on separate mats, with one or two of their intimate friends near them. They were married according to the usual forms, accompanied by a prayer and an address on the duties of husbands and wives. They then retired to different apartments, to partake of the refreshments provided. After a little time, the bridegroom came with a few select friends and tied on the bride's neck the *tarley* (a small gold ornament designating married women) and threw a wedding cloth over her shoulders. We prevailed on them to take a piece of cake together, as a substitute for smoking, which is common among them,—the wife taking the cigar after the husband. After a little time they went to her mother's abode, about two miles, he walking with his friends and she with hers, and then took other refreshments before going to the house of his family, where they are to reside. On their near approach to the latter his sister came to meet them, and put ear-rings into the bride's ears,—a mark of affection and respect very gratifying. They both wore their dress and ornaments several days, exchanging visits with their friends, and then returned to their usual habits. We hope to see more simplicity and more conformity to our own customs on these occasions after a while, but should be thankful that we have already been able to effect a beneficial change in many respects, besides that of introducing a christian form of marriage instead of absurd and idolatrous ceremonies.

Among the heathen the parties are not even consulted: every thing is settled without their consent, and perhaps without their knowledge. Of course they know little of domestic happiness.

"MRS. JANE TRUMBULL."

"OODOOVILLE, October 13, 1830.

"MY DEAR PARENTS,—This has been an auspicious day for the female boarding-school. Elizabeth Appleton and Louisa Hawes were married. A large number of spectators were present in the church, and more than one hundred men eat rice and curry on the premises. The girls felt sadly at leaving, so that we were almost obliged to force them away. I hope and believe they will do much good to their own sex around them. May they in some measure make up my deficiencies. I see no way for females to be instructed extensively in christianity but from the girls of this school.

"Christian David once said to me, 'The conversion of one woman is of more importance among the Tamul people than that of six men,' and he, you know, is a Tamul man, (a pupil of Swartz,) and has spent his life among them. It is matter of much thankfulness that nearly all in the school are hopefully pious or particularly serious; but when they are away from the school, they are as lambs among wolves, and require peculiar grace. I need not say, Pray for them.

"17.—*Sabbath.*—Mr. W. preached at Manepy, and Mr. Woodward here. Charles told Mr. Woodward that he had a hope that he was a christian. I know not what to think of him. He is more ready of late to attend meetings, prays differently, and manifests much tenderness of conscience. He often weeps when christians weep, and talks as they talk; but I fear he does not know the evil of his heart.

"*November* 16.—Your letters are received. We are greatly favored that you continue to write so fully, and that our younger sisters do their part so well. I cannot now more than thank you for their letters, and allude to E.'s prospect of engaging in the missionary work. It is no doubt too late to advise, and perhaps if not, it might be indiscreet; yet I could almost wish she had not agitated the question these *four years.* She is in *years* too young, and if she should soon be engaged in such a work, I hope she will feel that this deficiency must be made up, so far as is possible, in increase of grace—in humility, and daily and hourly leaning with her whole soul on Christ. Dear E——, my heart is more than full when I think of it; go to Jesus—let him direct you *altogether*—lean not to your own understanding. Your friends can help you to know yourself—take their advice in what they do know, especially your parents and those who are older than yourself; and after all, *wait on the Lord* as a little child blind and helpless. If you go to the heathen, why should you not come to your sister? There are certainly reasons why it should be so; but in this, too, I dare say but little."

We now approach the period when the hearts of the missionaries were again cheered by the *descent of the Holy Spirit.* How ardently Mrs. W. desired, and with what joy she welcomed this blessing, appears in the following communications to her parents, the first of which was dated as early as July.

"Mr. Spaulding is here. We have had a large congregation; more than seventy men and women, besides about forty beggars, the boarding-school, and about three hundred children from the out-schools. But, Oh! how they hear that word by which they are to be acquitted or condemned. Shall we say that 'the Lord's hand is shortened that it cannot save?' or shall we say that he had no designs of mercy towards this people when he called us up hither? or shall we conclude that we have forsaken our post, and are not such as he can employ in his service? Oh that he would show us what hindereth, and make us such as he would have us to be; that we could see his glory as we have seen it. When will it once be?

"A class of thirty lads are about to enter the seminary from the preparatory school, *only one* of whom is a member of the church. Where, then, are the patrons of these youths? Surely they do not hold up our hands as they once did, or this could not be. The Lord would hear their prayer if he cannot hear ours.

"There is an advance in some things; such as the writing and distributing of Tracts, which are extensively read; additional school-books, which have been much needed; increased numbers of readers, catechists, &c.; but almost no apparent progress in the influences of the Holy Spirit on the hearts of sinners. Cloud after cloud has appeared, and we have thought it spreading over the horizon, and almost seen the rain descend; but alas! each one has soon been scattered, and we must still plead, 'Oh that thou wouldst rend the heavens and come down!'

"Is it still so with you, dear parents, brothers, and sisters? Are you still unrefreshed by the showers of grace which water other parts of our favored country? But then it is not, as with us, midnight darkness around you. You cannot feel that you are in the midst of Satan's dominion, where he reigns over the head and heart of his subjects with almost undisturbed subtlety and power. There is, however, a Rock to which our minds turn, on which we build all our hope, and from which we derive all our consolation. May we cling to it more and more."

"OODOOVILLE, November, 1830.

"MY DEAR PARENTS,—During nearly the whole of this year we have been, I think, more strongly convinced than ever, that without the Spirit of God all is vain; and we have been led more earnestly to seek his divine aid, with anxious desire to have every hinderance in ourselves removed. The prayer-meeting in October was very interesting. A number of our own children were present, and were particularly addressed. It was followed by a season of fasting and prayer at all our stations. The quarterly meeting, three weeks after, was also unusually solemn, and at the close of the sermon, and during the administration of the Lord's supper, there was evidence of the special presence of the Holy Spirit. Two of the brethren were induced from the appearance of things to go that evening to Batticotta, where they found much encouragement to labor in *the seminary* on Friday and Saturday. One of them remained over the Sabbath. On Monday Mr. W. went to Batticotta, and found many in the seminary awakened, and some under strong convictions. He spent the day with them. In the evening there was a prayer-meeting with the mission families there. It was an occasion long to be remembered. The two oldest children of the mission, H. B. M. and M. A. P. resolved to give themselves to the Saviour, and there is reason to hope that they did so. The same day one of the native assistants came from Tillipally to Oodooville, and held several meetings with the church members, girls in the school, and domestics. Every thing evinced that the Lord was near. A work of grace was evidently begun in some hearts. Our native helpers, Goodrich and Niles, appeared quite awake, and many of the girls were aroused.

"We were saying a few days before, that we never expected to see Goodrich feel much; it seemed not his allotment. But could you hear him speak and pray now, you would be melted, and give thanks to God, with a full heart, for one such preacher to this benighted people. He is not, I trust, the only one from whom words now come with power to Christians and to the impenitent. The concert of prayer this month was a season of earnest supplication, and we have had some evening prayer-meetings of exceeding interest.

"*November* 3.—Mr. W. had a meeting with the native helpers, girls, and domestics. Goodrich had spent the day at Batticotta. He told what he had seen amongst his old companions in the seminary. Some, he said, who have been possessed with evil spirits, are now sitting clothed and in their right mind; some who have been exceedingly opposed to the truth, who have held meetings to ridicule the Bible and those who love it, and have committed sins too bad to be mentioned, are now with many tears crying to God for mercy. 'No one who has not lived with them as I have,' he added, 'and known them thoroughly, can conceive the alteration.' He had also been at a meeting of the children of the missionaries, heard their sobs, and groans, and prayers. Mentioning this he turned to Charles, and addressed him with much feeling, and I hope with effect. Poor C. thought it new times to be exhorted thus by a native, and was quite overcome. I felt thankful, and that we had increased reason to hope that our children will be brought into the kingdom of God.

"4th.—*Fast-day.* It rained violently, but was a very solemn season; observed more or less by all on the premises. They are new times indeed, when every one readily leaves work and play, and resorts to the house of prayer.

"*Monday* 8.—We have had a union prayer-meeting this evening of the church members at Manepy and Oodooville, with some inquirers from both stations; and such a time as we never saw before. There were about fifty adults present, besides the girls of the school. Addresses and confessions were made by sixteen or seventeen men. Many wept; indeed I should think nearly all. We have never, perhaps, had more evidence of the presence of God, by his Spirit. *Bailey*, who teaches an English school here, was perhaps the most pathetic. He said that he had been a long time like one sinking in a great ocean, where the sharks on every hand were coming at him with open mouths trying to catch him, and each crying, he is mine, he is mine; when a boat was let down from a ship for his deliverance; but instead of jumping into it, he had kicked it away, and remained struggling for life, till in great compassion the master of the ship had again let down the boat just in time to save him! Now he hoped that he was safely in the boat, and he wanted all others to get in; to quench not the Spirit, but accept of mercy while it was offered. He then begged leave to pray, and seemed to pour out his soul in thanksgiving and humble supplication to be kept by the mighty power of God. This description was the more moving, as it was known to be so accurate an account of his experience in resisting conviction of sin.

"9.—To-day an old gray-headed schoolmaster who was present last evening, and had never perhaps felt any concern for his soul before, came and said that he could get no rest last night on account of distress for his sins. Our domestics are all more or less affected, and we hope some of them deeply. The church members are most of them awake. Now, at ten o'clock, singing is heard from Goodrich's bungalow and from the girls' rooms. The latter have been in meeting since seven o'clock.

"10.—A prayer-meeting here this evening, in reference to a public meeting to be held in Jaffna to-morrow. The woman who assists me in the care of the girls says she has been long asleep, but is now aroused. She has at times appeared well, and then again we have feared for her. On my inquiring if she thought the girls much altered, she said, 'Does not *Amma* see that they are reading and praying all the time. There is no playing, as before.'

"12.—Yesterday the brethren had a very encouraging day at Jaffna. To-day Mr. W. is at Batticotta, and Dr. Scudder has been here. He thinks there is much feeling in those around us. A note this morning from Mr. Spaulding says, 'I never saw so much to encourage me.'

"13.—A number of schoolmasters, girls, and others, think that they have made an entire surrender of themselves and their all to the Saviour. We have had many meetings, public and private, and the voice of prayer has, I trust, been heard in heaven from old and young. He who hears the cry of the ravens will not reject the least sincere prayer of these little ones. Mr. W. returned this evening. He sees no cases of declension in the seminary. Every one is in some degree affected. Some who have been much opposed, some who have long halted, and others who have been like Lot's wife, are now apparently all of one mind. How wonderful the goodness of God! Shall we ever distrust him again? Shall we ever say, 'His hand is shortened that it cannot save?'

" 14.—Our inquiry-meeting at noon was very full. A young man connected with some of the first families in the district, and who has been the subject of many prayers, and hopes, and fears, gave an account of his experience, which was very encouraging. He was at one time a candidate for admission to the church, but turned back, through fear of his relatives.

" 15.—An interesting meeting at Manepy, similar to the one here last week. The young man mentioned above stated his feelings and hopes more particularly. He seems like one really born again. Among other things, he said that he had often wondered why the missionaries read the Bible so much, and the same things over and over again; but supposed that they were obliged to do so, as a form connected with their religion. Now, however, he sees that the Bible is different from all other books; that it is like food to the christian; he loves it, and sees new beauties in it every day.

"21.—To-day we had a large congregation of about twenty women and more than twice that number of men, with a church full of children. Mr. W. invited those who wished to unite with the church to come to his room after meeting. About forty, nearly half of them boys from the English school, and girls from the boarding-school, accepted the invitation.

"22.—Another union prayer-meeting was held at Oodooville. No one has been more interesting. A church member, who had lately fallen into the sin of lying, made a voluntary confession in a most humble and affecting manner; and prayed to God for pardon, with many tears. Oh, what shall we say of the goodness and mercy of the Lord!"

Mrs. W. was here prevented by ill health from continuing the narrative. In general this attention to religion was similar to that of 1824, though a larger proportion of the converts were adult heathen It commenced in the seminary, and though there was no noise or fanaticism, the feeling of deep anxiety among the students was soon so great that study was for a few days nearly suspended. The study rooms and small "*prayer houses*" were frequently seen lighted up until near midnight, and occupied by individuals or little companies engaged in prayer, reading the Scriptures, and singing praises to God. A quarterly meeting of the schoolmasters, attended by about one hundred teachers and visiters of the schools in connection with the American and church missions, held at Batticotta, was one of much solemnity. The meeting was addressed by all the missionaries and some of the native assistants. Many were "convinced of sin, of righteousness, and of judgment." A very interesting meeting was also held at Oodooville of the more forward children in the schools. About *eight hundred* of both sexes were present, who were able, more or less, to read the Scriptures. Short and affecting addresses were made to them by the missionaries and christian teachers, and many of the children expressed a resolution to forsake idolatry and seek salvation in Christ. Evening meetings in the villages, especially in the school-bungalows, attended by large numbers of the villagers, and addressed by several speakers in succession, became common, and served to hold forth the "word of life" more steadily than most other means to the attention of the perishing idolaters. By the more free circulation of the Bible and religious Tracts, the continued operation of the schools, the better acquaintance of the missionaries with the language and customs of the natives, and the increased number of their assistants, there was *a preparation* for an extension of this work into the domains of heathenism greater than at any previous time, and it was accordingly more *aggressive.*

At the "*quarterly communion,*" held at Oodooville, April 21, (the missionaries and members at the several stations still constituting but one church,) *thirty-four* natives made a public profession of their faith. Most of them were from the seminary. There were two girls of the Female Central School, a few women, and seven schoolmasters. It was a most interesting occasion. A very large and attentive audience of natives, many of them the most respectable in the vicinity, witnessed the exercises.

Three months later than this, at Batticotta, most of the remaining converts, *twenty-seven* in number, were received to communion. The two oldest children of the missionaries, who have been mentioned, were among them. One of these, Harriet B. Meigs, a lovely young christian, died a few days after, rejoicing that she had been allowed to profess her faith in Christ before the heathen, and quietly yielding her spirit into the hands of that Saviour whom she had so recently found.

In January, 1831, *Niles* and *Goodrich* were

licensed as native preachers. After receiving a charge and public designation to their work, they went into the pulpit of the church at Tillipally, and Goodrich having read and expounded a portion of Scripture, Niles preached a very impressive sermon from the text, "Oh, Lord God, behold I cannot speak, for I am a child." He gave an account, with deep feeling, of the manner in which he had been taken up, when a poor boy, brought forward, supported and educated by the missionaries, and converted, as he hoped, by the Spirit of God, so as to be prepared to stand there as a preacher of the Gospel. Looking around the church, in which were some very large stone pillars, about to be removed on account of their obstructing the view of the congregation, and their place to be supplied by wooden posts, he said, "The missionaries who are now among us, like these strong pillars, may be all taken away, and the church left to stand on us poor native preachers, who are only as wooden posts; but if the Lord gives us grace, we will stand in our lot, come life or come death; and, trusting in him, I will not say, 'I am a child.' I can do all things through Christ, which strengtheneth me." He then turned round, and taking his native brother by the hand, addressed him in English, expressing his fellowship, and calling upon him to make an entire consecration of himself to the Lord.

They both wept. It was affecting to see them then, and at other times, standing among their countrymen, with something of the feeling which Paul had for his brethren, his "kindred according to the flesh," and saying, "Now then, we are ambassadors for Christ, as though God did beseech you by us, we pray you in Christ's stead, be ye reconciled unto God."

On the 30th of April the mission sustained a serious loss by the burning of its buildings at Manepy, including the church, house, study, and a large bungalow, with most of the effects of the mission family.

"Oodooville, June, 1831.

"And where are most of my early friends; and perhaps *my dear father?* Surely we need not wish to return to America, for if *home* is where 'our friends and kindred dwell,' we must soon look for them above. I never calculate on long life, but now it seems only a step to where I hope I may eventually see all I have most loved on earth. Yes, *all*, what a privilege! And 'shall we receive good at the hand of the Lord, and not evil?' If we loved our Saviour as much as we ought for all the mercies we have through him, what christians we should be."

"July 21, 1831.

"My dear afflicted Mother,—I have now the

painful task of saying that your letters, containing the intelligence of dear father's death, have come to hand. And is he indeed gone? Gone to make one of that multitude who cast their crowns before Him who sitteth on the throne, saying, Holy, holy, holy, Lord God of hosts? Can it be that all his doubts, and fears, and cares have ceased for ever? Is my beloved mother a widow, and have we no father? I cannot realize that it is so, and yet it has been long expected. But what shall I say to you, my dear mother? How can I tell you, at this distance, how I feel, or help you to bear the heavy burden? It would be vain to attempt either, and I rejoice and give thanks that you are comforted and strengthened by Him who alone is able to help you. You are very solitary. Oh! how little can I conceive how difficult it may often be for you to say, 'Thy will be done;' but do, my beloved mother, be comforted by thinking that it is in kindness to you that you are bereaved, not in judgment. Think of the joys of those who see Jesus as he is. Could you not, when our dear father lived, bear almost any pain cheerfully while you saw him exempt from it; and was it not your happiness to see him happy? How much more, then, may you now rejoice because his joy is full!

" *October* 2.—We rejoice in the great news of revivals of religion in our own *dear* America; but what means so much controversy, even among the best of men. I hope it will do some good, though I am afraid not enough to balance the attendant evils. The arrival of a ship which may convey Charles to America is now daily expected; and I do not see a letter come in but my heart beats quickly till I have ascertained whence it came. Dear boy, he too feels his time to be with us is short. He told Mrs. S. (when making a little visit at Tillipally,) 'I do very well through the day, but when night comes I think of dear mother.' May he have a better friend always at hand. This is, I can almost say, *all my desire.* He appears more serious and conscientious of late, expresses a strong wish to join the church; but he needs to know himself better. I trust that when father and mother forsake him, then the Lord will take him up.

"*November* 24.—We have observed this as a day of thanksgiving. A very pleasant time. In meeting with the church members, after explaining the object of the day and making some remarks on our obligations to thankfulness, Mr. W. gave the native members opportunity to speak. Among them was Niles, who, with feelings which sometimes prevented his utterance, related some of the special causes which he had found for gratitude. He went back to one of the greatest mercies that he had experienced, when at fifteen years of age, after the death of his father, he came to Mr. W. to ask employment, seeking, as he said, 'a *shell* in which he had since found a *pearl.*' Instead of being left, as native boys usually are after the death of a father, having none to rule and guide them, to go in the broad road to destruction, a father was provided to guide his youthful steps, and to lead him to seek a better portion than any in this vain world. Here he spoke of some peculiar dangers to which he had been exposed, and seemed quite overwhelmed with a sense of the blessings he had experienced, in being 'plucked as a brand from the burning.' You may recollect that he is Mr. W.'s assistant in Tamul, having more knowledge of the language and more Tamul learning than any other one around us.

"*December* 17.—Could you look in upon us at this time, you would see and believe that we are really in earnest about sending our beloved Charles to America. We have looked for intelligence of the arrival of the 'Star' at Madras for two months past, and expected to have two months at least in which to prepare him and ourselves for his departure; but instead of this, we heard five days ago that the vessel had reached Calcutta, (not having stopped at Madras,) and that C. must be at the latter place on the 10th January. This makes it necessary for him to leave us a fortnight before that time. Mr. W. expected to accompany him and a son of Mr. Woodward, but Mr Spaulding will go in his place, as the mission wish Mr. W. to go to Colombo, to wait on the new Governor and confer with him about the restrictions on our mission. The dear boy is pleased with the prospect of going, as he has always been, but he says, 'Mamma, when we talked about it, it was not certain, but now since it is certain, I feel differently.' Mother can say the same. I have no misgivings of judgment, but my feelings as a mother, none but a mother can know. It is unnatural for parents to send a child of his age from them, with little expectation of seeing him again; and it was, perhaps, unnatural for us to leave our parents; but I have no more doubt of my *duty* in this case than I had in that, and I think that I thus give the strongest proof of love to my child.

"He has of late been unusually serious, and appeared to try to live as a christian; but he goes into the wide world at eleven years of age alone. Should he be qualified by education and grace to return a missionary to this people, our highest wishes will be accomplished, and for this our prayer is to the God of heaven."

It will be seen that the subject of this memoir felt most deeply the trial of thus parting with an only and first-born son; but the reasons which induced all the missionaries to consider such a course necessary, in regard to their children, were entirely satisfactory to her mind. Some of the principal are, 1, The children cannot be *properly educated* in Ceylon. 2, The state of society endangers *their moral and religious character.* 3, They cannot be furnished with proper *employment* to give them habits of early and thorough *industry.* 4, They are unable to earn *the means of their subsistence,* and must be *supported* by their parents. 5, There are not opportunities for their forming *suitable connections in marriage.* 6, They cannot, as a general thing, remain in the country with the *prospect of usefulness and happiness.*

These reasons might be extended to show why the children of the missionaries in Ceylon, and in other places where circumstances are similar, cannot be kept with their parents and settled around them in the manner of a colony. Southern Asia is no place for northern people to *colonize.* They dwindle away under a tropical sun. Besides, there is no room for them ; the country is already *full* of inhabitants to whom they cannot assimilate. They may, as foreign residents, carrying with them an established character, do much good ; but their posterity, born and educated in the country, instead of aiding to elevate the natives, would, in all probability, gradually sink to their level. Some have already done so in a few generations; and there are instances where they have sunk even below the Hindoos themselves.

The children of the missionaries, if pious, might, some of them, be employed in the mission; but to be respected by the people there, and to have the confidence of the churches at home, they need to be educated in the midst of those churches. They cannot be missionaries by *birth*, nor will they be worthy of the office unless "called of God, as was Aaron." They are not, therefore, sent to America to be educated and return to their parents, except they do so as missionary laborers—but to find a *home;* to enjoy their *birth-right* as Americans, (of which the voluntary exile of their parents ought not to deprive them,) and to remain in this happy land, which is "even as the garden of the Lord," until they are willing and joyful to leave it for the service of their Saviour in other climes.

In reference to the third reason above mentioned, Mrs. W. some two years previous, wrote as follows:

"If we ever send a daughter to America, I think it must be before her habits are formed for this country. I feel it to be a serious evil that our daughters can do so little work. Our domestics are men, from whom girls must be far removed. How then can they cook? And how can they do many other things which they might if at home? I fear and dread *indolence* more than almost any thing in my daughters, and see scarcely any girls here industrious. The happiness of the natives consists in sitting perfectly idle, without employment for body or mind."

"*December* 30.—Our dear Charles left us the day before yesterday, as we expected when I wrote; and oh what a blank there is in our little family. I fear I do not feel as I ought, though I certainly would not call him back. His own feelings were a good deal tried, even so as to affect his health, and he went away unwell. We trust, however, that the sea air will soon restore him. You will find his mind and body very intimately connected, and I am sure will love him none the less for his strong attachments. I try to feel that we have given him to the Lord, and sent him away in obedience to his will; but yet the thought comes across me sometimes, that we have thrust him from us, and cast him, at the most susceptible age, upon the wide world; and if I could not plead with some hope that my God will be his God, I should sink."

"Oodooville, (Jaffna,) Jan. 3, 1832.

"My dear Catherine,—You may be surprised to know that I write to send by our dear oldest child and only son, now on his way to Madras, to embark for America in the ship 'Star,' of Philadelphia. Perhaps you wonder how we can do so; or are you enough acquainted with our situation among this heathen people, to agree with us that we cannot do otherwise without incurring great guilt. We hope and pray that he may be qualified to return a missionary to the people among whom he was born. But if he be not pious he must seek his bread in the land of his fathers.

"Will you not pray for him, that this our desire and his may be accomplished? He speaks Tamul well, and has considerable acquaintance with the customs of the people, which would be a great advantage if he should return. The attachment towards him manifested by many natives on his departure, shows that he would be received by them as a teacher far more cordially than a stranger; but oh, my friend, this separation and anxiety concerning all the uncertainty of his life and character, has cost his mother what you can but little conceive of. My trust is in the living God."

"Oodooville, December 28, 1831.

"My dear Son Charles,—After you left us this morning, we were all sad enough for a time, but I hope were satisfied with your being gone, believing as we do that it is for your best good. I heard a number of persons praying for you, some in English and some in Tamul, and have no doubt that many will continue to pray for you daily. I trust that you, in turn, will not forget to pray for these poor people as well as for all your friends here. You will be glad to know that I feel comforted and thankful for the pleasant manner in which you left us, and for the prospect you have of being before long in the happy land of your fathers. My dear child, I hope you are comforted by the Spirit of God. Trust at all times in your Saviour. Cleave to him. Whatever else you do, never forsake or be ashamed of him.

"I feel anxious about you at all times; but when I go and pray, I feel better, for I know that God can take care of you. You must not think too much of my being troubled at your absence. I can do any thing for your good, and am glad to suffer for your sake if necessary.

"*January* 24.—We were glad indeed to receive the letters written on the 13th and 17th instant at Madras. Had been expecting them very anxiously. You are now, we trust, on the water, on your way to America. Your notes, my dear child, are very precious; the more so because I see from them that you love to give your parents pleasure. Always be willing to take trouble and make sacrifices for this; it will add to your own happiness. I hope that you will live in the constant fear and love of God; if you do you will be gentle and kind, and thus make friends wherever you go. I feel an inexpressible desire to have you give yourself *wholly* to Jesus, that he may keep you from that 'roaring lion which goeth about seeking whom he may devour.'

"Your ever affectionate

"MOTHER."

"OODOOVILLE, April 25, 1832.

"MY DEAR SON CHARLES,—I wrote you last week, and sent my letter to Colombo for Henry and William Scudder to carry to America. This morning I came from Panditeripo, where I have been to see Mrs. Scudder in her trial in parting with her dear boys. It was very pleasant to talk about you, and to pray for you and them together. We feel that you will all be exposed to great temptations on board the ship and after you get home; and that if you do not look to the Lord for his strength to keep you, you will fall into sin, grieve the Holy Spirit, and wound that blessed Saviour who has done so much that you may be saved from all sin and sorrow, and be made holy and happy with him. I am afraid, my dear boy, that you do not think enough of your own weakness; that you think you are strong, and can do this or that without any help. But you can do nothing, not even think a right thought or speak a right word without help from God. And you must not forget that he is always ready to help those who look to him. None *ever seek his face in vain.*

"28.—My beloved boy, a mother's prayers follow you every day and every hour; do not forget or neglect to pray for yourself. 'Seek the Lord while he may be found; call upon him while he is near.' Nothing would give me so much joy as to know that you are 'born again;' no, not even to see your face, and once more to embrace you in my arms. I hope you will tell me every thing you can about yourself, after you get home, as well as while in the ship. Tell me what you do wrong, as well as what you try to do right, and then I can better pray for you that the Lord will pardon your sins and keep you from sin.

"*May* 18.—Your papa is absent with Mr. Spaulding near Point Pedro, to preach and distribute Tracts. I am very glad to have him able to go, though it leaves me very lonely; I think so much more of you when he is gone. Not that I am sorry to have you go to America, for I believe it is for your best good; and I always endeavor not to regret what I have done, after having asked the Lord to direct me, and tried to do his will. But I have no more of those precious evenings when we sat down together at my table, and read and prayed together. The clock strikes twelve, and I must say good night. May angels guard my beloved boy. May the blessed Jesus wash his soul from all sin in his own blood, and may he be prepared to sleep the sleep of death, and awake to a glorious immortality beyond the grave.

"24.—We have had a visit from Mr. and Mrs. Spaulding and the dear children. Elizabeth has a new song put into her mouth. She was for some days much distressed in thinking of her many sins, and that she had so often grieved the Holy Spirit. Now she hopes that her sins are pardoned, and that her name is written in the Lamb's book of life. She talks, and sings, and prays like one who loves the Saviour.

"26.—*Saturday evening.*—My dear Charles will not, I trust, forget what used to be the employments of this evening; and although you cannot kneel by your mother's side and offer your prayers, you may at a great distance pray to the same God, and find him as near as he was here; and you may always be sure that she too is offering her prayers for her dear son. When you are settled in school, or wherever you may be, I shall wish you to tell me when you can each day think of Oodooville, and be engaged in prayer for your dear friends here as well as for yourself; and I shall endeavor at the same time to pray for you. It is pleasant to have stated seasons of prayer for each other. I watch carefully the shrub which you put out a few days before you went away. It grows finely, and bears a beautiful flower.

"I hope, my dear son, that you will give your beloved grandmother that place in your confidence which I used to hold, and go to her at all times with any thing you wish to communicate. She has had three sons, who always went to her with their joys and sorrows as their best earthly friend, even before any of their school-fellows and companions. She will love you more if you do so, and it will be very useful to you."

Early in 1832 Mr. W. visited Colombo, to seek an interview with Sir Robert Wilmot Horton, recently appointed governor of the island, and obtain permission to have the mission enlarged. The feeble health of a daughter induced Mrs. W. to accompany him. Finding that the governor was at *Newera Ellia*, in the interior of the island, Mr. W. followed him there; Mrs. W. remaining at *Cotta*, six miles from Colombo, with Mr. and Mrs. Lambrick, of the Church Missionary Society. Passing through *Kandy*, where he was cordially welcomed by Mr. and Mrs. Browning, English missionaries, and ascending to an elevation supposed to be 6,000 feet above the level of the ocean, amid scenery inimitably beautiful and magnificent, the thermometer at sunrise being but

42°, and seeming a retreat formed for the fainting missionary,* Mr. W. reached Newera Ellia, and had a most gratifying interview with the Governor. On all the subjects brought before him his excellency manifested the greatest kindness; signified his intention of giving some pecuniary assistance to the mission; and expressed his regret that they had been so long embarrassed by governmental restrictions.

The object of the visit was thus happily secured; calling forth the special thanksgivings of the mis-

* Among the beautiful natural productions of the interior of the island, one of the most splendid is the *talipot* (*corypha umbraculifera*) or large fan-palm. The body of the tree is 60 or 70 feet in height, and straight as a ship's mast; without a limb or leaf until you reach the top, where is an immense tuft of fan-leaves, so large that each one may cover eight or ten men. The stalk of these leaves clasps the body of the tree and inclines outwards, the long leaves bending over in a graceful curve. This vast crown of evergreen, surrounding such a shaft, is itself very grand; but when the tree is about fifty years old there rises from its centre a cone several feet in height, which gradually enlarges until at length it bursts with a loud explosion, and a vast conical flower, fifteen or twenty feet in height, and ten or twelve in breadth, stands exposed in almost incredible magnificence. It is yellow, and formed of numberless blossoms, so arranged on a giant stem and innumerable branches or tassels, as to appear over the elevated tuft of leaves as a gorgeous diadem on the head of this queen of the forest. The tree blossoms but once, and then dies.

sion to God, and giving Mrs. W. the opportunity to write as follows to an esteemed female friend:

"My dear Laura,—Your very precious letter came to me just as we were leaving home to pay our respects to the governor and lady lately arrived. Mr. W.'s object was to request permission for more missionaries to join us, and mine to obtain health for our little H. Through mercy both were accomplished.

"We now look forward with the hope of seeing the faces of missionary friends from our beloved native land. It is *thirteen* years since we were thus privileged; and we had become so accustomed to the thought that we must labor alone, that the expectation of its being otherwise excites strong emotions. We shall certainly be overjoyed, and I hope thankful. It will be pleasant if they are personally acquainted with some of our dear friends, but above every thing else, I hope they will have the qualifications of *good temper, common sense, and ardent piety*.

"My school has been small of late, owing in part to some of the girls having been married; but last week we made up all deficiencies by adding twenty-eight, making now *fifty-three;* so that my hands are full. We are greatly favored in being permitted to regard all the older ones as christians, and to see those who have married adorn their profession, though living among the heathen."

"OODOOVILLE, June 19, 1832.

"MY DEAR MOTHER,—Our Maternal Association has met here to-day. It is an encouraging fact, that all the children over *fourteen*, whose character we know—for some are in England—are hopefully pious; and some of the younger ones have at times appeared very serious. There are fourteen members of the Society, and about sixty children connected with it. I think there is more than a hope in the minds of most of us, that not one of these dear ones will fail of eternal life.

"*July* 11.—The last three days have been devoted to special services for the benefit of this benighted people. From six to half past seven in the morning was a prayer-meeting in Tamul, in the church; from that hour until half past eight a prayer-meeting of the brethren and sisters, and such of their children as were present; then breakfast. At half past nine a meeting with the larger children of the village schools, both girls and boys. At eleven, one with schoolmasters, and others who were disposed to come. At one o'clock another prayer-meeting by ourselves; and at four two meetings—one with women and the girls of the school, and another with church members. In the evening a general meeting of all who desired to attend; and many have been so disposed.

"This evening, especially, the church was, I think, better filled with respectable people than ever before. *The court Moodeliar*, of Mallagum, has been out every evening, and appeared very attentive. There seem many advantages in addressing the people in this way, which there are not when they are found at their houses, or in small circles. They see that the missionaries are in earnest when they leave home and make so much effort to address them; and they are obliged to be quiet, and to hear what is said, without one and another making remarks, or asking questions which divert the attention and excite ridicule, as is very common on other occasions. More than once I thought, how would friends at home rejoice to see so many heathen listening attentively to the word of life; to hear the earnest, affectionate exhortations of the missionaries and their assistants, or the fervent prayers and addresses of such natives as know, in some degree, the worth of the soul; to observe the effect of truth in the moistened eye and anxious countenance of many hearers; and to join in the prayers of the brethren for wisdom and grace to perform their most solemn duties. It was a high privilege, for which I feel under renewed obligation to live for God.

"*August* 11.—We have had another interesting week; special services being held at Batticotta. It was good thus to wait upon the Lord, with one accord, in one place. Many attended the evening meetings who could never before be induced to attend any place of christian worship. The Moodeliar, of whom I spoke, has since openly, and before many friends and foes, avowed his full belief in christianity; has visited Mr. W. to receive instruction, and has been furnished with the Bible and other books, which he spends much time in reading. His influence is such that his conversion would seem like that of a host. There is much inquiry at Oodooville and in the surrounding villages. Some say, 'Why, the Moodeliar talks to us, even when about his business in court; he says christianity is true; he is going to be a christian; nobody now can doubt about these things.' His friends persecute him much, and he seems aware that he shall suffer greatly from them if he perseveres."

The *Moodeliar*, mentioned in this letter, was from the most influential family in the district, and is himself a man of great respectability. After much inquiry, and many struggles, he became a decided convert, and was received to the church. On account of the opposition of his numerous and powerful friends, who would probably have used force to keep him back, his admission was private; but as though the birds of the air told the matter, his wife heard of it almost as soon as he had returned home. Immediately she collected together almost every thing valuable which she could carry off, and left him. A young lad, a nephew, whom he had adopted, as he had no children, and to whom he had given most of his property, was taken away by his father. His servants left him. No respectable man would go near his house, or drink water from his well. He was deserted by all. But in the midst of many trials he strove to maintain his integrity, and was enabled to adorn his profession.

CHAPTER IX.

Decease of her Son in America—results of labor—sudden death—character.

Arrival and death of her son in America—private reflections on parting with him—letters—brief sketch of his life—cheering results of missionary labor—last letter to her mother—renewed dedication of herself and family to God—sudden death—character—tribute to her memory—death of sisters.

In the autumn of 1832 the afflictive tidings were received of the death of that son who had been the object of so much solicitude and hope. A kind and consoling letter from one of the secretaries of the Board gave at once the intelligence of his arrival in America, and his early removal from the world. The previous solicitude of his mother concerning him, and how far she was prepared for this trial, may be in part understood by a few extracts from her private journal.

"*April* 22, 1832.—Near the close of the last year we were called to prepare our beloved son to go to America. Many a heart-rending pang did I experience; but I think I was graciously supported by Him who *can* do all things, and does visit the sinful also with his consolations. This trial was long contemplated, but never, till it was very near, did I expect to live to see it. I think I could scarcely bear another such. Charles' feelings were much exercised. Never can I forget some seasons when we were together at the throne of grace. How did he *plead* that his parents might be 'supported and comforted when he should be gone,' and 'that he might come back and preach to the poor heathen;' but 'if we should not meet on earth, that we might meet in heaven.' Oh, my Father, who didst so support me that I could endure it all, I thank thee for these seasons; I thank thee for my hope that this darling boy is one of the lambs of thy fold.

"*May* 27.—The burden of my effusions at the last date, is my burden still. Many hours of grief and care have been allotted me; but I hope that I can trust in the Lord to do all things well. To-day has been our communion—Mr. and Mrs. Woodward and the Manepy church members were here. I was much disappointed in being occupied with little H. who was quite ill this morning all the time before breakfast, and especially as I had reason to think that the other brethren and sisters were then praying for us; but I found, as I have done before, that when there is from *necessity* a want of preparation, the Lord is pleased to show that the preparation of the heart is from *him;* and that in the performance of *duty* we may safely expect comfort and consolation. My season at the communion-table was precious. It was sweet to look upward to a crucified Saviour, and forward to a place at his right hand. I was peculiarly impressed with the boundless love of God. How delightful the theme! Mr. W. met my mind and heart in all he said. I felt no embarrassment from a foreign language. Since I could not renew my private dedication in the morning, as I intended, have done so this evening. May I never forget my obligations. It has been a calm, a holy day. Praise the Lord, O my soul.

"*July* 8, *Sabbath.*—I have been greatly concerned for a few days about our dear Charles, since reading the account of some severe storms after his sailing. All my prayers for him are now, *if alive*, which I used scarcely to mention. I do feel that we gave him to our heavenly Father according to his will. That we did not send him forth without bidding; and did not commit him to the winds nor to the waves, nor even to our dear country and friends, but to the Lord.

"*December* 16.—The Lord has come very near to us since I last wrote, and we have realized in part what was then so much dreaded. Dear Charles is no longer an inhabitant of earth; but is, I trust, before the throne of God and the Lamb. The shock was what few can conceive. Oh, how we loved him. How our expectations were raised concerning his usefulness. But the Lord has not seen as we see. He has cut him down, and, I doubt not, for the best and wisest reasons. Perhaps no affliction has ever been more needed, and I humbly hope it has done us much good. It has drawn our thoughts and feelings upward, and made us, for the time at least, less earthly. It has made the Saviour more precious. Indeed, I think that new views of his character, and of my relation to him, have been given me."

"OODOOVILLE, November 2, 1832.

"MY MOST BELOVED MOTHER,—I scarcely dare trust myself to commence a letter to you; and yet I feel that I must tell you, that we have received the mournful intelligence which has made our hearts bleed as they never did before. The boy who carried my last letter for you, and as I thought for Charles also, to the post-office, on the 4th ult. returned with the heavy tidings. Oh, the anguish of my first feelings! We had feared that the vessel might be lost, but that he should, so soon after reaching our friends, be taken away, I had not for a moment anticipated. Still the Lord is good, and all his dispensations are right; and I know not that I would alter any of them if I could, severe as they may sometimes seem. Perhaps we loved our child too much, and were too much delighted in the thought that he might be qualified to return as a missionary to this people; and make up, in some measure, the deficiencies of his parents. He has, I trust, a purer service above, one more acceptable to his heavenly Father; and for him I greatly rejoice.'

"*November* 10.—I have written but a few lines since the intelligence reached us that our beloved Charles had so early finished his course; not, my dear mother, that I loved you or others less, or that I had nothing to say, but because it is not easy to clothe in language the heart's deep sorrow. I never felt the chastening hand of God so heavy upon me; though I trust I can say, 'It is good for me that I have been afflicted.' It was a seasonable warning. I am thankful that our heavenly Father thus graciously aroused me; that he did not leave me to be wholly engrossed by my dear earthly ones; but reminded me that this is not my rest. My earnest desire and prayer is, that he will draw me to himself, and fix my wandering heart upon him who is 'the chiefest among ten thousand.' Had I chosen the form of discipline, it would have been different; but doubtless this is best. May it accomplish all for which it was sent. It is consoling to think of one so dear as having escaped the pollutions of the world and joined the company of heaven. There, we hope, are *five* of our little ones. Surely we have reason to think of our treasures above.

"*December* 10.—I hoped to fill a long letter to my dear mother, but have not been well, and have been writing to dear F. a few particulars about Charles. Shall begin another sheet, to be finished, I hope, about a month hence by Mr. W. when I may be unable to write. The more frequent contemplation of another world, occasioned by dear C.'s death, and I hope, also, some nearer approaches than usual to Him who is altogether lovely, have made it seem *an easier thing for me to die* than has been common. I feel, however, strong ties to life, and hope and trust it will please the Lord to spare me still.

"The cholera prevails to an alarming extent in the district. Very many have been carried off by it, and the consternation of the people exceeds all that I have known among them before. It is a grievous scourge; not only as cutting down so many in their sins, but as the fear of it operates upon those who are spared, to keep them shut up at home. Many schools are scattered. The people will not attend preaching, and violent rains make it very difficult for the missionaries to go out amongst them to any extent. There are, however, nearly twenty candidates for admission to the church at our next quarterly communion."

Some passages from the sketch of her son to which she alludes above, and which was published in a small memoir of him, may illustrate the character of Mrs. W. as a mother, and her influence in forming the mind and habits of this promising child, who died at his uncle's in New-York only three weeks after his arrival in America, at the age of a little more than eleven years.

"Oodooville, November 23, 1832.

"My dear Sister F——, We learn that the 'Star' will touch at Madras next month, and as, just at this time, I feel that what I do must be done quickly, I commence a sheet, the first object of which shall be to give you some facts of our lamented Charles.

"I think that a desire to please his parents, and add to their comfort, more powerfully influenced him to duty than any other motive. When he had done wrong, nothing would so soon fill his eyes with tears as to see us grieve. Our sorrows touched his heart as though they were his own, and when he had occasioned them, it was to him doubly trying.

"His *purity of mind* was such as, in this polluted atmosphere, we could not too much prize.

"He was *obedient*—never, that I recollect, wilfully disobeying his parents; and his word was seldom, if ever, doubted. He was much impressed with the words, 'The eye that mocketh at his father, and despiseth to obey his mother, the ravens of the valley shall pluck it out, and the young eagles shall eat it,' and he meditated on them with a kind of horror. He also knew that 'liars shall have their part in the lake which burneth with fire and brimstone.'

"The poor beggars were objects of his great compassion. For two years or more he was in the constant habit of accompanying me to give them rice, &c. and to spend some time in communicating religious instruction. He often exhorted them to repent. Indeed he seemed for some time particularly desirous to be useful to the heathen, and often admonished such as came to the house. One old woman (the mother of a schoolmaster) since his death has reminded me of a number of instances when, said she, I stood by that door or sat on the mat there, and he said, 'You must repent now, you are an old woman, and will die soon; you must think of what Jesus Christ has said and done for you, and love him.' The girls in the school he often admonished and exhorted; one evening, in particular, they will never forget: it was during the last revival of religion, when he was more deeply impressed than ever before, and thought that he had himself accepted the terms of salvation. We were absent. After seeing the little ones asleep, he proposed to have a meeting with the girls, it being the evening on which I usually held a meeting with them, and he was generally present. He prayed and exhorted them, as they afterwards said, with a seriousness and earnestness such as they had rarely witnessed. It was somewhat characteristic of him that he said nothing of it to us after our return, and we should not have known it but from others.

"He had, at quite an early age, a good knowledge of Scripture history. Long before he could read himself, I commenced reading to him the Old Testament, omitting some portions, and explaining or simplifying the history so that he could understand it. His first reading for himself was to go on with what I had begun, in connection with studying Emerson's Scripture Catechism,—which, indeed, was scarcely a study, as he had the facts in mind from his reading. The Bible was in this way his most pleasant reading-book; and he had the principal historical facts in the Old and New Testament treasured in his mind when he had read but little else—and any text of Scripture that, in reading or otherwise, had conveyed a distinct thought to his mind, was never forgotten, but often referred to and quoted in conversation. Indeed I never knew him to forget any thing that he had once *distinctly understood.* Committing to memory what he did not understand was a task, and was seldom required of him. His evenings were generally spent with me alone in reading and conversation,—when quite young till eight o'clock, and afterwards till nine and half-past nine,—and these are the seasons on which more than all others my memory delights to dwell, when he gladly turned aside from the common amusements of children, and especially of boys, to sit down in a retired room with his mother, open his mind to her instruction, and into her bosom pour all his heart. Here he confessed his sins and wept over them, and here I felt that I had an influence which no precepts nor threatenings could give me under other circumstances. He never seemed so happy as in evenings thus spent.

"In his seasons of more than usual seriousness, which towards the close of the time of his stay with us were frequent, he seemed aware of the danger of their not being permanent, and with many tears used to pray that he might 'not be suffered to grieve the Holy Spirit.' It was his usual practice to pray alone in the morning, and with me in the evening, after our reading a portion of Scripture together. On Sabbath evenings he recited to his father, after which they had a season of prayer and religious conversation together, and we have often remarked that his prayers were the language of a mature christian, sometimes very affecting to us, and seeming to proceed from an overflowing heart. The burden of them was, that he might hate sin more and more, and be holy as Jesus was holy, and this with the strongest expressions of sorrow for sin, and longing to be freed from it, and washed clean in the Saviour's blood.

'There is a fountain filled with blood,' &c.

was a favorite hymn, to which he often alluded in his prayers. The first time he expressed a decided hope to me, was, I think, when he had been ill. I intimated my belief that he was better, but added, 'It may be that God will send a severer sickness upon you, to make you feel that you are in danger of death, and lead you to prepare for it.' He immediately burst into tears and said, 'Mamma, I am not afraid to die; I am sure God has not given me up.' He was then too weak to say much in explanation of his feelings, but the simple fact that he was not afraid to die was some evidence of a change of heart; as *death* to children in this country appears usually in the most forbidding forms.

"He however seemed to think of his sins as much as of his exposure to danger and to sudden death. One evening, I well recollect, he was so affected with a view of his sins that he begged me to pray with him, and himself prayed alone with me three or four times, appearing to feel that he could not sleep till his sins were pardoned and he had a new heart. Another time at a quarterly meeting, during the sermon and the administration of the Lord's supper, he sobbed and wept much. On my inquiring why he did so, he said that he felt as he never did before, and wanted to come to the Lord's supper. This desire he often afterwards expressed, and regularly attended the meetings at the station which were held for inquirers and those who wished to make a public profession of their faith in Christ. This was the more observable, as he always avoided any unnecessary exhibition of his feelings;

many times brushing the tears from his eyes and turning his head away when he thought he might be observed."

It may be added that this son of many prayers gave pleasing evidence to his friends in America of being truly a child of God. In his journal at sea he frequently mentions his religious enjoyment. In one of his communications to his parents he says, "I still feel that I have given myself to God;" and one of the last sentences that he uttered while he retained his reason was, "*I think the Lord seems to comfort me very much.*"

It is evident in the preceding pages that, during the *thirteen years* in which Mrs. W. was permitted to toil on heathen shores, *many cheering results* gladdened her heart—an earnest of richer blessings which have already descended, especially in the enlargement of the mission, and its wide extension on the continent; and which, in the fulfilment of the purposes of mercy to a fallen world, shall yet be granted to the prayer of faith and the labors and sacrifices of christian love.

For some years previous to her sudden removal, the *native free schools*, eighty or ninety in number, had contained *from three to four thousand* children, of whom more than five hundred were girls. The system on which they were conducted having been gradually improved, they had become much more strictly *christian schools*—christian books, prepared by the missionaries in Tamul, were extensively used; and each school was virtually a depository for Bibles and Tracts, and a little chapel in which the word of God was preached, from time to time, to the parents of the children and other villagers. Nearly one half of the teachers had become hopefully pious, among whom was a heathen girl, taught in one of the schools, who became a faithful teacher of forty or fifty of her own sex—an interesting train, that from Sabbath to Sabbath might be seen following her through the rice-fields as she brought them up with her to the house of God.

The *preparatory school*, into which the free boarding establishments had been concentrated, embraced more than *one hundred lads*—prejudice having so much given way, that when on one occasion notice was given that a few select lads would be received, more than *one hundred and fifty*, many of them from leading families, were brought to the missionaries and strongly urged upon their acceptance. On a similar occasion, when it was proposed to receive into the Female Central School about twenty *girls*, more than *seventy* were brought by mothers and other female friends, all saying, you *must* receive our children, we cannot take them home again.

The *Mission Seminary*, at the close of 1832, contained *one hundred and forty-two students*, including a theological class of twenty-five; and of the whole number fifty-three were members of the church. The public annual examinations in English were attended not only by missionaries of other denominations and friends in the vicinity, but by many gentlemen connected with the government, among whom was Sir Richard Ottley, in honor of whom the principal building was named Ottley Hall; and the examinations in Tamul drew together many of the more respectable natives, before whom dissertations relating to the solar system, and illustrating the great practical points in European knowledge, as well as on the truth and evidences of christianity, were read; and mathematical demonstrations and ocular experiments, with views of the heavenly bodies through the telescope, were presented—all throwing the light of true science on some of the deformed features of the puranic systems, and shaking the foundations of a false *religion* as well as of a false *philosophy*. Of the forty-three who had completed their studies in the seminary, twenty-three had gone into the service of the mission; eight remained in the seminary as teachers and students of theology; four or five were employed by other missions; and eight or nine by the government as interpreters in the courts, or assistants in the medical or surveyor's departments. Dr. Scudder had also always one or more assistants in his practice among the natives, whom he instructed as circumstances allowed in the medical art, a knowledge of which is of great importance among the heathen.

Permission for the establishment of the American mission *press*, which has since issued so many millions of pages, had been very recently obtained; but by means of the Church mission press established in 1825, catechisms and other *books for schools* and more than fifty *Tracts* had been printed; copies of the *Bible*, which was translated into Tamul a century before by the Danish missionaries at Tranquebar, had been procured from Madras and Colombo; and by the distribution of these publications much light and truth had gone forth amidst darkness and error, and had been evidently blessed in the conversion of some individuals. One of these, *Katheraman*, who was brought by one who received a Tract, to the house of God, himself brought many others; and at length met such as he could induce to attend, at a prayer-house every morning regularly, for reading the Scriptures and prayer, until fifteen or sixteen had joined the church, and others were inquiring.

At each of the five stations of the mission, from three to six hundred were generally present at the public *ministry of the word* on the Sabbath, of whom about one fourth were adults, and the remainder children from the schools. United meetings for special services were also held, not only at the mission stations, but in the midst of populous heathen villages; at which numbers of the heathen were often collected under favorable circumstances, to hear from successive speakers the most impressive truths, brought to bear with concentrated force upon their hearts and consciences, while united prayer was offered for the descent of the Holy Spirit. The Gospel was also proclaimed from house to house, and tours made for preaching and the distribution of books both on the island and the continent. In August, 1831, *one hundred and seventeen* who had been connected with the boarding establishments, *thirty* schoolmasters, and fifty villagers, including some domestics, had been admitted to the church; and in the following year thirty were added, of whom a still larger proportion were adults.

It was easy for the eye of faith to anticipate results far more glorious, as the prayer of the Great Intercessor for the progress of his kingdom should be fulfilled; and there is delightful evidence that the subject of this memoir could commit all to him, whether he would still employ her here, or call her to be "with him where he is," that she might "behold his glory."

The following unfinished letter is the last commenced by Mrs. W. to her ever dear mother:

"January 3, 1833.

"MY BELOVED MOTHER,—I did not intend to delay beginning a letter to you, as promised in my last, till this time; but you will excuse it. Most anxiously have I been looking and waiting for letters to come 'by another ship in a few days.' I long to know how you have been supported in the severe disappointment concerning dear Charles. We are still surrounded by the dead and dying, as the cholera is raging with perhaps no abatement; but hitherto our families and the church members have been preserved, except in the case of one young man who had left the mission and was living in the town. Several have been ill, but have been restored to health.

"I have felt much reproved this evening for some of my anxieties concerning our children. When shall I learn to cast all my burdens on Him who is able to sustain them? I think I have more delight in trusting him of late; but still 'come short.' Have been reading Mrs. Graham's life with new pleasure, and I hope profit. Believe I have read it three times since coming to Jaffna. Have also been engaged with the memoir of Isabella Campbell; another precious example of one who lived 'by faith on the Son of God.'

None I am sure can read it without profiting by such an exhibition of simple trust in Christ.

"In regard to our children, if I had the means I should not wish them put wholly in a boarding-school, but in such a place that, by uniting habits of domestic labor and economy with cultivation of mind, they could be qualified for happiness and usefulness in life. I seek not great things for them. Indeed I hope I can say, with Mrs. Graham, that I put a *blank* into the Lord's hands as to all their temporal concerns; seeking only this *one thing* with *all my soul*, that they may have their portion with the people of God."

The last night of the year 1832 was spent in prayer at Oodooville by the members of the mission, who remained in supplication and intercession until midnight; and then greeted the new year with thanksgiving. The uncertainty that life would be continued to all through the year was of course contemplated; and if uncommon fitness for death had been considered as an intimation of its near approach, a presentiment might have been felt that the subject of this memoir was keeping that "*watch-night*" for the last time. But no one, except perhaps herself, heard the voice which seemed to say, "the Master is come and calleth for thee."

In expectation of her confinement, concerning

which she was, for no apparent reason, uncommonly doubtful, she made her preparations much as she would have done had she known the result, and that she should be unable at last even to bid any one farewell. All the concerns of the boarding-school as well as the affairs of her household and of the station, as far as under her management, were arranged in the most careful manner, and written directions were left concerning them. There was also a paper of hints concerning her children, and a farewell letter to her husband. Nor was her soul neglected. She had laid up fresh provision for passing over Jordan. Her affliction, by weaning her from the world—by making the Bible and the throne of grace more precious—by causing her to look to a compassionate Saviour with more steady faith, and to appropriate to herself more than ever before the precious promises of his word, so changed the current of her religious feelings, and so carried them upward, that she often spoke of them as almost entirely new.

On Saturday evening, January 12, a few hours before her death, though much occupied with other concerns, she found time to express some of her feelings and desires in her private diary. The greatest part of what she wrote is given, as the last record of her experience—the dying testimony of her faith and love.

"*January* 12, 1833.—My time for writing is nearly gone, at least for the present; and my dear Charles' birth-day reminds me that I owe it to the Lord for his merciful affliction to say more than I have of what I hope it has done for me. I have even thought, at times, that had I appeared before Him previous to this stroke, I should have had my portion with hypocrites and unbelievers. I have thought, Is it possible that, after so long a life of profession, after many unspeakably precious seasons at the throne of grace, after so long feeling assured that my poor prayers were heard and answered, after experiencing in many trials that 'good is the will of the Lord,' and rejoicing to have him rule and reign, and after hours, weeks and months of bitter agony and abhorrence of myself on account of sin, and counting the holiness of heaven more to be desired than all the world can offer—I have never before submitted to Jesus as my Lord and Saviour? —never before embraced the Gospel as a little child?—never come unto Jesus so as to be saved? Oh, can it be?—and yet, sure I am that I never before saw the Saviour so lovely, so desirable,—never considered as now the length, and breadth, and height, and depth of that love which passeth knowledge—the value of that fountain which is set open for sin and uncleanness;—never saw the whole plan of salvation so perfect, so wonderful;

—never with such feelings could say, 'my Lord and my God.' And while this view of the subject has seemed greatly to endear the fond object whose removal has been the means, I have been thankful that the Lord did not wholly forsake me, and did not leave me to compass myself about with sparks of my own kindling, to strive to work out my own righteousness by tears and groans for sin. Oh, I bless him for this chastisement, and long that it should bring forth more fruit.

"Sometimes heaven has seemed very near, and as though it would be easy to die. At other times I have had less confidence, and more fear whether all is yet right between me and my God. Should I now be called from my little family, from my dear husband, oh my Saviour, let me rest in thine arms; carry me all the Jordan through. Oh be with me, even as I cannot ask or think. Support, sustain my sinking feet. Oh uphold me * * * * * * *. Be thou my Saviour in that dark hour; and do thou most graciously bless my dear, dear husband. Uphold him with thine everlasting arms. * * * * * My dear babes! may they be thine, thine only, and that for ever. Oh my Saviour, enable me this night to give myself unto thee, and do thou receive me in that well ordered covenant which thou didst die to secure."

She was interrupted and did not record her petitions for the school, the station, and the brethren and sisters of the mission, as, from other circumstances, it is evident was in her heart. The closing scene will be best given in a communication written at the time.

"OODOOVILLE, January 17, 1833.

"MY EVER DEAR AND BELOVED MOTHER,—The Lord has often come very near unto you, and removed, one after another, your earthly comforts, until perhaps you feel that you are almost desolate, and that the sources of consolation below are nearly dried up. But has not heavenly consolation descended into your soul in proportion as earthly comforts have failed? I doubt not that this has been the case, and that you are still able to say, 'It is good for me that I have been afflicted.' How trying in your widowed state to look upon our dear Charles only when nature was failing, or when he was laid out for the tomb. After all your hopes and expectations of clasping often to your arms the first-born of your beloved Harriet, and of seeing your eldest daughter in her eldest child, how trying the disappointment! Yet you could say, It is well, for the Lord hath done it.

"And what Providence is there, however trying, however it may wither and blast our hopes, and scathe our very hearts, concerning which, as the will of God, we cannot say, 'It is well?' Yet alas, we are weak; and unless supported from on high, there are dispensations of Providence which we cannot bear. We sink beneath great waters. Such an affliction has come upon me; and such, my dearly beloved mother, has come upon you. We are mutually and most deeply afflicted; for your and my beloved Harriet is gone. Yes, the wife of my youth, the partner of all my joys and sorrows, the mother of my three, now motherless children, is gone. That tender, that most affectionate heart, has ceased to beat; and all her anxious cares concerning those whom she loved as her own soul are over. She has passed the Jordan; and is, I doubt not, in the heavenly Canaan, rejoicing with joy unspeakable and full of glory. She is now in that world of 'spirits bright' where no sin nor sorrow can enter. My dear afflicted mother, do not mourn, but rejoice. Our too dear Harriet is with her Saviour, whom she loved better than all here, though she loved us very much.

"But I must give you a few particulars. On Sabbath she was somewhat ill; but went to church both forenoon and afternoon. I tried rather to dissuade her from going in the afternoon, and she at first concluded to stay at home; but as the children wished it, she went, and seemed comfortable. On her return she was a little fatigued, and lay down a short time; after which she rose and went out to tea. We then had family prayers. I read the forty-sixth Psalm, and made some remarks upon it, which appeared to interest her; and we conversed on the privilege of casting all our burdens upon the Lord Afterwards she went to her room, heard the little girls repeat their hymns and lessons, and directed their devotions for the night.

"I went out to my study, but not being so well as usual, came in early. Finding the door of her room shut, and having a sick head-ache, I lay down on a couch. This was very unusual for me, and caused her to inquire a little anxiously about my health when she came from her room. She said, 'I cannot bear to see you so unwell;' and soon added, 'I do not feel so well myself. I have a peculiar sensation in my breast.' I requested her to be as quiet as possible, and recommended that she should take a little laudanum, and lie down. She did so, and went to sleep; but in a short time awoke, feeling the same distress in her breast. I then immediately sent for Dr. Scudder and Mrs. Spaulding, supposing that she was about to be confined. She was partially relieved of the distress, but continued very uneasy and unable to rest in any position. She frequently requested me to pray for her.

"Dr. Scudder arrived about two o'clock in the morning. He bled her freely, and she became so much relieved that she lay down quietly and said that she felt quite at ease. She took a little coffee; and before she went to sleep called me (as Mrs. Spaulding was taking care of her) and insisted on my lying down on the couch on account of my being unwell, saying at the same time, 'Do you know, my dear, how good it is to be perfectly at ease after severe pain?' I said, 'You feel thankful.' Her reply was, 'Yes, I think I do. How good is the Lord.' She then very pleasantly bade me good night, and fell quietly asleep. This was probably the last she knew on earth.

"After a short time Mrs. S. noticed a peculiarity in her breathing, and attempted to wake her. As she did not succeed, she called Dr. S. and myself; but as the sleep was quiet and pulse regular, there seemed to be no danger. We again left the room; but were soon called back to witness slight spasmodic affections of the eyes and face, which were, ere long, followed by a convulsive fit. We were then greatly alarmed, and Dr. S. used every exertion to prevent a recurrence of the spasms. All was without success, and after two or three returns of the convulsions the breath of my beloved wife grew shorter and shorter, and a little before six o'clock on Monday morning, the 14th instant, she peacefully resigned her spirit.

"The funeral took place at five o'clock P. M. of the same day. We sang at the house,

'Why should we mourn departing friends,' &c.

And at the grave,

'Unveil thy bosom, faithful tomb,' &c.

And I believe all felt that those hymns expressed our sentiments, our feelings, and our hopes. The mortal remains were deposited in the church near those of our dear George;—thus was one babe by the *side*, and one in the *arms*, of the fond mother; and the spirits of *six* are, I trust, with her before the throne. Oh! how she loved them; how she prayed for them; how assured she was of their final salvation. She was indeed a precious mother as well as wife and missionary.

"Our departed Harriet had for the last few months been fast ripening for heaven; especially since we heard of Charles' death. How severe was that stroke! But what rich blessings did it bring! It made her lean more entirely on her Saviour. She had, under that affliction, new and peculiar evidence of the life of faith in her soul. On Saturday evening she expressed her feelings in her diary; and on Sabbath noon renewed her covenant with God—a covenant made twenty-five years before. *This was her finishing work.* It was the last time she wrote her name. As she had no opportunity for preparation after she became ill, it is most gratifying and consoling that she left these last memorials of her unwavering trust in God. She had, in every respect, set her 'house in order,' as though she fully anticipated being thus removed, almost in an instant, from all these scenes. But I did not at all expect, nor was I at all prepared for the shock. Much had I anticipated my own death; little had I thought that the desire of my eyes would be taken away as with a stroke. Yet it has been done by the hand of a Father; I dare not, I cannot murmur. I bless his holy name that he took my beloved so gently, and that she met the enemy without knowing of his approach; for he was disarmed. Should the Lord spare my life, I propose to send you another letter soon. I now write in haste, and with a bleeding heart.

"Your ever affectionate,

"though afflicted son,

"M. WINSLOW."

A joint letter from the mission adds, "The funeral was attended by all our number, and by our missionary friends in Jaffnapatam. The mother and babe were buried in the Oodooville church, amidst the tears, not only of the immediate mourners, but of the bereaved children of the school, the native members of our churches, and of many people around who could not but feel their loss.

"The following week on Thursday, being the time of our quarterly communion at Oodooville, a funeral sermon was preached by Mr. Poor, from the text—'And his disciples came, and took up the body and buried it, and went and told Jesus.' He described the deceased as like John, a 'burning and a shining light.' This description, though it made us weep the more for our loss, and for the loss of the natives around us, caused us also to rejoice for the grace conferred on our departed sister while here, and for the assurance that she is now enjoying the unveiled presence and glory of her Saviour in a better world."

We have thus accompanied our missionary friend through her brief but useful life. If her pathway was frequently thorny, the light of heaven was often let down upon it, to illuminate and cheer her steps. She was happy even in a distant land and amidst the heathen; and at last, how short was her passage through the dark valley to brighter regions; how sudden the transition from suffering, sinful mortality, to beatified immortality. All that remains, is to notice a few traits in her character, selected principally to excite imitation, or show the abounding grace of God to one who felt that she had nothing of her own but sin.

Mrs. Winslow, in her person, was above the usual size and stature; and with a fine dark eye, a pure white skin, and an elevated and expanded forehead shaded with dark locks, had an engaging countenance,

> "Where dawns the high expression of a mind:"

while she undoubtedly possessed "a nicer adjustment both of the intellectual and moral powers than is ordinarily to be found." Neat and tasteful in her apparel; affable and yet dignified in her manners; and, in her social intercourse, frank, candid, and sincere—always putting the best construction on the language and deportment of those around her, while her careful *self-scrutiny* made her acquainted with the hearts of others—she found easy access to persons in every department of life, and was a favorite in every circle which love of her Saviour did not forbid her to enter.

In her school-days she had great fondness for mathematical studies, and the effect was seen in after life, in her discipline of mind and regard for strict order and system. Perhaps this also contributed, in connection with her native strength of intellect, to form her uncommon *decision of character.* Such were her habits of thought that she could not but rest steadily in the fixed decisions of her judgment; and her determination on important subjects was often such as to lead to the most untiring perseverance. Difficulties seldom overcame her. It was a maxim from her childhood not to say, "I can't;" but "I'll try." She generally finished what she undertook, and was remarkably *thorough.* She had great *industry* as well as energy, and did most things with a *facility* which enabled her, though subject to very frequent illness, to accomplish more than do most persons in continued health. In addition to the care of her family when abroad, the education of her children, the charge generally of a large boarding establishment, the keeping of pecuniary accounts for the station, and various direct missionary labors, she maintained a frequent correspondence with many friends, and did much writing for the mission.

With these traits of her character were united much *delicacy of taste,* and an unusual degree of *sensibility.* Her feelings were all acute and tender, rendering her peculiarly susceptible to sorrow or to joy; but she studied, and to a good degree attained, in these as in other respects, *self-control.* It was her rule, in regard to all wrong habits, mental or moral, to strive for the victory over them, and never to give up the conflict from the impression that they were unalterably confirmed.

It is perhaps frequently the case that the leading features of religious character are stamped at the time of the new birth. It is certainly remarkable in Mrs. W. that *concern for the souls of others* mingled largely with her earliest religious impressions. She was imbued with the missionary spirit in her first sanctification and sealing by the Holy Ghost. From the beginning she was an *active* christian. Her benevolence sprung from a deep fountain of christian love, opened by the Spirit in her soul, and kept full by free communication with the "river of the water of life." Thus qualified, she could be faithful in reproving and seeking the eternal welfare of others, and seldom give offence; and rarely failed in her attempts to gain access, even in circumstances the most forbidding. Her growth in grace was perhaps more manifest from the increase of *love* than of any other fruit of the Spirit. In one of her last letters she says, "I have often of late thought that it is not sufficiently considered that our religion is a religion of *love;* and there is nothing which I have more frequently resolved to aim at, especially when coming up from the banks of Jordan, than to have love to God and love to man the leading principle of my spared life"

While her piety was active it was also *meditative.* She abounded in self-examination. Mason on Self-Knowledge was a constant manual. It was her practice, at different periods, to keep a written account of her *deficiencies*, and in her examinations to dwell principally on those things in which she had come short. She kept at times a list of the principal faults, both of omission and commission, to which she felt herself exposed, on which she noticed her delinquencies, and kept the account for her subsequent inspection. At her seasons of fasting and prayer she sometimes recorded at length these and other sins as they occurred to her mind. For instance, at one time she began her devotional exercises by noting her sins against God—against her husband—against her children—against her domestics—against the brethren and sisters of the mission—against her friends at home, and against the heathen. Under these heads some pages are written, which show the minuteness and severity of her examination, and her awful sense of the strictness of the divine law. Among the *sins against God* she in one instance records:

"Not meditating upon God at stated seasons, and constantly going to him to guide, uphold, and deliver—not waiting on him in *faith*, to keep me from temptation, and to give me the victory over my besetting sins—not desiring more earnestly to be with him to behold his glory—not being more thankful for the mercies I experience, and doing more cheerfully to the Lord whatsoever my hands find to do—not committing myself and my all to him with entire submission and a desire only that his name may be glorified—not trusting in him at all times before any created one, and making him my chief good before husband and children—not desiring life for *his* sake, that I may labor for him among the heathen, rather than for the love of the world or of friends—not constantly recommending the Gospel by a meek and quiet spirit before the heathen, from whom he only has made me to differ—not thinking enough of the exceeding love of Jesus, and feeling my obligations to him—not giving more honor to the Holy Spirit by thankfully receiving his influences, giving him a throne in my heart, and obeying his teachings."

She also at such seasons reviewed her *resolutions*, which were made when her views of divine things were clearest; and according as she had been enabled to keep them or had broken them, she gave thanks to God, or humbled herself before him. It appeared to be her sincere endeavor to act in that manner which had seemed to her best when she made the closest approaches to

God. If she could not afterwards recall the *emotions* excited at such times, she would have the benefit of the *opinions* formed, and rules of life laid down, when farthest from earth and nearest to heaven. She desired it to be, as she often said, her *daily business* to make progress in the divine life.

Her habits of *devotion* gave soul and life to her piety. It was her frequent practice to have specific subjects of prayer on each day of the week, and also for different parts of the day. Indeed, in a good measure, she obeyed the injunction, "praying always with all prayer and supplication in the Spirit," and her *intercessions* were often most fervent and prevalent. The instances are numerous in which manifest answers to her prayers were granted; some of them in the conversion of individuals, both at home and abroad, who were apparently very far from God. No one can easily conceive how great was her anxiety at times, and how earnest her petitions, for the girls of the school, for her domestics and others at the station, and for all connected with the mission; nor can any one tell how much they were indebted to her prayers. No domestic lived in her family any number of years without becoming a christian. At the time of her death *five*, assisting in the care of her numerous household, were all members of the church, though they came to her *heathen*. In the devout and diligent *reading of the Scriptures* she had frequent communion with God. The Bible became more and more precious to her as she became more and more spiritually-minded; and meditating on its truths until they assumed form and substance, she obtained great peace of mind, which often shed its lustre on all around her. In one instance, in expressing her wishes for the day, she says, "I desire especially to walk softly before God; and to this end I would be *moderate in all things*—*not hasty* in speaking or acting—*kind to all*—*not talkative*—*not noisy*—*thoughtful*—*grave*—and *much in ejaculatory prayer*."

In regard to all her anxieties *as a mother* and the mistress of a family, as well as a missionary laborer, she endeavored to roll her burdens on the Lord, but felt her responsibilities so deeply as to be often "pressed in spirit beyond measure." Though few are more frequently occupied in contemplating the divine perfections, her views of Jesus as a Saviour, or rather as *her* Saviour, were not always equally distinct with those of her deficiency and guilt, and she groaned being burdened. But when through grace she was accustomed to look more steadily at the cross of Christ, and was more sensible of the actings of faith within her, and of her *union* to Christ as her head, she looked away from herself, and rejoiced in hope of the glory of God.

Her progress in the spiritual life is happily described by Mr. Spaulding, in a letter to her mother, with which we close this short review of her estimable character.

"Your dear Harriet in her religious and social feelings continued, for the first five or six years of her missionary life, much as when you last saw her. She suffered frequently from bad health, and was eventually obliged, as you know, to take a voyage to Calcutta. Though she always delighted to spend her whole strength, sometimes laboring even beyond her strength; still the growth of her religious affections and her *enjoyment* in religion and in the missionary work have been increased since her return in 1826 This may have arisen in part from better health. but I think she had somewhat clearer views than before of herself and her Saviour. The intelligence of Charles' death was more than nature alone could bear, and with the aid of grace it seemed difficult for her to recover at once from the suddenness and severity of the shock. Yet, though cast down, she was not forsaken. She mourned bitterly, but submissively, silently and in hope.

"In one of my last conversations with her, we were speaking of the ill health of some of her children, when she remarked that she felt that she must do all she could for them while spared to her, as they seemed to be lent but for a little season.* Her conversation for the last two or three months was not only heavenward, but she seemed to get new views of Christ, and of salvation by faith in him. All the more meek, lowly and gentle graces of the Spirit seemed to have taken a new and rapid growth. She talked of that love which Jesus manifested, and still manifests for us, and of 'forbearing one another in love;' and mourned more than ever over those dissonant feelings among christians which unhappily are sometimes exhibited. In a word, her conversation and feelings seemed to be those of one who enjoyed a frequent and solitary walk along the banks of Jordan; who looked with unusual interest at the prospect on the other side, especially at the loveliness and glory of the Saviour, as he seemed to hold out his hands towards her and say, 'Come, heavy laden and afflicted, I will give you rest.' These feelings seemed to be new, and almost strange to herself; and while she pondered them in her heart, wondering what they could mean, she suddenly 'overstepped the grave,' and is not, for God hath taken her.

"She is no more with us, but she lives in our hearts. She lives in the affections of relatives,

* Her three surviving daughters were brought by their father to this country, and each adopted into an estimable christian family.

and friends, and christians at home. She lives and will long live in her labors of love among the Tamul people. In this providence there is much of comfort as well as of affliction. Even the suddenness and unexpectedness of it was full of mercy to her, as she had always some fear in view of death. This seemed to be regarded by our kind and sympathizing Saviour, who so ordered it that she should take rest in a sweet and quiet sleep; and putting off the body and mortality in that very sleep, 'awake in his likeness.'"

The following affectionate tribute to the memory of Mrs. W. is from the highly gifted pen of Mrs. SIGOURNEY, who was a friend and companion of her early days.

TO THE MEMORY OF

MRS. HARRIET L. WINSLOW.

"Thy name hath power like magic.
"Back it brings
"The earliest pictures hung in memory's halls,
"Tinting them freshly o'er; the rugged cliff,
"The towering trees,—the wintry walk to school,
"The page so often conn'd, the needle's task
"Achieved with weariness,—the hour of sport
"Well-earned and dearly prized,—the sparkling brook
"Making its clear cascade,—the darker rush
"Of the pent river through its rocky pass,—

"Our violet-gatherings 'mid the vernal banks,—
"When our young hearts did ope their crystal gates
"To every simple joy.
"I little deem'd,
"'Mid all that gay and gentle fellowship,
"That Asia's sun would beam upon thy grave,—
"Though even then, from thy calm, serious eye,
"There was a glancing forth of serious thought,
"That scorn'd earth's vanities.
"I saw thee stand
"With but a few brief summers o'er thy head,
"And in the consecrated courts of God
"Confess thy Saviour's name. And they who mark'd
"The deep devotion, and the high resolve
"Of that scarce half-blown bud,—did wondering ask
"What its full bloom must be.
"But now thy bed
"Is with thine infant train,—where the sad voice
"Of the young Ceylon mother tells her child
"Of all thy prayers and labors. Yes, thy rest
"Is in the bosom of that fragrant isle
"Where heathen man, with lavish nature, strives
"To blot the lesson she would teach of God.
"—Thy pensive sisters pause upon thy tomb
"To catch the spirit that did bear thee through
"All tribulation; till thy robes were white,
"To join the angelic train.
"And so farewell,
"My childhood's playmate, and my sainted friend,—
"Whose bright example, not without rebuke,
"Admonisheth, that home, and ease, and wealth,
"And native land,—are well exchang'd for heaven."
"L. H. S.

"HARTFORD, (Conn.) March 17, 1835."

The influence of Mrs. W. in forming the character of her sisters, to whom Mrs. Sigourney so beautifully alludes—one of whom, who yet survives, received, on arriving at Ceylon, the first intelligence of her death—claims the following brief notice of the two others, who had scarcely entered on their labors among the heathen when they were called to higher services above.

Mrs. Charlotte H. Cherry, the eldest of the three, having for some years, in her native land, sought with great fidelity and success the eternal welfare of souls, especially those under her charge in Sabbath and other schools, and whom she met in her Tract distribution, reached Ceylon in April, 1837, expecting to be stationed on the continent; but, after a painful illness, died, November 4 of the same year, aged 26. Eight days before her departure she wrote in pencil:

"I am still spared, although very low. Yes, dear friends, our good Dr. Ward thinks the earthly house of this tabernacle will soon be dissolved. Well, if the Lord's will be so, is it not far better to be with Christ? I think the Lord sent me here; and though it were but to die, I do not regret coming at his bidding. Many, many thanks to dear mother and sister, who, in my childhood, taught me *to prize the Bible*, and to learn many passages from its holy pages, which now cheer my fainting spirit."

During her severe illness she was an example of patience—cheerful, submissive, happy. Often, when in anguish of body, she would say,

"This sorrow, touched by Thee, grows bright
"With more than rapture's ray."

A few hours before her departure she said, "Is this death? Yes, this is death. It is a solemn thing to die. I want to tell you, that Jesus Christ is my all—*my all.* I am a lost, vile, undone sinner, but Jesus Christ is my all." Then after a pause—"'Have not I commanded thee?' 'Have not I commanded?' I believe the Lord commanded us; and tell them at home I am not sorry we came here, because I believe we came at the Lord's command. Do not let them say I have done much. I have done nothing. It was all the Lord Jesus Christ. Farewell."

On the stone which marks where her dust is deposited by the side of her two sisters at Oodooville, is written *in Tamul*, "Her dying words were, '*Jesus Christ is my all. He is my precious Advocate with the Father.*'"

Mrs. HARRIET JOANNA PERRY, the youngest sister, who arrived in Ceylon September, 1835, was suddenly removed (three days after her husband, both by cholera) March 13, 1838, aged 22; leaving an orphan daughter at the tender age of a little more than one year. A part of the letter from the only surviving sister, which bore the intelligence to their widowed mother, may close this narrative of the dispensations of a wonder-working God.

"OODOOVILLE, March 19, 1838.

"MY DEAREST MOTHER,—We have sometimes lately said to each other, 'Perhaps the Lord will have spared our dear mother the pain of hearing of the death of dear Charlotte, and have taken her to meet her and other loved ones before the throne of God and the Lamb ere the news reached home.' But why need we say that? Cannot He who has sustained you in six troubles, support you in this also? And can He not even fill you with joy at the thought of your precious ones multiplying in heaven? I feel that it is so, and that you are enabled

'To rise within the veil, and see
'The saints above, how great their joys,
'How bright their glories be!'

"Mrs. Spaulding and I, as we sit here this evening, have been naming those we know and love among the blessed company. They seem a precious, happy band—and we almost feel that it would be a privilege to join them.

"The cholera is now prevailing in some parts of this district. The poor heathen, in their alarm, fly with new zeal to their gods, their ceremonies, and their incantations.

"The Lord drew near to us, and laid his hand on *one of our brethren.* We had all felt for some time that we needed chastisement; that those which have been sent upon us had not been improved as they ought. But He who said, 'I will visit with the rod,' 'nevertheless my loving-kindness will I not take from them,' mingled tender mercies with the affliction, and permitted us to see the sufferer filled with resignation, peace, joy, and confidence in God. He was dear to us, but dearer to Him who died for him. Do not mourn, dearest mother, that he has taken *brother Perry* to himself.

"Do not mourn, *even on dear Harriet's account.* I was wholly unprepared for the stroke, and felt that she would be; and while I hastened to her after receiving the intelligence, I dreaded to meet her. But after I had seen her, I ceased to weep for her. Even then she was 'kept in perfect peace;' and if you could witness, dear mother, the *joy* with which she is filled *now*, you would be overwhelmed with gratitude for the grace bestowed on her. God has wiped away tears from her eyes, and put a new song into her mouth, even *praise* to her God. She is spared the sorrows of widowhood in India. She is reunited to her beloved husband—her body rests by the side of his.

"The first words she said to me were, 'Precious sister, I have wanted to see you. I have thought all day that I should soon go to join his happy spirit before the throne.' It was a pleasure to attend her in her short sickness, and to hear her continual expressions of peace and joy in believing in the Saviour. She talked of HIM, and almost of Him only. I would, if I could, make you see and hear her; but it is impossible to give any but those who were around her an idea of such a scene.

"A little before her death two Tamul women came in to see her, and she told me to say to them for her, 'I expect to die in a few hours. I go happily. I desire very much that when you die, you may be as happy as I am. But you cannot, unless you believe and love the Lord Jesus Christ, who died for you.'

"Afterwards her countenance became filled with joy, and she tried to sing. At first she could articulate nothing, but continued to make a cheerful sound, till it appeared that she was singing, 'Hallelujah, Hallelujah.' She seemed for a long time engaged in this exercise; and we thought from her manner that she supposed she was mingling her songs with those in heaven."

Lines suggested by reading the Memoir of Mrs Winslow on the anniversary of her birth.

" Thou measurest not thy life by years,
" By change of night and day;
" Nor by the drops of ceaseless tears
" That wash our bloom away;

" But on the dial-plate above,
" Which blessed seraphs scan,
" Thou seest eternity roll on
" As when it first began.

" Thou wanderest from thy home no more,
" Where sprung thy childhood fair,
" To pitch upon a heathen shore
" Thy mission-tent of care.

" No more the insatiate grave shall feed
" With what thy bosom reared—
" Nor feel thine inmost spirit bleed
" Till every vein is seared.

" Are they not there,—those infant souls,—
" Are they not by thy side,—
" For whom thy sleepless prayer arose,
" For whom thy Saviour died?

" And do we still, with blinded grief,
" Lament thy lot sublime,
" High raised above the countless fears,
" The countless ills of time?

' Is it thy voice that makes response
" In tone so sweet and free?
" Weep for yourselves, my dearest friends,
" But weep no more for me.

" L. H. S.

" HARTFORD, April 9, 1837."

THE END.